Guide to
CLASSROOM TEACHING

Edited by Robert McNergney

Curry School of Education,
University of Virginia

with the assistance of
Michael Caldwell and Donald Medley

ALLYN AND BACON, INC.

BOSTON   LONDON   SYDNEY   TORONTO

To Donald Medley
with respect and gratitude

Copyright © 1988 by Allyn and Bacon, Inc.
A Division of Simon & Schuster
160 Gould Street
Needham Heights, Massachusetts 02194

Library of Congress Cataloging-in-Publication Data

Guide to classroom teaching / edited by Robert McNergney, with the
assistance of Michael Caldwell and Donald Medley.

    ISBN 0-205-11418-0
    Includes index.
    1. Teaching. 2. Classroom management—United States.
I. McNergney, Robert F. II. Caldwell, Michael F. III. Medley,
Donald M. (Donald Matthias)
LB1025.2.G84   1988
371.1′02—dc19   87–31856
                                            CIP

Printed in the United States of America

10 9 8 7 6 5 4 3 2 1 92 91 90 89 88

detra housear

Contents

Preface   v

Acknowledgments   vii

Foreword, by Thomas L. Good   ix

1. TEACHING IN CONTEXT   1
   Joanne Herbert and Elizabeth Pitt

2. PLANNING   23
   Robert McNergney

3. REINFORCEMENT   43
   Sandra B. Cohen and Donna Hearn

4. CONSISTENT RULES   67
   Ruth Anne McLaughlin

5. ACADEMIC LEARNING TIME   81
   Ruth Anne McLaughlin

6. ACCOUNTABILITY   97
   Martin Aylesworth

7. CLOSE SUPERVISION   109
   Jeremy Burnham

8. AWARENESS   121
   George M. Bass and Roger R. Ries

9. QUESTIONING SKILL   145
   James Mackey and Deborah Appleman

10. CLARITY OF STRUCTURE   167
    Pauline Pagliocca

11. MEANINGFULNESS   193
    Stephanie Hinson

12. INDIVIDUAL DIFFERENCES   211
    Jean Coolican

13. LEARNER SELF-CONCEPT   231
    Kathleen Anne Dunne

14.   AFFECTIVE CLIMATE   247
         Susan O'Connor

15.   EVALUATION   263
         Harvey Carmichael and Michael Caldwell

         Index   285

Preface

This book is written to help teachers, particularly new teachers, as they begin to translate knowledge about teaching and learning into practice in their classrooms. Like other professionals, teachers must possess special knowledge about their field and be able to use it when situations warrant. By leaning heavily but not exclusively on research that has examined connections between teaching and learning, the authors present some of the best pedagogical knowledge available.

The book should be of interest to teacher educators who work with prospective or experienced teachers as well as to teachers themselves. The material that follows can be used to form the nucleus of a preservice or inservice teacher education program. This is more than wishful thinking or idle speculation, for an earlier version of this text has been used successfully with hundreds of beginning teachers in a highly organized statewide program of teacher assistance. Although the teachers served by this program were all relatively inexperienced, some more mature teachers can be expected to learn from reading these chapters and working through the exercises provided.

Two assumptions underlie this text. First, teachers do not become master professionals overnight; they need time, experience, and support. This book points in one direction that reasonable support might take, but only one. Second, there has always been a lot to be said for learning by doing. Thus, the authors have tried to encourage readers to use ideas, not merely to read about them—an approach that should help teachers attach practical meaning to the ideas in this book.

Even though people have been establishing teaching standards and teacher education programs for a long time, some would argue persuasively that the knowledge base for the kind of teacher education this book promotes is weak at best. It would be foolish to assert anything beyond the fact that the knowledge base used to make decisions about teaching practice is only now emerging from careful study of life in classrooms. As the knowledge grows, so, too, will conceptions of how teaching competence and teaching excellence can be fostered. Indeed, it is almost as if Lewis Thomas were thinking of educational research instead of inquiry in biomedical science when he wrote:

> The thing to do, to get us through the short run, the years just ahead, is to celebrate our ignorance. Instead of presenting the body of human knowledge as a mountainous structure of coherent information

capable of explaining everything about everything if we could only master all the details, we should be acknowledging that it is, in real life, still a very modest mound of puzzlements that do not fit together at all. . . . Get us through the next few years, I say, just get us safely out of this century and into the next, and then watch what we can do.[1]

The book is organized into fifteen chapters. Chapter 1 sets the stage by encouraging thought about the context in which professional knowledge must be applied. The remaining chapters present knowledge about teaching and learning as if such knowledge can be separated neatly into discrete components. In practice, of course, there is considerable overlap among the ideas. For example, to be able to plan for instruction, a teacher must know something about individual differences among students, about evaluation, and so forth. Recognizing that various kinds of professional knowledge tend to cluster in particular instructional situations and that certain contextual factors (for example, grade level and subject matter) may influence behavior is one thing; writing about the complexity of these interactions in a way that is understandable is quite another. By treating each chapter as a self-contained unit, able to stand independently, we hope to provide material that is understandable and useful to practicing educators.

Each chapter, with the exception of Chapter 1, follows the same general pattern. First, a *definition* of the teaching knowledge covered in the chapter is presented. Next, the *purpose* of the chapter, or a statement of what people can expect to gain as a result of working through the chapter, is explained. In the *background knowledge* sections relevant literature is discussed; various *practice activities* designed to build one's practical knowledge are interspersed. Not only do these activities provide opportunities for the reader to practice new skills, they also encourage the exploration of educational policies and procedures and the examination of one's own attitudes and values. A complete list of *references* is also included at the end of each chapter, along with a list of additional, uncited sources in some cases.

RFM

---

[1]Thomas, Lewis (1980). *Late night thoughts on listening to Mahler's Ninth Symphony.* Toronto: Bantam Books, p. 163.

Acknowledgments

Special thanks go to numerous individuals and groups for their help with the development of the Beginning Teacher Assistance Program (BTAP), the program from which this document emerged.

The following members of the BTAP Advisory Committee have provided challenging, thoughtful counsel throughout the course of program development: Judith Whittemore (Chair), Joan Bloomer, Vincent Cibbarelli, Brenda Cloyd, Victor Culver, Howell Gruver, George Gum, Marie Keritsis, Barbara Mann, James Oglesby, Jerry Owens, Joe Roberts, Lois Rubin, Steve Sailer, Don Shirley, Loretta Small, Ulysses Spiva, Ann Sweet, Russell Watson, Rachel Wilson, and Elaine Witty.

Representatives of the Virginia State Education Department have been skillful in clarifying and implementing public policy with respect to the BTAP. Mention must be made of Nancy Vance, E. B. Howerton, William Helton, James Patton, Sara Irby, Byrd Latham, Sue Parsons, Diane Lantor, Joan Murphy of the Attorney General's Office, and James Macmillan, a consultant from Virginia Commonwealth University.

Colleagues at the University of Virginia have served as program development team members and have selflessly contributed time, energy, and a wealth of ideas to the BTAP. These include Donald Ball, Michael Caldwell, Robert Covert, Brenda Loyd, Donald Medley, and Elizabeth Rosenblum. During early phases of the program the team benefited from discussions with Terry Wildman, Hilda Borko, Ruth Anne McLaughlin, and Rosary Lalik of Virginia Polytechnic Institute and State University.

Numerous people have served as consultants to the BTAP during the past several years, providing valuable insight into the problems of assessing teacher performance and of supporting teachers' professional development. Among these have been David Berliner, Carolyn Evertson, Betty Fry, Thomas Good, Gary Griffin, Richard Jaeger, Jason Millman, Barak Rosenshine, Lee Shulman, B. O. Smith, Robert Soar, Les Solomon, and Joseph Stulac. We especially thank Robert Spaulding for his helpful criticism of an earlier version of this manuscript.

The following graduate students in the Curry School of Education at the University of Virginia have worked on the BTAP: Mark Dewalt, Francis Doherty, Barry Ehrlich, Patricia Francis, Clarice Gressard, Luree Hays, Joanne Herbert, Stephanie Hinson, Susan Lopez, Donna Murphy, Judy Pearce, Betty Pitt, and William Scarbrough.

Wei Li Fang produced the photographs used in this book. We are grateful to the students and staffs of Johnson Elementary School, Buford Middle School, and Charlottesville High School—all in Charlottesville, Virginia—for cooperating with Ms. Fang.

Without the clerical support of Louise Chinnis, Alice Giannini, Mary Rolfe, and Sandy Sherman this project would never have been completed.

The fact that these people and many others have contributed in one way or another to the Beginning Teacher Assistance Program does not, of course, imply their endorsement of the program or of this document.

RFM

Foreword

Classroom teaching is not easy, in part because classrooms are complex social environments in which teachers often must make quick and difficult decisions on the basis of incomplete information. Many things happen simultaneously in classrooms. During a discussion, a teacher not only listens and helps improve students' answers, but also monitors students who did not respond for signs of comprehension and tries to keep the lesson moving at a good pace. A single event can have multiple consequences. Waiting a few seconds for one student to answer a question may positively affect that student's motivation but negatively influence another student who would like to respond, and it may unnecessarily slow the pace of the lesson for the entire class.

The transition from preservice to inservice teaching can be a traumatic experience as teachers move from the college classroom or a training program and into the reality of everyday teaching. New teachers may experience some problems because they have had only general training (understandably so), and many are therefore not ready to teach in the contexts to which they are assigned. For example, a preservice teacher may teach in an inner-city first-grade classroom and then be assigned to teach full-time in a sixth-grade class in a suburban district.

There are other reasons why teachers may have difficulties when they start to teach, and teachers cannot prepare for some "problems" in advance. For example, first-year teachers not only become teachers and learn to deal with students, parents, and colleagues, they also assume new responsibilities (make new friends, pay off loans, and so forth). Thus, some anxiety and role conflict are to be expected when one becomes a full-time teacher.

Research conducted in the 1970s and 1980s provides convincing data about the complicated, fast-moving conditions of teaching. At one time, teaching was frequently characterized as a relatively simple and straightforward task, and in the 1960s and earlier many social scientists were quite negative about the quality of teachers and teaching. However, because in the 1970s researchers began to study classrooms (fast-moving and complex interaction in social settings), most educators and social scientists realize that teaching is sophisticated cognitive activity that demands many decision-making skills, as well as teaching skills and sophisticated knowledge about students and subject matter. To be successful in the classroom, teachers also need to possess advanced skills for identifying students' problems and dealing with individual students in a social setting.

Although those associated with education realize the complexity of teaching, the job of the beginning teacher is seldom altered accordingly. A beginning teacher is responsible for an entire class—and must perform the job well if students and teacher alike are to survive in the classroom. In contrast, beginners in other professions often have reduced work loads or support staff to facilitate their entry into the field. For example, beginning lawyers have secretaries to prepare their correspondence, legal assistants to do research, and assistants to help prepare trial notes. Furthermore, beginning lawyers do not deal with all types of cases; rather, they specialize in one area. In contrast, beginning teachers often must teach unaided and deal with the wide range of behavior problems and academic skills associated with teaching (from teaching complicated geometry proofs to dealing with student misbehavior in the cafeteria, to career counseling of students who are trying to decide which college they want to attend to individualizing instruction, and the like).

Fortunately, there is growing interest in programs that provide assistance to teachers, especially first-year teachers. Proponents of these programs argue that, because of the assistance beginning teachers receive, education will be significantly improved. These induction programs strive to help teachers remain in teaching and adapt to its demands. The retention of promising beginning teachers is extremely important, because when these teachers leave the profession, a large investment of time and resources is lost. Indeed, this book was developed as one part of a state-mandated assessment program.

The Beginning Teacher Assistance Program resulted in the useful chapters that constitute these integrated readings. Robert McNergney has organized a collection of chapters that identify key skills and information that teachers must know if they are to be successful. The book provides detailed information on planning, teacher awareness, presenting information, and evaluating student performance and includes realistic activities to practice and use that information. I believe that students who read these fifteen chapters will understand much of the research that has been conducted on teaching effectiveness in the past fifteen years. Although the readings describe teaching skills and specific strategies that might be effective, they emphasize that teachers need to be reflective and to understand when and how to apply teaching skills to classrooms. In this sense, I especially enjoyed reading Chapter 1, "Teaching in Context," which describes the complexity of teaching and emphasizes that there are multiple ways to be effective in the classroom.

Beginning teacher programs need to do more than assess beginning teachers in order to remove incompetent teachers or to remediate weak teaching. Although teachers need research information and feedback about their skill in performing basic and important teaching competencies, teachers also need support and structures that help them reflect on classroom knowledge and grow as professionals. These programs also help good teachers become even better, by learning from colleagues and using resources intelligently. That is, the most helpful teacher induction programs stress the need to help teachers grow as professionals in school settings.

To this end, the state department in Virginia has expressed some interest in sharing recent and helpful information with teachers in order to expand their views of teaching. The mentor program, one part of the BTAP, attempts to use research information to improve a teacher's ability to think and to apply that information in appropriate ways, according to the context in which he or she teaches (see Wildman & Niles, 1987)[1]. I am especially pleased that my own work, *Looking in Classrooms* (Good & Brophy, 1987),[2] has been useful and provided a base for helping teachers to reflect about appropriate practice.

In my judgment, the Virginia State Department of Education, under the leadership of Nancy Vance, has started to build a responsive induction program that takes the needs of beginning teachers quite seriously and attempts to help teachers develop appropriate skills and knowledge to cope with the problems they face. State-mandated assessment of teachers is still the key part of the present program. I hope that in subsequent work Virginia and other state departments of education and local school districts can take the next important step, going beyond assessment and investing more directly in teacher development. Beginning teachers need materials, activities, and professional norms that encourage them to become autonomous, reflective, and effective practitioners.

Robert McNergney's book provides an initial and useful return on the investment of funds by the Virginia State Department of Education. The book is responsive to the instruction needs of beginning teachers. In my opinion, the information in these chapters, when adjusted to a particular situation and used in a responsive school environment that encourages teachers to collaborate (and provides beginning teachers with the opportunity to talk to successful role models), can play a significant and positive role in helping teachers to adjust successfully to classroom demands.

THOMAS L. GOOD

---

[1]Wildman, T., and Niles, J. (1987). Reflective teachers: Tensions between abstractions and realities. *Journal of Teacher Education 38*, 25–31.

[2]Good, T., and Brophy J. (1987). *Looking in classrooms* (4th ed.). New York: Harper & Row.

Chapter One

Teaching in Context

Joanne Herbert and **Elizabeth Pitt**
University of Virginia

To be a teacher and a professional means being able to bring special-ized knowledge to bear on problems of educating others. This book is about facing all kinds of problems in all kinds of classrooms and applying knowledge that is derived largely from research on teaching and learning. Make no mistake; research results cannot be applied directly to resolve all or probably even most classroom problems. But if teachers use knowledge from careful systematic study of teaching and learning—apply it, think about it, compare it to their own experi-ences—they can change their thinking about life in classrooms when need be and help themselves and their students succeed.

To be a teacher and to be a professional is first to be a person who understands oneself. David Hunt (1987) has argued forcefully on practical grounds that teachers need to begin their professional odysseys with themselves by asking questions about teaching and learning that are filtered through their own experiences: Are ideas offered as "help" truly helpful in everyday life? Do these ideas fit with my own experiences as a teacher or as a learner? Asking such questions, Hunt contends, demands that we hold theoretical and re-search criteria in abeyance while considering the practicality of ideas. Ultimately, the value of any idea, then, must be defended at least in part on the basis of its practical worth as defined personally or "from the inside out." So it is with the material in this book.

But one's professional identity is formed in no small measure by others, or as Hunt would say, "from the outside in." This thought can be paralyzing. Teachers who are caught in the grip of this realization can grow cautious, predictable, even frightened, subject always to self-fulfilling prophecies that are anything but flattering. Unfortunately for some, it is all too easy to forget the Emersonian warning against a foolish consistency, that "hobgoblin of little minds" that traps people in rigid patterns of behavior.

But for many teachers their conceptions of themselves as professionals can and do change over time as a result of interacting with others and reflecting on their own experiences. As some veteran teachers will argue, the fact that they are stretched by others again and again is, day to day, the most rewarding part of their careers.

If teachers are to continue learning from their experiences, to create and respond to challenges in their careers, it seems sensible to begin by thinking about what it means to be a teacher, and then to consider life in schools from students' points of view. It also seems reasonable to expend some effort exploring schools—those places where teachers and students come together—to acquire some sense of the social contexts in which teaching occurs.

Teachers

Who are these people called "teachers?" What drives them to try to help others learn? Why do some temporarily suffer public rebuke only to trade in their erasers for implements of more lucrative fields, while others revel in the many demands of classroom life? How is the profession and your place in it likely to evolve in the years ahead?

There are, of course, no ready responses to these questions. There may be as many different answers as there are people who call themselves teachers. But when one examines teachers' pasts, it is often possible to find some clues to the future of pedagogical life, a life that promises to be nothing if not challenging.

Most teachers have been women, and they have come most often from middle-class and lower-middle-class families. The stereotypes from novels, television, and comics—Mr. Chips, Miss Brooks, Miss Grundy—are humorously outdated now, yet curiously prescient about some values shared by many teachers today. Through the years teachers have been people who "worked their way up." Their fathers have been farmers and tradesmen; until recently, few have been upper- or even upper-middle-class professionals. Some half-century ago, Waller (1932) observed that teaching was a "respectable" way to a better life for thousands of Americans.

Since Waller's time, teachers as a group have remained remarkably similar in some ways and yet have changed rather significantly in others. Plisko and Stern (1985) report that for the period 1961–83 the demographic characteristics of teachers have remained fairly constant, with 67 percent being female and 88 percent being white. While teaching used to be for the young, in recent years there has been a gradual graying of the teaching force. The median age of male teachers rose from thirty-four to thirty-nine from 1961 to 1981, while

the median age for women decreased from forty-six to thirty-three in 1978 and then rose to thirty-nine in 1983. About two-thirds of the nation's teachers have at least ten years' experience, while about 3 percent have less than two years' experience. The number of beginning teachers has diminished in recent years.

There may be many reasons fewer young people are choosing to enter teaching. The National Commission on Excellence in Education in its now widely discussed report entitled "A Nation at Risk" (1983) was alarmed by the severe shortage of qualified teachers, particularly in science and mathematics. It laid part of the blame for the shortage at the feet of those who control the educational purse strings for holding teachers' salaries down. It recommended that grants and low-interest loans be provided to entice bright, creative people into teaching. After all, the argument goes, why should people be expected to enter teaching when they could make more money and attain higher prestige in other sectors of the marketplace?

The shortage of qualified teachers in certain disciplines and in various geographical areas of the country has given rise to what Albert Shanker (1985) has called the "dirty little secret" in the profession. According to a recent survey, there may be large numbers of teachers throughout the United States who are "misassigned" or teaching outside the field for which they were prepared (Robinson, 1985). In Utah in 1983–84, for example, about 76 percent of the teachers with major assignments in general science had neither a college major nor a minor in general science. Although the effects of misassignment on students are difficult to calculate, the practice is unlikely to enhance students' or the general public's perceptions of teachers. Teaching in an area for which he or she was not academically prepared probably does nothing to enhance a teacher's perception of his or her place in the profession either.

Like most other workers in the world, teachers are not particularly pleased with the money they make. In 1985–86, the average public school teacher—one with about fifteen years' experience—earned $25,257 a year (National Education Association, 1986). Nearly 62 percent of private school teachers and 55 percent of public school teachers have expressed dissatisfaction with their pay. But when asked whether they would leave their teaching job for one in another field that paid at least $5,000 more per year, nearly two-thirds said they would rather keep their teaching jobs (Feistritzer, 1986).

Because teachers value the opportunity to work with young people and play a part in their development over monetary gain, Emily Feistritzer contends that teachers are "a breed apart" from other workers in society, a breed that wants and should have "greater freedom to exercise their own creativity in choosing and designing what they teach. Individuality itself needs to be encouraged, and rewarded with higher pay and more responsibility" (1986, p. 68).

These days such conclusions are hardly random, isolated events. The National Governors' Association captured headlines in the fall of 1986 when it advocated higher salaries and greater professional freedom for teachers and administrators, but not without an educational price: The governors wanted better-educated students in return for added benefits for educators. Teachers, the governors argued, would have to meet national professional standards and be accountable for their performance and that of their students. In return, they would have greater say over how money was spent, how time was allocated, and how curriculum was selected (National Governors' Association Center for Policy Research and Analysis, 1986). With teachers gaining greater control over educational matters, then, will come heightened demands for accountability.

Where teachers had previously closed their classroom doors and operated fairly autonomously, in the future teachers may assume collective responsibility for the quality of their work. Some school systems are already moving to establish greater freedom for teachers from the vertical hierarchy. Lortie (1986) reports, for instance, that in Northfield, Minnesota, teachers and administrators have been working together to establish mutually agreed-upon criteria for the identification of "good" teaching and to create methods for applying these criteria in the supervision of classroom teachers. In Taylors Falls, Minnesota, a group of five teachers will be the first in the nation to implement a recommendation of the Carnegie Forum on Education and the Economy by assuming collectively the responsibility for administering a school (Rodman, 1987). Presently there are many other examples of efforts to alter old patterns for decision making and accountability in schools (Wise et al., 1984).

If recent reports are to be taken at face value, teachers are showing increasing dissatisfaction with extrinsic rewards, such things as salary, prestige, and influence. Kottcamp, Provenzo, and Cohen (1986) suggest that twice as many teachers today, as opposed to twenty years ago, receive no satisfaction from those rewards typically thought to be status accruing, such as the respect of others or opportunity to wield influence. They report that the majority of the teachers they studied place a premium on what might be characterized as psychic or intrinsic rewards. About 87 percent of their respondents said that what mattered most to them were "the times I know that I have reached a student or group of students, and they have learned."

It would seem that there could be many teachers who are reaping such rewards. Feistritzer's (1986) data led her to conclude that, in the main, teachers were happy with their jobs. Nearly 84 percent of the public school teachers and 95 percent of the private school teachers she surveyed expressed satisfaction with their jobs, with greatest satisfaction being derived from relationships with other teachers, followed by relationships with principals and students' parents. Teachers in Feistritzer's sample also seemed reasonably content with curriculum, textbooks, and general working conditions.

In the future, teachers who not only survive but prosper are likely to be those who view teaching as a job worth thinking about, a job that requires intellectual nimbleness and appreciation for the conceptual complexity of human interaction. They will most likely be facing more rigorous entrance and exit examinations during their years of formal professional preparation. Their training program will probably also be longer than programs have been in the past. If even some of the educational reforms of the 1980s stick, teachers of the future, as true professionals, will be able to do things for their students that the untrained cannot do. As teachers begin to master the emerging knowledge base underlying teaching and learning, represented in part by the chapters that follow, they will be empowered to control their own professional destiny.

Practice Activity 1-1

As the 3:00 P.M. bell sounded, Robert Benson gathered his briefcase and jacket and assumed his post at the doorway to his classroom. He noticed with irritation that few of the other teachers were on duty as the students began to stream by, laughing and jostling each other on their way to the outside exits. Yesterday he had collared two students fighting in the hall and spent ten minutes restraining them before the assistant principal could intervene. Consequently Robert had been late for tennis practice. All he needed was for one of the players to get injured while unsupervised and have a parent charge him with negligence!

A young black man, Robert was one of the mere handful of minority staff members who had been hired to teach mathematics at Midmont High School. The school was for students in grades eight through twelve and served mostly middle- to upper-class families. About 75 percent of the graduates were college bound—a statistic particularly appealing to Robert, who was an honor graduate himself.

Many of Robert's college classmates and teachers had encouraged him to use his strong mathematical skills to go into computer programming or other business fields. Robert, however, had wanted to be a teacher for as long as he could remember. He enjoyed working with people and felt that teaching would offer him the challenges and rewards that he had been seeking.

When the principal met in August with the eight members of the mathematics department, Robert learned that he would be teaching three classes of basic math and one class each of calculus and trigonometry. Knowing the school makeup, Robert was surprised at the heavy load of basic math students he would be carrying. He interpreted the assignment as a vote of confidence in his ability to teach, particularly after he was approached by the principal at the end of the meeting and asked to serve on the planning committee for the school evaluation project.

Robert's school day was structured so that he met with his basic math students during the first, second, and sixth periods of the day. Students in these groups needed work on addition and subtraction, division, fractions, and other skills normally covered in elementary school. Robert would typically introduce a skill, work examples on the board, and then assign problems for the students to work on during the class period. Few were motivated to complete home assignments, and the in-class work period gave Robert an opportunity to monitor the students and give help where needed. Even though the students were relatively well-behaved, Robert was frustrated because their long-term memory for math skills was so poor. He would think the majority of the class had mastered a concept, move on to a new one, then find that students were unable to apply previously learned skills because they were already forgotten.

Students in these three groups had met with failure in the past. Robert knew that simply using positive reinforcement was not enough; he needed a teaching technique that produced understanding. In the spring several students would be taking the Examination of Minimal Competence, and Robert was pessimistic about their chances of passing. Of equal concern to Robert was the lack of interest shown by parents of students from these three groups. Parents seldom responded to the notes he sent home regarding poor school work or misbehavior, and few showed up for parent–teacher meetings.

Robert's next two classes of calculus and trigonometry were quite different. Both classes were composed of many bright and capable students, including the daughter of the school board chairperson. The girl's parents, as well as many other parents, had been present at the first parent–teacher meeting in October and had raised many questions about Robert's goals and objectives for the year. Robert knew that these parents were worried about the upcoming SATs, wanting their children to be accepted at the most prestigious colleges and universities. Robert was not intimidated by the parents because he felt confident in being able to challenge and stretch these bright students.

In his own student teaching, Robert had been fortunate to work with a supervising teacher who had a wealth of knowledge about ways to motivate and challenge students. She had shared many of her supplementary materials with Robert and involved him in a math workshop where he had learned about individualized instruction and use of contract plans. Robert found himself wishing he could use some of the ideas for his lower-level groups. He felt that he was doing less than half his teaching job.

By December Robert wondered whether he could make it through the rest of the school year. Behavior problems were becoming more prevalent, particularly in his sixth-period basic math class. Rita, an attractive sixteen-year-old student, seemed to cause a commotion no matter where she was placed in the classroom. Rita made Robert very uncomfortable; he wondered whether she was as difficult with other teachers. He tried ignoring her but was continually distracted by her behavior.

January and February went more smoothly. Rita was sullen and subdued in her behavior, the two advanced classes were making excellent progress, and students in the three basic classes were beginning to show slight gains. Robert began offering a before-school tutoring session that several students attended—sometimes for math help and at other times just to talk. It was the one time in the day that Robert felt he could relax and get to know his students as individuals.

In the spring he signed up to be the coach for the boys' tennis team. Robert had been a strong college player and had taught lessons for the city recreation department during his summer vacations for the past three years. Although the school days were already long, he needed the extra money, particularly since he and his wife were expecting their first child.

Aside from the hassles with the track and baseball coaches over insufficient locker space for his team, Robert enjoyed the afternoon practices. The matches proved to be long, however, and the games at other schools required extensive travel. The $500 supplement seemed meager in comparison to the time Robert was investing in the team activities.

Robert assumed he was in the "spring slump" his colleagues had been complaining about. Between the painting and decorating of the nursery at home and his long school day, Robert found he hardly had energy to read the newspaper or talk with his wife before collapsing into bed.

Spring vacation came as a welcome break. After a couple days of relaxation, Robert began looking over his plans for the last few weeks of school. At his request the school psychologist had recently been in twice to observe Rita and to give Robert feedback including her observations and suggestions for dealing with Rita's increasingly overt misbehavior. As Robert mulled over the psychologist's notes, he realized how different teaching was from what he had expected.

The range of abilities and needs among his students had taken him by surprise. He wondered whether the students in his basic math classes had mastered previous skills or had merely been given social promotions. There were also several students in those classes who seemed capable of performing at a higher level—students who appeared to be misplaced.

Robert returned to school after spring break with many unanswered questions.

Study Questions 1-1

The questions that follow, like most that teachers face, do not have right and wrong answers. Professional literature, knowledge born of experience, and common sense suggest some responses that would seem more promising than others. Take some time to think about the questions and discuss them with a colleague if you have an opportunity. Speculate on possible responses but try to withhold judgment on a "best answer." As you read the chapters that follow, more ideas will come to you. Your task in this activity, as in the others in this chapter, is simply to generate ideas and opinions.

1. Put yourself in Robert Benson's shoes. What single word describes better than any other how he feels about his own place in teaching? Why? Do you think Robert will stay in the classroom? If so, what will keep him there? If not, what will be the most influential factor in his leaving? If you could give Robert one bit of advice, what would you offer?
2. Robert found his basic math students frustrating to work with. How might he have been able to meet the varying needs and abilities of these children? Would permanent records have been of help? Why, or why not? Could these students' former teachers have been of help? How might the students have "told" him about themselves?

3. Who could have helped Robert modify the ideas and materials from his student teaching days to suit the needs of these students?

4. How should teachers deal with the "Ritas" in their classrooms? Who besides the school psychologist could be of help?

5. High school teachers are often expected to sponsor one of the various teams or clubs that meet after school. What are the pros and cons of this extra duty?

6. Few parents of students in the lower-level classes came for conferences. How important is parent contact? How can a teacher encourage home–school communication?

With the rapidly changing demographics of U.S. public schools, teachers are challenged to work effectively with a diverse group of students: 14 percent are illegitimate; 40 percent will be living with a single parent by their eighteenth birthday; 30 percent are latchkey children; 20 percent live in poverty; 15 percent do not speak English; 15 percent have physical or mental handicaps; 10 percent have poorly educated parents (Fischer, 1986–87). Differences in age, sex, ethnicity, responsibility, and maturity add to the diversity of the classroom,

as does the increasing number of exceptional students. Stubbornly clinging to the belief that all students can succeed, we ready ourselves for the task of meeting the wide array of interests, needs, and abilities of the approximately forty-six million students in our schools.

Nowhere is the diversity of students more apparent than in large cities. Whereas minority enrollment as a percentage of the total enrollment rose from 21 to 27 percent between 1970 and 1980, the minority representation in several large cities—among them Boston, Denver, Seattle, San Diego, and Portland—doubled. By 1982 some cities, such as Atlanta and the District of Columbia, had minority enrollments exceeding 90 percent of the school population (Plisko and Stern, 1985). A graphic example of this diversity is found in the District of Columbia, where students represent 132 different countries and speak 91 different languages.

Of concern to educators is the fact that many of these minority students are educationally disadvantaged. They often come from poverty backgrounds or face language and cultural barriers to learning. In addition, critics of current educational reform feel that these exceptional students are left in the cold by proposed methods for improving educational performance: "Competency standards, increased requirements, longer school days and years—those do not address the crisis of the educationally disadvantaged child" (Hollifield, 1986).

Minority students, particularly those who are Hispanic or black, weigh heavily in the numbers of students failing to graduate from high school. These students also tend to come from single-parent families in which the mothers work outside of the home, lack formal education, and have low educational expectations for their children (Strother, 1986). The one student in four who drops out may do so for a variety of reasons: frustration with school work, lack of interest in school, and economic reasons, marriage and pregnancy being among those cited most frequently (Boyer, 1983). The Children's Defense Fund campaign to prevent "Children Having Children," for example, notes that 40 percent of teenage girls who drop out of school do so because of pregnancy or marriage, and that only half of all teenagers who become parents before age 18 graduate from school (Tugend, 1986).

There has been a surge of concern among educators and political leaders over what is to be done for these "at-risk" students who are growing in number each year. More recently, the Governors' Task Force on Readiness has proposed two sets of recommendations for cutting the dropout rate. The first includes early intervention measures, providing, for example, assistance for first-time, low-income parents of high-risk infants; kindergarten for all five-year-olds; high-quality developmental programs for all four-year-old (and where feasible, three-year-old) children at risk; and information on effective parenting practices to all parents of preschool children. The second recommendation is intended to help at-risk children and youth meet the new educational standards from school entry through graduation.

Examples of proposed state initiatives include providing extra help in basic skills for students who have major deficiencies; developing incentives, technical assistance, and training for teachers and principals to encourage the use of effective school and classroom procedures; establishing alternative programs for high school dropouts and potential dropouts; and establishing a method for state intervention when school districts fail to make progress with low-achieving students.

The boldness of these recommendations and others indicates the level of concern for the plight of those who leave school before graduation. Not only are they poorly equipped to face the demands of an increasingly complex society, but they are also considered a burden to taxpayers. According to Mary Hatwood Futrell, president of the National Education Association, 60 percent of all prison inmates in the United States are high school dropouts. In addition, dropouts cost taxpayers an estimated $75 billion annually in welfare benefits and lost revenues (Futrell, 1986).

At the other end of the educational spectrum, we find students labeled "gifted" and "talented." Though they seem to contrast sharply with at-risk students, they may in fact include minorities, handicapped persons, persons with limited English-speaking proficiency, and migrants. Gifted children may demonstrate high performance in one or more of the following: general intellectual ability, specific academic aptitude, creative or productive thinking, leadership, visual and performing arts, and psychomotor ability (Gage & Berliner, 1984). The Marland Report, produced by the U.S. commissioner of education in 1972, states well the challenge of working with gifted young people (p. 17):

> Gifted and talented children are those identified by professionally qualified persons who, by virtue of outstanding abilities, are capable of high performance. These are children who require differential educational programs and/or services beyond those provided by the regular school program in order to realize their contribution to self and the society.

More recently, the Regulations for the Educational Security Act of 1984 described the gifted student as one who demonstrates actually or potentially high performance capability in the fields of mathematics, science, foreign languages, or computer learning. Such a definition highlights the fact that the schools often define giftedness in terms of the needs of society. Likewise, cultural and socioeconomic factors influence our definitions: "[What] is creative for a child in the barrio or on the reservation, where different value systems are in operation, will not be the same as for the child who grows up in the suburbs" (Bernal, 1974).

Just as the definitions for giftedness vary, so, too, do the means for meeting the needs of the gifted and talented. The two basic approaches used for helping these students in their areas of high ability, however, are acceleration and enrichment.

Students who are accelerated may skip grades; attend special schools; be granted early admission to, or concurrent enrollment in, high school and college; and be allowed rapid advancement in specific subjects. In contrast, those participating in enrichment programs are provided with experiences that enhance the regular classroom instruction, that is, special interest clubs or organizations, resource rooms, independent study, field trips, summer camps, and mentor programs.

Another type of exceptional student encountered in the classroom is the one labeled "handicapped." This student may be learning disabled, speech impaired, mentally retarded, emotionally disturbed, hard of hearing or deaf, multihandicapped, orthopedically or otherwise health impaired, visually handicapped, or deaf and blind.

Since the enactment of Public Law 94-142, the Education for All Handicapped Children Act, public schools have been charged with the task of providing education for handicapped students in the "least restrictive environment." Not surprisingly, the number of handicapped students in public schools has grown. Between 1976 and 1984 there was an increase of 3 percent, with handicapped students representing approximately 11 percent of the total school population (Plisko and Stern, 1985). As with other exceptional groups, the percentage of handicapped students varies from state to state. Massachusetts and Delaware, for example, have numbers in excess of 16 percent of their school population, while California, Colorado, District of Columbia, and Idaho report their numbers as being between 8 and 9 percent of the total (U.S. Department of Education, 1986).

Of those handicapped students accounted for by state agencies in 1982–83, 78 percent of the learning disabled, 93 percent of the speech impaired, and 29 percent of the mentally retarded children—the three largest groups—spent most of the day in the regular classroom (Plisko and Stern, 1985). The goals of such mainstreaming were more than "placing" exceptional students among their peers. Mainstreaming was viewed as a means by which children could interact with other students and become better prepared to get along well in the environment outside of the school setting.

Practice Activity 1-2

Rita fingered the detention slip in her pocket as she stepped off the bus and sprinted toward her mother's apartment. The bus was running late again, and Rita had to hurry home to take care of her younger brother so that her mother could leave for work.

At first, Rita had loved babysitting for Shawn; she could take him wherever her friends were playing, plop him on a blanket, and join in the fun. But now that Shawn was two, Rita had less freedom. Shawn had to be watched every minute; he never seemed to stay in one place for more than five seconds. Shawn was also getting more picky about eating, so the evening chore of fixing dinner for him was becoming a hassle.

Since the age of five, Rita had experienced a tumultuous home life. There were frequent fights between her parents, often ending with Rita's mother taking the children and moving to a relative's or friend's house. Within two months they would return, things would be calm for a few days, and then chaos would begin anew.

Though bright, Rita had little opportunity to cultivate her talents. For one reason, with the frequent moves, Rita had little continuity in her education. Also, Rita's mother was so distraught with their home situation that Rita's education took a backseat to stopgap efforts at making life more tolerable. Consequently, when the moves were to areas outside the school district, Rita would often miss one or two weeks of school before her mother would register her at the new location.

During this difficult period, Rita had frequently been an offender of school rules. Notes were often sent home charging Rita with disrespect, poor attitude, aggression toward other children, and the like. Report cards also showed Rita as performing below grade level. Rita's substandard work, and the recent abusive nature of Rita's father, spurred the mother to file for divorce and move with Rita to another state. Rita was then thirteen years old, and her mother was five months pregnant with a third child.

Study Questions 1-2

1. What can a classroom teacher do to keep a student like Rita from "falling through the cracks"? Which staff members might provide resource help or advice on ways to make Rita's school experience more positive and productive?
2. Why might cooperative learning experiences versus individualized or competitive learning situations be better for a student like Rita?
3. What services might the school social worker (visiting teacher) be able to provide? How is a teacher to find out about such services?

Schools

The history of public schools in the United States is a rich and complex story of changing and increasing expectations. The idea from which schooling has grown is the Jeffersonian assumption that public education has the responsibility to reflect and benefit the society it serves. As our society has changed, so have the concomitant expectations for our schools.

In its early days, public education was expected to develop a strong, rather rigid moral, behavioral, and intellectual discipline in students. Those students who could not meet the expected standards left school; most were able to integrate themselves into the then predominantly agricultural economy in jobs that required little academic training.

The demand for unskilled labor began to decline significantly in the years following the Civil War. Increasing technological advances called for workers with some practical education. The number of schools grew. Supporting and sustaining this growth in public education was a 1874 ruling that state legislatures could empower local communities to levy taxes to support schools.

In many cities the influx of foreign immigrant groups added to the pressure on schools to help people prepare themselves for participation in the U.S. economy. These demands for schools to play a role in acculturating new members in the society, coupled with demands for practical education to help meet the needs of the growing technological sector, brought about a broadening of the curriculum.

The twentieth century has seen a rapid and expanding evolution of societal expectations for schools. Since World War II the structure of U.S. society has undergone significant change at an accelerated rate. As women entered the work force in increasing numbers, family roles and economic expectations began to change. The size and composition of families was altered. Advancing technology has made a society in which the illiterate or semiliterate are greatly disadvantaged economically. Political and judicial changes in areas like women's rights and civil rights have had a major impact on the obligations of our public schools.

The increased legal rights of women, minorities, the handicapped, and the economically disadvantaged have introduced new programs and sensitivities in our schools.

Thomas Jefferson introduced his "Bill for the More General Diffusion of Knowledge" to the Virginia legislature in 1779 because he believed that the state had a responsibility to educate a citizenry that could fulfill its responsibilities to a democratic society. His basic proposal provided for three years of elementary education in reading, writing, arithmetic, and history to all white children in Virginia. How far have we come since then?

One major dimension of change is the perception of education as a right and not just a privilege available to a wealthy few. Secondary and postsecondary education are viewed as reasonable expectations for the majority of U.S. citizens. The result is a heterogeneous school population undreamed of a century ago.

In addition to meeting the academic, emotional, physical, and career needs of an extraordinarily broad range of students, schools are expected to meet a host of other demands. Schools are viewed as a copartner of the family in providing training in life skills; indeed, at times the schools seem to have a greater responsibility than the fam-

ily in meeting the needs of students in this area. The schools are called upon to instill desirable attitudes and values in all students.

Sensitive "moral" responsibilities are increasingly delegated to the schools. When students have trouble academically or socially, schools are supposed to provide counseling and/or crisis intervention or some new program to meet the special needs that have arisen. Schools are expected both to discipline and to encourage students. Clearly, no faculty of teachers trained only in reading, writing, arithmetic, and history could begin to cope adequately with all these responsibilities!

Even supposing schools ever really did teach average children typical things in usual ways, that is no longer the case. As more mothers become "working mothers," reliable, quality child care is a high-priority concern for schools. More attention is being directed to four-year-old school programs and to before-school and after-school care and activities for elementary school children. At the other end of the spectrum, secondary schools are expanding their existing adult education and equivalency programs by forming teams or partnerships with community and four-year colleges to ensure a smoother, more successful continuum in the educational experiences of their students.

Public schools have endeavored to meet the needs of many and, at the same time, serve as the agents of the larger society. By attempting to minimize ethnic, religious, and socioeconomic differences, the school is the "emancipator of the child from the family" (Coleman & Hoffer, 1987). Private schools have traditionally been established to preserve the values, culture, and religion of specific communities. They are extensions of functional and value communities and, as such, act *in loco parentis*. The "intergenerational closure" that private schools can provide is highly valued by their clients (Coleman & Hoffer, 1987).

The Bureau of the Census shows that in 1983 approximately 10 percent of secondary school students aged fourteen to seventeen were enrolled in private schools, elementary enrollment in private schools was nearly triple the number in private secondary schools, and one fifth of all kindergarten students aged three to five were enrolled in private schools (Grant & Snyder, 1986). What are some of the characteristics of private schools that attract such a substantial number of families away from the public schools?

Financial constraints usually result in private schools being smaller, with less diversified programs. The positive aspect to restricted size is increased student–teacher interaction brought about by smaller classes and more intense participation in extracurricular activities by both students and teachers.

Increased student achievement is often cited as the reason for choosing a private school. Data show that among the private schools, Catholic schools show evidence of greater achievement growth in verbal skills and mathematics, compared to public schools, but they show no evidence of greater growth in science knowledge or civics. Other private schools have demonstrated effectiveness only in verbal skills equal to that of the Catholic schools (Coleman & Hoffer, 1987).

In matters of discipline, Catholic schools are notable for their highly effective implementation of rules and standards. Their attendance patterns are extremely good, and student involvement in school activities grows during the high school years (Coleman, Hoffer, & Kilgore, 1982).

Private schools, especially Catholic schools, are not necessarily racially, culturally, or socioeconomically homogeneous. They do represent, however, a community of common values: a functional community. This commonality may result in increased parental involvement and in increased parental support of the principal. Highly effective principals have an "implicit or explicit" philosophy of education that includes an image of what it means to be educated; this image is "consistent with the values of the larger public served by the school" (Austin & Garber, 1985). Together, public and private schools strive to meet the challenges facing education today.

Schools today must attend to a multitude of concerns, but they can still be, and indisputably are, effective. There is a growing sense of what it means for schools to function as viable organizational units, independent but not isolated from the contexts in which they exist. As Purkey and Smith contend, "an academically effective school is distinguished by its culture: a structure, process, and climate of values and norms that emphasize successful teaching and learning" (1983, p. 442).

At the elementary level, these schools are characterized by their freedom from disciplinary problems and vandalism. Teachers communicate the expectation that all students can achieve. Schools emphasize basic skills instruction and provide for high levels of student time-on-task. Instructional objectives are clear and students' progress is monitored. The school principal is a strong programmatic leader "who sets school goals, maintains student discipline, frequently observes classrooms, and creates incentives for learning" (Bossert, 1985, p. 39).

Research at the secondary level produces only a slightly different image. Effective secondary schools are managed by principals who have the authority and power to take action in response to problems. These people play important roles in articulating school philosophy and curriculum, setting goals, and supporting staff. There may be some schoolwide staff development, and parental involvement is evident. Academic success is prized, and time for learning is maximized. Collaboration and collegiality are the rule, not the exception. Goals are clear; expectations are high. And there is support for the school at the district level (Corcoran, 1985).

What lies ahead for schools, both public and private, whether effective or ineffective? Will the state eventually provide cradle-to-grave care and education for its citizens? Should it do so? With the projected shortage of teachers in the 1990s, is the video classroom going to be a viable alternative? How far will the responsibility and influence of the schools eventually extend in the teaching and counseling of our society's children? Is it possible for schools to provide everything that society expects?

Practice Activity 1-3

A view of the first hour of the day at a large metropolitan high school as seen by a visitor:

8:15 A.M.   I wait patiently behind a line of student cars to pull into the parking lot at Midmont High School. Once parked, I ask one of the students why so many of them drive instead of taking the school bus. His response is courteous but hurried. His name is Greg and he says many of the students stay after school for athletic practices and games, club activities, and makeup tests, or to get extra help on material they don't understand; others leave early to earn credits in a cooperative work-study program. The few buses the school runs for activities just aren't very convenient. He rushes off to arrive at his homeroom class before the last bell: He has already been tardy once; another tardy and he will have to serve a detention after school.

8:19 A.M.   Students are disappearing from the halls into their homeroom classes as I go to check in at the principal's office. One couple remains in the hall, holding hands and exchanging a long final kiss as the last bell rings. The girl slips into the nearby classroom and the boy sprints down the hall to his homeroom and sneaks in. I wonder whether he has been noticed by his teacher.

8:22 A.M.   The principal welcomes me and apologizes for any time I might have had to wait for him. He has been in conference with a student and her parents. The student had been suspended for fighting with another girl and then cursing at the teacher who intervened. To be readmitted, she had to come to school with her parents after the two-day suspension. As the parents leave, I notice the mother looking worriedly at her watch.

8:25 A.M.   With my visitor's pass in hand, I begin to walk around the school building. A student, Gayle, who is assigned as an office runner first period, accompanies me. It is the middle of the homeroom period. Gayle explains that home room has been extended today to allow enough time for teachers to collect materials the students are turning in with next year's selection of classes. We pass a home room and peek inside: The teacher seems to be counseling a student who has a problem in his schedule; that settled, he takes attendance and sends a student to the office with the absentee list. During the last minutes of the home room the P.A. system has been on with the daily announcements: That day's baseball game has been rescheduled because of rain; students who sold candy to raise money for the prom should turn in their money and receipts to Mrs. Blake before noon; prom tickets will be on sale during lunch at $12 a pair; the French Club will meet after school to finalize its plans for the club's contribution to the International Dinner; students needing a work permit for a summer job should report to the office during lunch . . . I look around the room and notice that several students are chatting quietly; five are busy doing homework and the rest are listening absentmindedly to the announcements. The bell rings. As the students leave and others enter, the teacher talks to many of them, asking specific questions about yesterday's biology test or a missed homework assignment or commenting on a new haircut. As the students arrive, they sit down and begin working on the geometry problem the teacher wrote on the board before school.

8:37 A.M.   Students are in the halls on their way to their first-period classes. A teacher with a cart loaded with books bumps into me and apologizes; she "floats" from classroom to classroom and is in a hurry to get to her class before the tardy bell for the students!

8:42 A.M.   Gayle shows me the classroom of her favorite English teacher, Mrs. Hornberger. The students are acting out, in their own words and then in the real text, several of the important scenes from *Romeo and Juliet*. After a brief discussion of some of the words the students didn't understand, Mrs. Hornberger asks them to tell whether they have seen a similar scene in a TV show. As we leave, she is pulling together the students' comments into an introduction for the film version of *Romeo and Juliet* that they are going to watch in class on TV.

8:50 A.M.   Gayle takes me to Ms. Shear's American history class. She is lecturing on the causes of the Civil War; the students are listening and taking notes. In a corner of the room, a Vietnamese student is working on a reading assignment in the textbook; she is being helped by another student. The conversation is partly in English, partly in French. When I ask the student about this, she tells me she is a student aide in the history class; she has been assigned as a special tutor for this student because she is also an advanced French student and can communicate with the Vietnamese girl who is in the transition phase of learning English.

9:00 A.M.   Out in the hall again, an assistant principal passes us in great haste and turns into a classroom at the end of the hall. As we pass the room, we can hear him complimenting the students on their behavior while no one was with them; he will stay with the class until the substitute arrives.

9:03 A.M.   Gayle takes me into the guidance office. I notice a number of students going into a conference room with a counselor. They close the door. When I ask about the group, the secretary tells me that it is a crisis counseling group. A student at Midmont was killed in a car accident the week before and the students who were her closest friends are in the group. She explains further that they don't often have to do this kind of counseling, but the counselor did take a special training class after another student had died of cancer the year before.

9:10 A.M.   Gayle and I return to the hallway to walk toward the wing of the building with the science laboratories when I notice a very young student entering the attendance office to check in because she has arrived late. She is noticeably pregnant and wears a T-shirt that says "Baby." We continue toward the science wing.

9:13 A.M.   We pass a general science classroom and stop to listen. The teacher is assigning book reports.

9:14 A.M.   We arrive at the chemistry laboratory. Mr. Chapnik has the students working at several stations, preparing to begin an experiment. As I get closer, I can see that they are working at portable computers; the program is a simulation of the experiment they are to conduct the next day in class.

9:20 A.M.   The fire alarm sounds! Students and teachers pour out of their classrooms and disappear quickly through various exits. I follow. Gayle wonders aloud whether there is a real fire because they don't usually do drills in the rain . . .

9:22 A.M.   It is just a drill. The all-clear bell sounds and the students return to their classes more slowly than they exited.

9:25 A.M.   I return to Mr. Chapnik's class with the students. Gayle tells me how to find my way back to the office and then leaves to collect her books and check in there herself before the end of the period. Mr. Chapnik looks discouraged at not being able to finish the preparation for the lab the next day. Since the experiment will take the whole period to complete, he postpones it for a day, telling the students they will finish the preparation tomorrow.

9:30 A.M.   As I return to the office, I run into Greg, the student in the parking lot. He introduces me to the man he is talking with, Mr. Benson, his tennis coach.

9:35 A.M. Mr. Benson has been telling me about his teaching assignment at Midmont High School. He received a degree in mathematics last summer and began teaching this year. Despite some discouragement with his teaching assignment, three classes of basic math and one class each of trigonometry and calculus, he speaks enthusiastically of his students and some of his successes with them. At the sound of the bell, he hurries off to his duty station as a hall monitor during the upcoming period.

9:40 A.M. I return to the office to thank the principal for his hospitality and say goodbye, but he is not in. He has been called to a hearing at juvenile court regarding a student at Midmont. I say goodbye to the secretary and leave the building. The sun has come out.

Study Questions 1-3

1. What do you think the philosophy of Midmont High School is? What specifically reflects this philosophy?
2. Do you feel that Midmont High School is likely to be an effective school? Why, or why not?
3. Which teachers do you think might be most effective? Why?
4. What are the strengths and weaknesses that you see in Midmont High School?
5. What impression do you get about the role of the principal in Midmont High?
6. Would you like to teach in this school? Why or why not?
7. Are the activities cited appropriate components of a school program? Which are or are not, and why?

References

Austin, G. R., & Garber, H. (Eds.) (1985). *Research on exemplary schools.* New York: Academic Press.

Bernal, E. M. (1974). Gifted Mexican American children: An ethnoscientific perspective. *California Journal of Educational Research, 25,* 261–73.

Bossert, S. T. (1985, May). Effective elementary schools. In R.M.J. Kyle (Ed.) *Reaching for excellence: An effective schools sourcebook* (pp. 39–53). Washington, D.C.: U.S. Government Printing Office.

Boyer, E. (1983). The high-risk student. *High school* (pp. 239–48). New York: Harper & Row.

Coleman, J. S. & Hoffer, T. (1987). *Public and private high schools: The impact of communities.* New York: Basic Books.

Coleman, J. S., Hoffer, T., & Kilgore, S. (1982). *High school achievement: Public, Catholic, and private schools compared.* New York: Basic Books.

Corcoran, T. B. (1985, May). Effective secondary schools. In R.M.J. Kyle (Ed.) *Reaching for excellence: An effective schools sourcebook* (71–97). Washington, D.C.: U.S. Government Printing Office.

Feistritzer, E. (1986). *Profile of teachers in the U.S.* Washington, D.C.: The National Center for Education Information.

Fisher, B. (Ed.) (1986–87). Students. *Today's Education, 5*(1), 22–27.

Futrell, M. H. (1986, April). It's a tragedy we cannot afford. *USA Today, 29*, p. 8-A.

Gage, N. L., & Berliner, D. C. (1984). Individual differences and the need for special education. *Educational Psychology* (3rd ed.) (pp. 240–42). Boston: Houghton Mifflin.

Grant, V., & Snyder, T. D. (1986). *Digest of education statistics 1985–86.* Washington, D.C.: U.S. Government Printing Office.

Hollifield, J. (1986, March). Educationally disadvantaged soon to become a majority of public school students. *R & D Preview, 1*(1), 2–5.

Hunt, D. E. (1987). *Beginning with ourselves: In practice, theory, and human affairs.* Cambridge, Mass.: Brookline Books; and Toronto: Ontario Institute for Studies in Education Press.

Kottcamp, R., Provenzo, E., Jr., & Cohn, M. (1986, April). Stability and change in a profession: Two decades of teacher attitudes, 1964–1984. *Phi Delta Kappan,* 559–67.

Lortie, D. (1986, April). Teacher status in Dade County: A case of structural strain? *Phi Delta Kappan, 67,* 568–75.

Marland, S. P. (1972). Education of the gifted and talented. *Report to the Congress of the United States by the U.S. Commissioner of Education.* Washington, D.C.: U.S. Government Printing Office.

National Commission on Excellence in Education (1983). *A nation at risk: The imperative for educational reform.* Washington, D.C.: U.S. Government Printing Office.

National Education Association (1986). *Estimates of school statistics, 1985–86.* Washington, D.C.: National Education Association.

National Governors' Association Center for Policy Research and Analysis. (1986, August). *Time for results: The governors' 1991 report on education.* Washington, D.C.: The National Governors' Association.

Plisko, V., & Stern, J. (Eds.). *The condition of education.* Washington, D.C.: U.S. Government Printing Office.

Purkey, S. C., & Smith, M. C. (1983, March). Effective schools: A review. *Elementary School Journal, 83*(4), 427–52.

Robinson, V. (1985). *Making do in the classroom: A report on the misassignment of teachers.* Washington, D.C.: Council for Basic Education and American Federation of Teachers.

Rodman, B. (1987, June 17). In Minnesota experiment committee of teachers replaces principal. *Education Week, 6*(38), 1 and 13.

Shanker, A. (1985). Statement by Albert Shanker. In Robinson, V. *Making do in the classroom: A report on the misassignment of teachers.* Washington, D.C.: Council for Basic Education and American Federation of Teachers.

Strother, D. B. (1986, December). Dropping out. *Phi Delta Kappan, 68*(4), 325–28.

Tugend, A. (1986, September). Youth issues rise in prominence on national agenda. *Education Week, 6*(2), 9–13.

U.S. Department of Education. (1986). *Eighth annual report to Congress on the implementation of the Education of the Handicapped Act, 1.* Washington, D.C.

Waller, W. (1932). *The sociology of teaching.* New York: Russell & Russell.

Wise, A., Darling-Hammond, L., McLaughlin, M., & Bernstein, H. (1984, June). *Teacher evaluation: A study of effective practices.* Santa Monica, Calif.: Rand.

Chapter Two

Planning

Robert McNergney
University of Virginia

Definition

The competent teacher knows the importance of deliberate and varied planning activities. Instructional planning should reflect the teacher's knowledge that (1) learning activities should match the instructional objectives, (2) learning is facilitated when ideas are communicated in more ways than one, (3) the current literature on the teaching profession should be consulted regularly, and (4) learners' scores on standardized tests contain important and useful information about the class as a group and about individual learners.

Purpose

The purpose of this chapter is to assist you in performing a number of activities typically associated with effective instructional planning. The material that follows encourages you to use test data—in particular standardized test data—to help define instructional objectives and to formulate strategies for teaching. It suggests how you might begin to identify relevant professional literature as you define objectives and how you might choose learning activities, content, or materials that are appropriate for your students. This section also addresses problems of defining objectives of instruction in measurable terms, of using information about test reliability, validity, and test norms, and of using different modes of delivery to reach learners with different needs and abilities.

Background Knowledge

Never mind what is said about the plans of mice and men; if you are a teacher, you are a lot better off with plans than without them. Educational theorists and practitioners have long recognized that the ability to plan, to make decisions that will shape the course of instruction, is an important part of teaching (Morrison, 1926; Tyler, 1950; Jackson, 1966; Eisner, 1967). Many teacher education courses and textbooks are devoted, at least in part, to developing teachers' abilities to plan, and research on planning has received increased attention in recent years.

No doubt when you assumed your first job you were given a plan book and encouraged to forecast your instruction well in advance. Some school divisions require teachers to plan for a period of weeks or months using such a book. The importance of the book is not in its form but in the idea behind it: Planning helps you organize instruction, keep records of events, and guide others who might observe your teaching or take over in your absence.

Teachers' plans can and do take many forms. Some are elaborate scripts, detailing what is to be done, by whom, when, and under what conditions. In contrast, others are cryptic scrawls closely resembling shopping lists—reminders of key ideas and events in teaching. Regardless of length and detail, the basic components of plans include goals or purposes, some sense of the needs of students in relation to these goals, procedures for moving students toward the goals, and some provision for deciding whether or not instruction was successful (Morine–Dershimer, 1977). Plans are no more and no less than indications of teachers' thinking about what is supposed to occur in classrooms.

As research and practice suggest, teachers are concerned about a variety of things when making instructional planning decisions. Researchers have been interested in trying to determine at what point teachers actually begin the process of planning and how much time and effort they spend on different kinds of planning decisions. Although studies of planning have yielded somewhat variable results, there are commonalities among the problems teachers face when planning instruction. As one might expect, early in their careers teachers are concerned about maintaining order in the classroom (Fuller, 1969). This concern may be reflected in plans by teachers' efforts to reduce their own uncertainty and anxiety (Yinger, 1978). McCutcheon (1980) concluded that one of the important functions of planning—beyond serving as a means of organizing instruction—is the sense of security and direction it provides teachers. (Remember this when you are inside on a beautiful Sunday planning for the upcoming week!)

As teachers gain experience, they become more concerned about the needs of students. Indeed, Taylor (1970) concluded that while teachers' approaches to planning vary widely, they seem to be concerned first about students, second about subject matter, third about goals, and finally about methods of teaching. Bloom's (1976) work suggests that learning is so heavily dependent on the abilities of children—both cognitive and affective—that diagnostic skills are among the most important for teachers to master. By knowing what students can reasonably be expected to accomplish and what is likely to interest and challenge them, a teacher will be able to plan in-class activities and seatwork or homework assignments that will truly encourage learning.

In one planning study, Zahorik (1970) found that the kind of planning decision that teachers made first was concerned with the selection of content, and the one made most often involved the selection of learning activities. Teachers in the Zahorik study were by comparison only quite minimally concerned with the objectives of instruction.

Often teacher education programs do not emphasize the importance of various planning activities in quite the same way as do practicing teachers and researchers. The prescriptive models stressed in some teacher education programs are typically modeled after objectives-based approaches to teaching and curriculum development. Although these approaches can appear quite reasonable and logical, results of research do not seem to support their popularity among

teachers. As noted above, teachers are often concerned about maintaining order, selecting content, and helping individual students.

Identifying Goals and Objectives

It is often tempting for teachers to create their own objectives and curriculum or to pick and choose parts of textbooks while ignoring other sections altogether. If you are a beginning teacher and you find yourself succumbing to this temptation, *don't*. As a beginner, don't take sole responsibility for deciding what should be taught and what should be neglected. When you do, you may well fail to help students attain important outcomes. The responsibility for deciding what should be taught belongs to curriculum committees and to school administrators. Beginning teachers should rely heavily on local and state curriculum guides and on textbooks for direction. Once you get your feet on the ground, there will be plenty of time for stretching and enriching your curricular and instructional decisions.

Of course you have a professional responsibility to take advantage of opportunities to teach your students about ideas and events that arise naturally every day and are not part of the standard curriculum. But you also have a responsibility to provide students with opportunities to master material that presumably has been selected with some care and reflects the values of the school and community.

Practice Activity 2-1

Did you know that many states are developing and refining curricular standards for all subjects taught in the public schools? In Virginia, for instance, these are called the Standards of Learning, or SOLs for short. Here is what S. John Davis, Superintendent of Public Instruction in Virginia, says about the Standards of Learning:

> The Standards of Learning Program is designed to identify what students are expected to accomplish, to provide a method for determining what has been learned, and to encourage teachers to give additional instruction when needed. It is not intended to reduce the total school program to a single list of objectives or to replace the curriculum that a school division already may have developed for its students. The staff in school divisions which already have such programs will need to examine them to ensure that the Standards of Learning Objectives are included (1983, p. 11).

Do you know whether your state has such standards? If not, go immediately to your nearest curriculum coordinator or administrative office and find out. As you read, ask yourself (and others in your building) how the standards are being used to guide instruction in your school district.

Don't be misled, objectives are important. If you don't know where students are supposed to go, how will you know whether and when they have arrived? You may recall from your own teacher education program that you spent considerable time studying the concept of instructional objectives, or behavioral instructional objectives (Mager, 1962). You probably also remember that some objectives are measurable—reasonably precise and possible to appraise somewhat objectively—and others are not. If you can state your objectives in unambiguous language, you have gone a long way toward making it possible to assess your instruction. At the same time, an objective that is measurable is not automatically worthwhile. Critics of the use (that is, the overuse) of behavioral objectives have rightly noted that efforts to make objective and quantify *all* learning can lead to trivialization. But as you move toward greater precision in planning and communicating your expectations for student performance, you will begin to realize how to identify appropriate objectives for learners.

Practice Activity 2-2

Which of the following objectives do you think might be measurable? If it is not measurable, do you know why?

1. Students will listen to a recording of Robert Frost's poetry and develop an appreciation for his work.
2. Given a crossword puzzle, each student will complete it within twenty minutes.
3. After the demonstration on electromagnets, the students will write a paper of at least one page in length in which they describe the three principal components of magnetism.
4. In a whole group discussion on drug abuse each student will be called upon at least twice to share his or her thoughts.
5. The teacher will read a story about a Native American tribe and students will learn about religious customs in their culture.
6. After the students have seen the film *People of the Northland*, they will analyze the factors associated with living in a polar environment.

Responses to Practice Activity 2-2

1. This objective may be desirable, but how the teacher might measure "appreciation" is unclear.
2. This objective is measurable. It is possible to determine whether each student has completed the puzzle within twenty minutes.
3. The criteria for success are clear: one page, three principles. This one is measurable.
4. This one is measurable but not necessarily worthwhile.
5. The phrase "will learn" is unclear; therefore, the objective is unmeasurable in this form.
6. The phrase "will analyze the factors" is fuzzy and thus the objective is not measurable.

Despite considerable latitude, teachers are not often left free to plan instruction in isolation from the social system in which they and their students operate. As Chapter 1 suggests, contextual factors dictate to a large extent how and why teachers plan as they do. It is fairly obvious that if you are in a departmentalized system, you can't plan an all-day field trip with your class without first consulting teachers of other classes that might be affected by your absence. It is somewhat less obvious, but certainly no less important to recognize, that a teacher who tries to teach concepts that have already been addressed by colleagues and mastered by students may well be wasting valuable instructional time. The teacher who relies heavily on his or her texts and on local curricular guidelines and policies will be in a professionally sound, defensible position.

Identifying Students' Needs

To the casual observer it may seem that teachers often neglect the information they have about students and about curriculum in their planning. But as Borko and her colleagues (1979) suggest, teachers can and do use information relevant to teaching and learning as they plan instruction for their students. From a series of studies on teachers' planning decisions, they found that teachers will estimate students' abilities when given some cues about learning needs, they will revise their readings of students when provided additional information, and their assessments of students' abilities will figure prominently in the decisions they make while planning instruction. The decisions teachers make may depend on different kinds of information relevant to the tasks to be accomplished.

Practice Activity 2-3

Let's examine some of the information about students that you might have at your disposal and see if you can interpret it. Table 2–1 contains information about children's scores on the Metropolitan Readiness Test, a test often given to kindergarten children. We'll use this table in some of our discussion. (Even if you happen to be a high school social studies teacher, you may want to try your hand at these activities. The concepts discussed are relevant to standardized testing regardless of grade level.)

1. Assume for a moment that you are a kindergarten teacher who has administered the Metropolitan Readiness Test and has recently received the results of scoring. Given your Class Record (Table 2–1), you must now decide how to interpret and use the information to make some instructional planning decisions. The following questions (and responses in the section below) have been adapted from the *Teacher's Manual for the Metropolitan Readiness Test* (Nurss & McGauvran, 1976):
   a. Who are the three slowest students in the class?
   b. How might these test scores be used to help you plan instruction for the group, and why do you think certain students receive the kinds of scores they do?

Table 2–1 *Class Record of Metropolitan Readiness Test Scores*[*]

Name	Auditory			Visual			Language				Pre-reading Skills Composite			Sex	Age Yrs.	Mths.
	1	2	3	4	T	Sta.	5	6	T	Sta.	Raw	%	Sta.			
1. Aileen W.	6^A	6^L	8^A	10^A	18	4^A	11^A	7^A	18	4^A	48	30	4^A	G	5	4
2. Nathaniel T.	10^A	13^H	11^H	13^A	24	7^H	14^H	11^H	25	9^H	72	95	8^H	B	5	9
3. Matthew S.	4^L	2^L	3^L	6^L	9	2^L	1^L	1^L	2	1^L	21	3	1^L	B	5	1
4. Lucas R.	8^A	5^H	11^H	10^A	21	5^A	13^A	10^H	23	7^H	57	48	5^A	B	5	9
5. Bernadette P.	4^L	10^A	10^A	12^A	22	6^A	14^H	8^A	22	6^A	58	51	5^A	G	5	3
6. Kyle N.	12^H	12^H	10^A	13^A	23	6^A	14^H	10^H	24	8^H	70	88	7^H	B	5	6
7. Cecile M.	10^A	11^A	11^H	14^H	25	$8\text{-}9^H$	13^A	11^H	24	8^H	70	88	7^H	G	5	5
8. Clarice M.	11^H	13^H	11^H	13^A	24	7^H	14^H	11^H	25	9^H	73	97	9^H	G	5	6
9. Jason L.	7^A	10^A	11^H	13^A	24	7^H	13^A	9^A	22	6^A	66	76	6^A	B	5	7
10. Frank K.	4^L	10^A	11^H	5^L	16	4^A	10^A	5^L	15	3^L	45	24	4^A	B	5	1
11. Dustin K.	7^A	7^A	6^A	3^L	9	2^L	10^A	4^L	14	3^L	37	13	3^L	B	5	6
12. Erica J.	3^L	7^A	5^A	10^A	15	4^A	9^L	6^A	15	3^L	45	24	4^A	G	5	7
13. Gabrielle H.	10^A	9^A	10^A	10^A	20	5^A	14^H	9^A	23	7^H	62	63	6^A	G	6	4
14. Helena G.	2^L	4^L	4^L	1^L	5	1^L	8^L	2^L	10	2^L	21	3	1^L	G	4	11
15. Irene F.	4^L	8^A	10^A	10^A	20	5^A	13^A	9^A	22	6^A	61	60	6^A	G	5	8
16. Cameron D.	7^A	11^A	11^H	14^H	25	$8\text{-}9^H$	13^A	10^H	23	7^H	66	76	6^A	B	5	7
17. Jessica D.	8^A	5^L	7^A	12^A	19	5^A	10^A	5^L	15	3^L	47	28	4^A	G	5	3
18. Brandon C.	8^A	9^A	11^H	14^H	25	$8\text{-}9^H$	14^H	9^A	23	7^H	63	66	6^A	B	5	3
19. Lauren B.	6^A	12^H	5^A	7^L	12	3^L	10^A	7^A	17	4^A	47	28	4^A	G	5	8
20. Adrian B.	6^A	13^H	10^A	12^A	22	6^A	15^H	10^H	25	9^H	66	76	6^A	B	5	5

[*]The letters "L," "A," and "H" represent ranges of stanines. L (low)=1-3. A (average)=4-6. H (high)=7-9.

c. Identify those students who may be ready to begin a reading program, that is, those students who have Pre-reading Skills Composite stanines and Visual and Language Skill Area stanines in the 7–9 range.

d. Identify those students who will need special attention for the purpose of trying to determine why they received low scores.

e. Which children should be able to begin communicating ideas by dictating words, phrases, or sentences?

f. What is a median?

2. Now let's turn our attention to a different set of test scores: those for one student, Jane Doe, on the SRA Achievement Series. (See Tables 2–2 and 2–3.) When Jane took this test she was in the eleventh grade in Smith's classroom in Horace Mann High School in the Acme County Schools. At the left of Table 2–2 are the names of the tests administered and the scores Jane earned on each. At the right is the national percentile ranking and its range plotted for each test.

Reading across the first horizontal line, Total Reading, you can see that Jane received a score or growth skill value (GSV) of 466. Her grade equivalent (G-E) is 12–9. This put her in the seventy-ninth national percentile (NPCT) and the seventh national stanine (NSTN). Jane's "true score" (as depicted in the columns at the right) fell somewhere between about the seventy-first and eighty-ninth percentiles on the national sample of students who took the test.

Assume for a moment you are planning a "career day" for students when college and business representatives will visit your classes. Before you encourage Jane to visit with a college representative, you have invited Jane's parents to see you to discuss her progress in school. They are concerned parents who want Jane to do her best so she might go to college on a scholarship. They have several questions about these test results and about Jane's overall progress. Try to answer their questions as best you can, then check your responses against those provided below. If you can't respond reasonably, you would be wise to seek additional information on standardized testing. *Remember:* Some of the best information you can find is available in the test manuals that accompany standardized tests.

a. "My Jane has always liked to read. I guess her trips to the library have paid off. Is it true that she really reads better than 79 percent of the other eleventh-graders in the nation?"

b. "I'm a little confused about this 12–9 grade equivalent. That can't mean Jane reads as well as a graduating senior, can it?"

c. "Other teachers have tried to explain to me what a stanine is, but I can't remember. Would you please refresh me?"

Table 2-2 *SRA Results*

Student Name: Doe, Jane
Date of Birth: 01/25/67
Grade: 11
Sex: F

Division: Acme County Schools
School: Horace Mann
Classroom: Smith
Test SRA Form 1/H—1978 Edition
Date of Test: March 1984

Test Title	GSV	G-E	NPCT	NSTM	Performance Profile Based on National Percentile
					50 60 70 80 90 95 99
Total Reading	466	12-9	79	7	----X----- (≈80)
Total Mathematics	577	12-9	92	8	-----X---- (≈92)
Total Language	569	12-9	99	9	----X (≈99)
Composite (R/M/L)	671	12-9	96	9	----X---- (≈96)
Reference Materials	478	12-9	70	6	-----X----- (≈70)
Social Studies	517	12-9	76	6	-----X----- (≈76)
Science	442	12-9	73	6	----X----- (≈73)
Survey Applied Skills	510	12-9	83	7	-----X---- (≈83)

	GSV	NPCT	NSTM	
Educ. Ability Series	583	80	7	----X---- (≈80)

Table 2–3 *SRA Skill Test Results*

Skill Title	National Average	Below	Obtained Aver.	Above
Reading Vocabulary	29.2/40		36	
—Literal Meanings	25.2/35		32	
—Nonliteral Meanings	4.0/ 5		4	
Reading Comprehension	35.0/50		42	
—Grasping Details	9.0/13		9	
—Summarizing	3.2/ 5		3	
—Perceiving Relationship	7.7/12		10	
—Drawing Conclusions	11.8/16			16
—Understanding Author	3.2/ 4		4	

d. "I can see Jane's score of 36 on vocabulary [Table 2–3] is in the average range, but what does that national average of 29.2/40 mean?"

Responses to Practice Activity 2-3

1. a. *Be careful:* You must resist labeling students on the basis of these test scores. The scores should alert you to the possible need for collecting more precise diagnostic information on particular students. Impressions of students based on these test scores can be misleading because the scores are subject to error. Students' performances can be influenced by a variety of factors. Generally, the Standard Error of Measurement for this test is about one stanine. This means that if a student has a stanine of 3, his or her "true" stanine falls somewhere in the range of 2 to 4 (or one stanine above the reported stanine and one below). Remember, a stanine is a translation of a raw score into a single-digit standard score having a range of 1 to 9, with 5 always representing the average performance of a group of students.

b. The test scores may help the teacher plan instruction by providing some indication of the extent to which students have acquired the skills measured by the test, by suggesting what skills students need to develop, and by making evident some instructional objectives that need to be modified. Students may score as they do for a variety of reasons beyond differences in abilities. For example, they may not have had opportunities to develop skills measured by the test. For some, English may not be their first language. Others may have certain learning disabilities. Still others may not have put forth their best efforts when taking the tests.

c. The students who may be ready to begin a reading program—based on their visual, language, and prereading skills composite stanines—are Nathaniel, Cecile, and Clarice. Kyle may also be considered, but his visual stanine was only in the average range. Once again, be careful in the use of these test scores to make such an instructional decision. If you were to identify the three or four students above and place them in a beginning reading program, while having other students do "prereading activities," you might discover at the end of the year, not surprisingly, that those who had been instructed could read and those who were not identified as ready, and thus were not taught, could not read. This could mean that the test is a good predictor, but it could also mean that because a teacher expects less from some students, they deliver less. You can protect against such possible negative effects by recognizing that testing can influence a teacher's expectations and thus his or her teaching behavior, and by assessing students periodically using a variety of devices.

d. The students who will need special attention in order to determine why they received low scores are Matthew, Dustin, and Helena.

Remember, low scores may indicate that students did not understand the task. If a student scores below 22, his or her abilities have not been adequately measured by the test. Low scores may also indicate a general lack of maturity. In this particular case, two of the three children are the youngest in the class.

e. The high language group—Nathaniel, Lucas, Kyle, Cecile, Clarice, Gabrielle, Cameron, Brandon, and Adrian—should be able to handle these activities.

f. The median is the point below which 50 percent of the scores fall.

2. a. "Well, Mr. and Mrs. Doe, that is not quite what the seventy-ninth percentile means, but you aren't far off the mark. As you can see at the right of Table 2–2, Jane's

score, designated by the *X*, falls within a range from about the seventy-first percentile to the eighty-ninth. This means her true score could fall anywhere in that range. The seventy-ninth percentile is the point below which 79 percent of the scores fall. You should also remember that not all eleventh-graders in the nation took this test. Jane is compared only with those who did."

b. "I can understand why you might be confused about grade-equivalent scores. They are tricky and easily misinterpreted. Let me try to explain by using an example. If Jane received a score on a test that was equal to the median or average score of the eleventh-graders taking the test in September, she would be given a grade equivalent of 11.0. If her score were equal to the median score of all twelfth-graders, she would be given a grade equivalent of 12.0. Because most school years consist of ten months, any score in between is expressed in terms of decimals; that is, 11.1 would refer to average performance of eleventh-graders in October.

"Just because Jane got a 12–9 (or 12.9) does not mean she reads as well as a graduating senior. The 12–9 is an estimation of the total reading skills measured by this test. An eleventh-grader with a 12–9 grade equivalent does not necessarily read as well as a graduating senior."

c. "Stanines are standard scores with a mean of 5 and a range of 1 to 9. Jane's stanine of 7 puts her in what the test makers often refer to as the 'high range'—those students who fall in the seventh, eighth, or ninth stanines."

d. "That's correct. Jane's score of 36 on vocabulary skill test (Table 2–3) is in the average range. The national average of 29.2/40 means that the average performance on this skill test was 29.2 correct out of 40 items."

Formulating Teaching Procedures

A procedures section of a teacher's plan typically outlines when and how certain events will occur. A lesson plan for one class period may be quite specific in this regard. Indeed, one beginning high school teacher used to write every word he intended to say in class, noting when he should be at certain points in his script! Certainly a better strategy would be to use an outline or structured overview, much like those discussed in Chapter 10, "Clarity of Structure."

The procedures section of a plan contains a teacher's thoughts about moving students toward lesson objectives. Often teachers will include statements about materials to be used at each step of a lesson and about time allocation to various activities. Sometimes a separate

"materials subsection" will be included so that ideas about what will be needed to conduct a lesson will not be buried in the procedures section and easily overlooked.

It is important to remember when establishing procedures that there is often more than one way to teach the same or similar concepts. You may need to try several approaches in order for students to succeed. Note in Box 2–1 that the teacher has planned two activities, varying somewhat in the amount of time required for completion, to address the same multiplication concept. The first activity might be used with children who have demonstrated some facility with multiplication; the second could be used with those who have had some difficulty with that process.

Your planning can be governed by any number of philosophies about teaching and learning, but there are three, for want of a better term, "general approaches" that are quite prevalent. These dictate to a large extent how the teacher will communicate his or her expectations to students. In varying degrees, your plans will probably try to (1) remediate students' deficiencies, (2) compensate for deficiencies that students possess and are likely never to be remediated, or (3) capitalize on the kinds of things students prefer to do and do well (Solomon, 1972). There is little information about how teachers spend the majority of their time with respect to these approaches, yet many seem to believe that the most frequently used approach is

---

Box 2–1 *Sample Outline for Teaching a Single Concept Using Two Different Approaches*

Sample 1—Teaching the commutative law deductively.

1. Write "a x b = b x a" on the chalkboard. Explain that the letters stand for numerals. Substitute various numerals for the letters.

2. Ask students to supply other examples. Write their suggestions on board.

3. Distribute worksheet containing examples and nonexamples of the commutative law and have students work independently to identify the examples.

Sample 2—Teaching the commutative law inductively.

1. Give students large stacks of paper cups (at least 100 in a stack).

2. Have students make three stacks of four cups each and then tell you how much 3 x 4 equals. Using the same cups, have students make four stacks of three cups each and then tell you how much 4 x 3 equals.

3. Encourage students to make other such groupings and to write down the examples they find which have the same answer.

4. After some time to work, see if you can get one of the students in the group to tell the class what "rule" he or she has discovered.

---

to try to remediate deficiencies, to fix the things students don't do very well. As you teach, you will communicate much to students by the general approach that has governed your thoughts during planning.

If you are always planning and teaching to remediate students' deficiencies, for instance, you must be careful to do so with a sense of providing opportunities for success by emphasizing what students can do, rather than stressing what they have not yet mastered. In other words, you would probably be wise to turn your thinking about the procedures section of a plan toward ways of encouraging students to tackle new challenges for which they are prepared, hurdles that may at times be difficult but that are clearly within the grasp of people who have accomplished so much.

When Things Go Wrong

Successful experienced teachers (and beginners who worry a lot) realize that planning, as an attempt to make "things go well" in the classroom, is a way to avoid problems. There are numerous planning decisions that, if made appropriately, can decrease the likelihood of having to face problems of student uninvolvement or disruption during teaching. For example, if teachers, anticipating which learners can work cooperatively on certain tasks, select content and activities that are interesting and challenging, then learners are less likely to become uninvolved or to misbehave. Likewise, when teachers sequence material and activities in reasonably logical progression and forecast a pace of instruction intended to maintain momentum in a lesson, students' chances for behaving as they are "supposed to" are improved.

Practice Activity 2-4

Yinger (1978) suggests that planning involves three activities: discovering problems, designing strategies to address these problems, and implementing, evaluating, and routinizing plans. For a moment, let's use his model to examine one of your daily lesson plans that didn't exactly work out as you had hoped.

1. Think of any day's plans that failed. (Elementary school teachers might choose a reading or mathematics lesson, while high school teachers might select a lesson from their specialty area.)
2. Describe what you wanted to happen in your class (not what went wrong).
3. What materials did you rely on to guide this activity?
4. How much time did you spend thinking about the information you wanted to share with your students?
5. How specific was your plan or script for the lesson?
6. What outcomes did you expect students to achieve?
7. Once you decided what you wanted to happen in the lesson, how much time did you spend deciding how you were going to conduct the lesson?
8. Describe what happened when you implemented the plan.
9. What did you do when you sensed the plan was going awry? Why did you behave this way?
10. In retrospect, what might you have done differently during the class as things began to falter?
11. Did this experience affect your future planning activities? If so, how?

Yinger suggests teachers spend most of their time on problem solving or identification and less on other steps of planning. If you changed plans in midstream, you may have been smart or lucky. According to Yinger, most teachers tend to stick with flawed initial plans to the bitter end. Also worth considering: If you answered all or even most of the questions above, you probably spent more time evaluating the usefulness of your plans than is typical. Remember, as a seasoned teacher once said, "An ounce of prevention expended planning instruction may save a pound of your flesh during the course of a lesson."

Clearly there are pitfalls in planning instruction that successful teachers try to avoid. In one of the most frequently cited studies of teacher planning, Zahorik (1970) noted that teachers who planned instruction (versus those who did not) were less likely to use student ideas in the course of instruction. Gage and Berliner (1975) noted the dangers of rigid planning:

> Planning can make teachers too rigid, too concerned about following their plan, and correspondingly less open to students' ideas. Teachers should beware of trying to achieve what they have planned at the expense of what students can contribute to the learning situation. Especially in the activity of extension, as compared with initiation and encouragement, teachers who plan their lessons should try to remain open and sensitive to their students' ideas. . . . Teachers should plan not only the goals, experiences, and evaluations of their students, but also their own interactive behavior. They should consciously plan to open up their classes' discussions, reflect upon student comments, and expand their ideas (p. 673).

When teachers must help learners master difficult, complex concepts and principles, a quite specific, orderly plan might produce achievement of the objectives. If students tend to divert the class from the main objectives of teaching and learning, then fairly rigid planning might be all to the good. Teachers who don't plan might appear to be receptive to students' ideas, but this may be because they have too few ideas of their own (Gage & Berliner, 1975).

Evaluating the Success of Instruction and Planning

Chapter 15 is devoted exclusively to evaluating instruction, so it is unnecessary to dwell on the subject here. Instead, let's consider several points raised briefly at the outset.

First, if planning does not help you determine when students are moving forward, something is wrong. Your plans should specify outcomes for students. At least some of the actual outcomes should be related to objectives of instruction, and it is often helpful for them to be measurable. It may be impossible to emphasize too strongly, however, that successful instruction can and should be defined in various ways. Indeed, many desirable outcomes of instruction may be difficult to anticipate. For example, students who develop confidence in themselves because of experiences they have in schools can be said to have learned something worthwhile. You might not write an objective for developing student confidence or test for it, but when you help students succeed at any of a variety of tasks, confidence is a logical and desirable outcome of instruction, and thus, in turn, an indication of your success as a teacher.

Second, because planning involves making decisions about overall strategies of teaching, when planning is done well it should help you feel and be organized. Although some organizational benefits of planning are readily apparent from the beginning of your career in the classroom, you may not appreciate fully how important planning skills are until you teach for a second year. Despite the cynicism of jokes about dusting off the old plans for a new year, there is much to be said on the positive side for trying some approaches in the classroom a second and third time. Once you have immersed yourself in the curricula for which you are responsible, you are simply better prepared to make teaching decisions the second time around.

Third, your old plans should provide sufficient detail to serve as records of teaching that succeeded and failed. Only when plans serve the record-keeping function can they help you do a better job in the future.

Fourth, good plans make it possible for observers to give you feedback about your performance. When such feedback is related directly to what you were trying to do in the classroom, it can be an invaluable aid in your professional development. If your plans do not imply directions for observers, you may need to elaborate. Good plans also provide enough detail to help substitute teachers take over in your absence without losing precious instructional time. This does not necessarily mean anyone unfamiliar with your class should be able to read your plans and to do things exactly as you would do them. But your plans should provide sufficient information for important objectives to be addressed in your absence.

So how might a teacher, particularly a beginner, demonstrate some acceptable level of knowledge about planning instruction? Essentially, he or she must address those components of plans that are commonly recognized as part of the process (that is, learners' needs and abilities; objectives; and teaching procedures, such as learning activities, utilization of time and materials, and methods of evaluation). You must also be able to defend your decisions. In other words, it is not enough for professionals to say they are going to teach certain things in certain ways; when called upon to do so, they must also explain why.

How might a teacher explain why plans are constructed in various ways? You should turn to sources of information about learners and curricula that are relevant to your situation. This information may take many forms: learners' scores on standardized tests, observational data and informal assessment results on students' needs and abilities, curriculum guides for a school and/or district, state guidelines for the formulation of instructional objectives, scope and sequence charts for textbook series, reports made by counselors and clinicians, results of research and evaluation studies, and so forth. Decisions for planning instruction that are based on knowledge from such sources are the decisions that are professionally most defensible. To be sure, the quantity and quality of such information may vary greatly from one situation to another, but professionals seek and use what information exists until it is supplanted by newer, fresher, more relevant information upon which to base instruction.

How might you seek newer, fresher, more relevant information beyond those ways already discussed? Perhaps one of the more beneficial ways is to read the professional literature regularly. One of the important attributes of a profession is that it has a body of knowledge upon which to base decisions, and the profession of teaching is now beginning to amass such knowledge.

You are busy, often tired beyond belief, and already stretched to do more than seems humanly possible. There is more than a hint of truth, however, in the cliché that knowledge is power. Only when you command knowledge will you be empowered to make the kinds of decisions you, as a teacher, should make—decisions that others may wish to make for you.

It is beyond the scope of this book to instruct you in methods of exploring the knowledge base on teaching and learning. But there are some good books that will get you started and point you toward some people who should be able to help you. One book is *Applying Educational Research: A Practical Guide for Teachers*, by Walter R. Borg (Longman, 1981). This is not the one and only book, and perhaps it is not even the best. But it is an excellent guide for you to begin cutting through the persuasive (and sometimes not so persuasive) prose that seems to dominate discussion in education. The methods Borg suggests are intended to get you down to bedrock information and to enable you to do so without possessing a Ph.D. in educational research.

You might also seek out people in higher education for leads on good, solid professional information upon which to plan your teaching. You need not enter a graduate program to do so, although for some this would be a wise idea. Advanced degrees, of course, do not automatically lead to competence in interpreting or even locating the kinds of information teachers need to make informed decisions in classrooms. Short of degree work, you can talk with researchers and people who translate research results into practice, many of whom you can identify through professional education organizations.

Some school districts and teachers' organizations, too, offer professional assistance through teacher centers. Centers can be ideal places for exploring information about teaching and learning. Typically, they provide settings where teachers feel free to express themselves and to help one another address common problems.

References

Bloom, B. S. (1976). *Human characteristics and school learning.* New York: McGraw-Hill.

Borg, W. R. (1981). *Applying educational research: A practical guide for teachers.* New York: Longman.

Borko, H., Cone, R., Atwood R., & Shavelson, R. J. (1979). Teachers' decision making. In P. L. Peterson & H. J. Walberg (Eds.), *Research on teaching: Concepts, findings, and implications* (pp. 136–60). Berkeley, Calif.: McCutchan.

Davis, S. J. (1983). *Standards of learning objectives for Virginia public schools.* Richmond, Va.: State Department of Education.

Eisner, E. W. (1967). Educational objectives: Help or hindrance. *School Review, 75,* 250–66.

Fuller, F. F. (1969). Concerns of teachers: A developmental conceptualization. *American Educational Research Journal, 6,* 207–26.

Gage, N. L., & Berliner, D. C. (1975). *Educational psychology.* Chicago: Rand McNally College.

Jackson, P. W. (1966). *The way teaching is.* Washington, D.C.: Association for Supervision and Curriculum Development.

Mager, R. F. (1962). *Preparing objectives for programmed instruction.* San Francisco: Fearon.

McCutcheon, G. (1980). How do elementary school teachers plan their courses? *Elementary School Journal, 81,* 4–23.

Morine–Dershimer, G. (1977). Instructional planning. In J. M. Cooper (Ed.), *Classroom teaching skills: A handbook* (pp. 20–75). Lexington, Mass.: D. C. Heath.

Morrison, H. C. (1926). *The practice of teaching in the secondary school.* Chicago: University of Chicago Press.

Nurss, J. R., & McGauvran, M. E. (1976). *Teacher's manual for the Metropolitan Readiness Tests, Part II: Interpretation and use of test results.* New York: Harcourt Brace Jovanovich.

Solomon, G. (1972). Heuristic models for the generation of aptitude-treatment interaction hypotheses. *Review of Educational Research, 42,* 327–43.

Taylor, P. H. (1970). *How teachers plan their courses.* Slough, U.K.: National Foundation for Educational Research in England and Wales.

Tyler, R. W. (1950). *Basic principles of curriculum and instruction.* Chicago: University of Chicago Press.

Yinger, R. J. (1978). *A study of teacher planning: Description and a model of preactive decision making.* Michigan State University Institute for Research on Teaching. (ERIC Document Reproductive Services No. ED 160 605)

Zahorik, J. A. (1970). The effect of planning in teaching. *Elementary School Journal, 71,* 143–51.

Chapter Three

Reinforcement

Sandra B. Cohen and **Donna Hearn**
University of Virginia

Definition

The competent teacher demonstrates awareness that the skillful use of reinforcement is an effective means of encouraging and discouraging particular behaviors. Establishing the importance of reinforcement in modifying human behavior and clarifying principles that govern its use are two of the principal achievements of research in learning.

Purpose

The overall goal of this chapter is to assist a teacher in acquiring knowledge of reinforcement theory. The intended outcome of such knowledge is the demonstrated application of reinforcement theory to classroom teaching and a resultant increase in student social and academic achievement. Review of the chapter material and practice activities will encourage the teacher to (1) provide students with frequent positive, rather than negative, feedback, (2) emphasize desirable behaviors, (3) clarify behavioral expectations through positive feedback, and (4) decrease or eliminate the use of punishment as a management strategy. The information contained in the chapter will provide a basic level of knowledge. However, instructional competence will be achieved only through actual practice of the specified principles within the classroom setting.

Background Information

A good teacher, like a good parent, knows that reinforcement is among the most effective teaching techniques. Although most reinforcement theorists do not agree on the exact techniques that should be applied to any specific situation, there is general agreement among experts on the value of reinforcement as a learning and behavior management tool. A large number of reinforcement techniques have been developed, empirically tested, and proven effective. These include, among others, verbal praise, modeling, token economy, self-management, and shaping. Additional procedures specifically designed to decrease a behavior that is deemed undesirable include removal of reinforcers, response cost, and punishment (Brophy, 1983). In contrast to many techniques, punishment (that is, the application of an aversive stimulus to decrease an inappropriate behavior) is not advocated as an effective procedure for promoting behavioral changes in most children. A full discussion of these terms, examples of their use within the classroom, and practice activities follow.

Reinforcement

Reinforcement theory has been developing over the past century. A major focus on educational applications has occurred during the past

fifty years. Historically, E. L. Thorndike was among the first researchers to use reinforcement as a behavior modification technique and to include it within educational research (Craig, 1967). Thorndike (1905) postulated two laws of science that have had a strong influence on our understanding and use of reinforcement. The Law of Effect, which essentially defines reinforcement, states that "Any act which in a given situation produces satisfaction becomes associated with that situation, so that when the situation recurs that act is more likely than before to recur also" (p. 203). The Law of Exercise includes the assertion that a response becomes associated with the situation in which it was made. A psychologist named J. B. Watson, working in the 1920s, advocated that only those human behaviors that could be directly observed, and therefore measured, be used as the basis of study. Watson is credited for originating the term *behaviorism* now commonly used in reinforcement theory.

Subsequently, B. F. Skinner, who has become the patriarch of behavioral psychology, built upon the works of his predecessors and refined behaviorism into the technical body of knowledge we now employ (for example, Skinner 1953; 1971). Skinner pursued the notion that a stimulus induces a response (that is, S–R, or stimulus–response, theory) and elaborated on what was known about conditioning. Specifically, he said that a favorable response to a stimulus could be expected to reinforce or strengthen a particular behavior. For example, a teacher who consistently recognizes (provides attention to) only those children who raise their hands will increase the likelihood of hands being raised to gain attention.

Several key behavioral techniques will prove highly useful to teachers. Each of us is aware of the consequences of our behaviors and whether or not these consequences are sufficiently rewarding to motivate future performance. In essence, these response consequences are reinforcers. A reinforcer can be precisely defined as any stimulus or event that follows a response and increases the occurrence of that response in the future. For instance, if a teacher praises a student's in-seat behavior, and as a result the student continues to remain seated during the rest of the morning, the teacher's praise has acted as a reinforcer. If, however, the teacher's praise does not result in the student's continuing to sit appropriately, the praise cannot be considered reinforcing. Another example is when a teacher writes praising comments on a student's written assignment. Most likely that student will try to repeat the same response patterns in the future.

The above examples illustrate a specific class of reinforcers known as *positive reinforcement*. A "desired" stimulus was presented immediately following the student's behavior/response. Generally speaking, this is the most applicable type of reinforcement for classroom settings. A second reinforcement class is called *negative reinforcement*. According to the definition of a reinforcer, negative reinforcement must increase the likelihood of a response's occurring in the future. This is accomplished through the removal of an aversive, or undesired, stimulus. Although limited in classroom use, there are times when negative reinforcement is appropriate within the school. Every teacher has had the experience of increasing attending behavior by closing the door and blocking out distracting noises. In this case, the hall noise functioned as an aversive stimulus that, when "removed," resulted in greater on-task performance.

Practice Activity 3-1

1. Tim, who usually never interacts in class, received a star for class participation yesterday. Today he willingly joined in the discussion.
   a. To what might you attribute the change in Tim's behavior?
   b. Is this a reinforcer?
   c. Why?
2. Mrs. Clack says "okay" a lot when she talks to her high school class. It is so annoying that several students choose not to listen to what she says. Ms. Allen, the supervisor, calls Mrs. Clack's attention to this behavior. Mrs. Clack stops saying "okay." Her students listen much more often.
   a. What is the reinforcer in this situation?
   b. What type of reinforcement is it?

Responses to Practice Activity 3-1

1. a. the star he was given
   b. yes
   c. It increased his participation in the future.
2. a. the reduction in the number of times Mrs. Clack said "okay"
   b. negative reinforcement

The management of student behavior through reinforcement is based on a complex structure of human needs. Primary reinforcers are those that have an actual biological importance to the individual. These are natural, unlearned reinforcers, such as food, touch, and shelter. Because of the introduction of such things as snacks into the classroom program, it is somewhat difficult to use primary reinforcers with great frequency. Some schools even have preestablished policies against such reinforcement. Teachers who judiciously use primary reinforcers, however, find they are very effective. Few elementary school teachers complete the year without using some popcorn, cookies, and/or drinks as rewards for good behavior or achievement on at least one Friday afternoon.

Secondary reinforcers are essentially social stimuli that have obtained strength through frequent pairing with a primary reinforcer. A secondary reinforcer is behaviorally linked to a primary reinforcer. As a consequence, a conditioned association of one to the other occurs. For example, verbal praise for a very young child frequently is paired with a hug from the parent or is given during feeding time. By the time most children enter school, many types of secondary reinforcers have been well established. These include praise, permission to engage in preferred activities, grades, stars, tokens, and the like. These are learned reinforcers that tend to be more appropriate and common than primary reinforcers in classroom situations. Some types of secondary reinforcers used by teachers often occur fairly naturally during teacher–student interactions. These social reinforcers demonstrate approval or attention, such as positive nonverbal expressions (for example, smiling), teacher proximity (nearness) to a student, and extension of school or classroom privileges. There may be a child in your class for whom secondary reinforcers have little or no value. In such a case you will need to establish a conditioned association between the secondary reinforcer and a primary reinforcer. There are two things to keep in mind: (1) Never present a primary reinforcer without pairing it with a secondary reinforcer, and (2) once the association occurs, gradually remove the primary reinforcer.

A specific form of secondary reinforcement that most teachers have at least heard about is token reinforcement. Tokens are nothing more than symbols that are exchangeable for a valued reinforcer. In the world of work, money is an excellent example of a token reinforcer; it is exchangeable for valued goods and services. Within the classroom, tokens can be money, stars, points, chips, or anything that can be used to "purchase" a reinforcer like a toy or free time. To work, a token system must provide four elements:

1. Tokens
2. A clear set of behavioral contingencies by which tokens can be earned
3. A backup reinforcer for which a student is willing to work
4. A system for exchanging tokens for reinforcement

The following are advantages of a token system:

1. Tokens provide intermediate reinforcement while a student is working toward a larger goal.
2. They allow differential valuing of behavior because different behaviors can earn different amounts of tokens.
3. They teach students to accept delayed gratification.
4. They are portable and easily distributed unobtrusively. (Ayllon & Azrin, 1968)

Token systems have proven to be particularly valuable when working with special education students. Token systems should be adapted to reflect the objectives of a particular class and the needs of the students involved.

There are some concerns related to using a token system. One concern often expressed by teachers is the expense of providing backup reinforcers of value. Many teachers have overcome this problem by using reinforcers that occur naturally in the school, home, or community. A second area of concern involves keeping track of the number of tokens each student receives. Teachers will need to devise a system for keeping accurate records. A simple way to record tokens is by posting a list of student names. As each student wins a token, a star or check is placed next to the appropriate name. This type of system is more teacher controlled (and therefore tends to be more accurate) than leaving the management of tokens up to students. Providing fairly frequent token exchanges helps to establish a token reinforcement program, but teachers should be aware of the potential for difficulty as the frequency of exchanges is reduced.

Teachers should also realize that token economies may reduce intrinsic motivation. This occurs when the tokens are more important to students than the satisfaction of having completed the targeted task. Under such circumstances, motivation becomes extrinsic, and students stop working when the economy is withdrawn. Moreover, if students begin to value the tokens more than the task for which the reinforcement has been given, the system may actually lead to stealing, bribing, and hoarding. (This is more likely to occur in large classes, where token systems are more difficult to monitor.) Teachers who establish token economies must therefore carefully keep track of the system. They should also be sure to pair social reinforcement with tokens and to decrease gradually the frequency of token exchanges.

Practice Activity 3-2

Over the next two or three days become aware of the types of reinforcers you use in your teaching routine. Make a list of all you have used and label each one as positive or negative reinforcement and as primary or secondary reinforcement. Remember to label fully each rewarding consequence (for example, a good grade is a positive secondary reinforcer).

Selecting Reinforcers

You should also note that reinforcement may need to be tailored to specific individuals. That which is reinforcing to one student may not be to another. In addition, some rewards are applicable to groups of students while others are not. Therefore, the first consideration is the selection of reinforcers. Invalid assumptions regarding what should be reinforcing to a student or students are frequently responsible for the failure of the behavioral program. It is advisable to offer a reinforcement menu (that is, reinforcement selection) that allows students to indicate which consequences are most rewarding to them. Creating personal profiles that students can complete (and update throughout the year) is one useful technique. An example of a reinforcement profile is given in Box 3–1. Be sure to examine the questions in order to select those that are age appropriate for the children you teach. You may wish to add questions of your own to get a more comprehensive picture of each student's preferences.

It is important to note that praise and some other social reinforcers often lose their greatest effectiveness after the lower primary grades. In addition, a teacher in a class of twenty-five or thirty students is bound to have trouble keeping track of all the desired behaviors that occur and at best can only do a hit-or-miss job of reinforcing.

Box 3–1 *Reinforcement Profile*

1. The thing I like best about school is _____

   _____.

2. I feel really good when someone tells me that I _____

   _____.

3. The school subject I like best is _____.

4. My favorite snack is _____.

5. If I could do anything in school that I wanted, I would _____

   _____.

6. If I could do anything at all that I wanted to, I would _____

   _____.

7. The thing that makes me enjoy school the most is _____

   _____.

8. In my free time I like to _____

   _____.

Therefore, a variety of reinforcement options should be established to match consequences with the preferences listed in the profile. Box 3–2 lists a number of reinforcers available in most teaching situations. Some are appropriate for a particular age level, while others generalize across all grades. You may want to add to this list any reinforcers you have found useful. As you go through the list, place an asterisk (∗) by the ones you feel would work within your situation.

Box 3–2   *Classroom Reinforcers*

receiving smiles, winks, etc.	assisting custodian, secretary, etc.
using the gym, library during unassigned time	
getting stamps, stickers	getting a snack
making a phone call home	choosing a special work spot
eating lunch with teacher	speaking over address system
bringing comic books to read	using a calculator
writing notes to a classmate	working at teacher's desk
being line leader	getting a soda from the lounge
getting a chance to solve codes, puzzles	using felt tip pens
getting time to spend in student lounge	spending a day interning with a local business
getting peer recognition	displaying progress
getting good grades	getting no homework
being hall monitor	assisting in another room, grade
getting a photo in newspaper	getting permission to miss a test
getting free time	participating in a special project
watching films	taking class roll
selecting time for completing assignments	using a tape recorder, microcomputer
videotaping	creating a bulletin board
working with a volunteer	having a class dance in the room
grading papers	other

Remember to check a student's reinforcement profile before selecting performance consequences.

Reinforcement Guidelines

There are some basic principles of reinforcement that can be used as guidelines when establishing a behavior change program. These are as follows:

- Concentrate on the use of positive reinforcement as a consequence of a desirable behavior or improvement in a desirable behavior.
- Deliver reinforcers immediately following the desirable behavior.
- Apply reinforcement directly to the target student (don't be subtle).
- Allow the child to select the reinforcer whenever possible.
- Use continuous reinforcement while establishing a behavior; then use intermittent (occasional) reinforcement to maintain it.
- Use large amounts of the reinforcer at first, slowly reducing it after the behavior is established.
- Reward small steps (improvements), with the goal of building toward more complex behaviors.

Increasing Desirable Behavior

Using a reinforcement system to manage a number of students who demonstrate a variety of target behaviors is a difficult task. Teachers recognize a need to motivate students to be responsible for their own behavior. One of the most positive outcomes of reinforcement is that students can learn to think about the personal consequences that result from their actions. Some of the more effective techniques for increasing student responsibility are contracting, prompting, modeling, and teaching self-management.

Behavioral Contracts

Contracting involves a written statement developed by the student and the teacher in which each agrees to act in certain ways. In general, a contract fits within an "if–then" statement that focuses a targeted behavior and the resulting consequence. Specific procedures for establishing a contract are given below, and a sample contract for a young child is presented in Figure 3–1. Secondary-level teachers who wish to use a contingency contract are encouraged to do so. For an older child a contract can be designed following the basic contracting principles but within a format similar to those of actual business agreements. The following are guidelines for designing a behavioral contract:

- Fit the terms of the contract to the model and state them clearly: "If first you do X, then you may do (or will get) Y."
- Specify the task, being concise about the criteria (for example, the amount of work the student must complete, the level of accuracy required, the time limits involved).
- Identify a reinforcer. The appropriateness of the reinforcer depends on the child's reinforcement history and the targeted task.
- Establish a method of checking progress.
- Sign the contract.
- Be sure that both you and the student meet the terms of the contract.

Contracting is helpful to teachers who wish to raise students' levels of awareness regarding their behavior. Contracting is most effective when (1) students are permitted to participate in the establishment of their behavioral goals and the corresponding contingencies, and (2) students and teachers refer periodically to their contracts.

The key to using contracts successfully is the selection of a task that is appropriate to the student's current level of performance. If the student is just acquiring a skill, be sure to include some instructional component, such as guided practice, that is, practice involving close supervision and immediate feedback. If the contract is to be

IF I AM A WIZ AT . . . .

_____

_____

_____

_____
(TASK)

THEN I CAN . . . .

_____

_____

_____

TO BE CHECKED . . . .

_____

_____

_____
STUDENT'S SIGNATURE   **DATE**

_____
TEACHER'S SIGNATURE   **DATE**

Figure 3–1   *Contract Format*

completed without teacher assistance, then do not select tasks beyond the child's independent level (90 percent accuracy rate). This will alleviate the problem of the student's agreeing to a contract she or he cannot keep and then "testing the system" to see what aversive consequences will occur. Proper selection of the contract tasks reduces the threat of failure and increases the positive consequences of success. Periodic renegotiation of the contract may be necessary to match the task with the appropriate objective.

Practice Activity 3-3

A classroom teacher has asked you to help design a contract for each of the following classroom situations. See if you can do it.

1. Jay is nine years old, active in sports, and has lots of friends. He is having trouble learning his multiplication tables. In the past, for basic computation he has relied on finger counting. Now the teacher wants to teach the rote skill of multiplication at an acceptable performance rate.

2. Wendy has been absent from high school a lot this year. Her teacher has told you that she is working at her mother's beauty salon on the days that she misses school. When you spoke to Wendy she seemed very excited about the status and the money she received by working.

Work plans.   To avoid some of the concerns associated with contracts, it may be preferable to choose the alternative procedure of work plans. Work plans are designed as collaborative agreements between students and the teacher. The teacher selects the goals and objectives to be completed in a given time period, while the student develops a plan of study and activities. After sharing the plan, the teacher and student negotiate the work schedule based on the student's original product. If renegotiation is necessary, the student should remain in control because the student is the one who requests the reassessment. No external reinforcement is provided. Instead, the student is rewarded by the opportunity to follow his or her own plan. Students who are self-directed and capable of taking on responsibility for their own work would be excellent candidates for a work plan program.

Prompting

Another technique intended to increase the probability that a behavior will occur is prompting. A prompt may occur in visual, physical, or verbal form and is best described as a supplemental stimulus that helps elicit a desired response from students. The teacher who holds up a flashcard (2 + 3 = [ ]) and says, "Two plus two equals four. Three is one more than two, so two plus three equals what?" is using a verbal prompt. A science teacher who writes critical vocabulary words and their definitions on the board for students to refer to during class is using a visual prompt. A prompt works as a support for a child who is in the initial stages of learning a skill or concept. According to Alberto and Troutman (1982), "The use of prompts increases teaching efficiency. Rather than waiting for the student to emit the desired behavior, the teacher uses extra cues to increase the number of correct responses to be reinforced" (p. 243).

Two specific examples of verbal prompts that teachers use often and at which they should be highly skilled are rules and directions. Rules are often given by teachers as a cue before asking a child to respond to a direct question ("*Q* is always followed by *U*. How do you spell *queen*?"). In other instances, a teacher will refer a child to a rule in order to correct an error ("A noun is a person, place, or thing. Is *run* a noun?"). Rules also apply to behavior, and a teacher can therefore prompt students about how to behave during a lesson ("I will only call on people who raise their hands"), on the playground ("Remember our playground safety rules"), or in any social situation ("Be sure to say hello and to shake hands").

"Follow the directions" is a common statement in any classroom. Yet as any teacher knows, not all children can, or do, follow directions when told to do so. Directions act as a verbal prompt only when a child's behavior is under the stimulus control of a direction. A child who does not respond appropriately to directions may need to be taught to follow detailed directions by breaking instructions into simple, precise units and reinforcing each successful step. The teacher may need to provide specific practice in following directions. For example, "Put your finger on the rectangle in the upper left-hand corner of your paper; now write your name in that space" is a direction that can eventually be reduced to "Write your name on the paper," once the child is brought under stimulus control.

Practice Activity 3-4

Mr. Ultra is teaching a seventh-grade American history lesson on governmental powers. He wants the students to learn that different branches of government exert different controls in the democratic process.

1. In his class, Mr. Ultra has both a very bright student, Pat, and a slow-achieving student, Lesley. When asked to state the three branches of the federal government Lesley hesitated and said, "Executive, legislative . . ." but was unable to go on. Mr. Ultra decided to prompt Lesley. What would be an appropriate prompt to use?

2. Later in the lesson, Pat was discussing the control of power when he said the veto was used by Congress. Mr. Ultra was sure Pat knew the correct answer and was just confused. What could the teacher say to prompt him?

3. Another fact Mr. Ultra wanted to be sure his students understood was the difference between the legislature's making the law and the judiciary's interpreting the law. Before calling on Ronny, an average student, Mr. Ultra cues him to be certain that Ronny will give the correct answer. What could Mr. Ultra say to reduce Ronny's chance of error?

4. Mr. Ultra has also been working with his class on outlining skills. After the government lesson, Mr. Ultra tells the class to outline what they know about each branch of government. To be sure they use the correct format, Mr. Ultra provides a prompt for the whole class. What type of prompt would be appropriate?

Responses to Practice Activity 3-4

These answers are given as examples only.

1. "The last branch of government involves the court system."
2. "The President can veto the Congress, but how does Congress check the presidential power?"
3. "The laws are made in Washington and carried out in the courts around the country."
4. A visual prompt showing a traditional outline format.

Modeling

Modeling is the demonstration of a behavior. When a child who is reading aloud stumbles across a word, most teachers provide the correct response, that is, they model the word. Modeling is particularly valuable when attempting to elicit behaviors that are completely new to the student or are of an advanced level of complexity. It is used when verbal or visual cues are insufficient, and it is therefore considered more intrusive than regular prompting. It should be clear that a demonstration is the technique of choice for a science teacher showing the use of lab equipment; there are also other times when a teacher will want to use modeling when less intrusive prompts have not led to the correct response. Most students are able to respond efficiently to instructions that include a model.

Teachers also need to be aware that students will imitate the behaviors of other classmates as well as of teachers. Peer imitation occurs throughout the grade levels and perhaps is strongest in the social grouping at the secondary level. Students will be more likely to imitate a model (person demonstrating the behavior) who (a) has high status, (b) is acknowledged to be competent, and (c) is similar to themselves.

Although students will often imitate even if they are not reinforced for following the model, adding reinforcement to the procedure can be effective. It is also important to note that when the model is reinforced, the likelihood of imitation occurring is increased. When reinforcing a peer model, the teacher should clearly specify what behavior of the model is being reinforced. For instance, if the teacher wants to increase hand-raising behavior and reduce talking-out, and Sheri raises her hand to answer, the teacher might say something like, "I'm glad you raised your hand before answering" rather than something vague like, "Good for you!" By specifying the behavior being reinforced, the teacher helps all of the students understand what constitutes the appropriate behavior.

Shaping and Fading

Prompts are often used to shape or develop a behavior and to assist the student in making the correct response so that reinforcement can be applied. By reinforcing a planned sequence of closer and closer approximations to the correct response, the teacher is more likely to guarantee that the student will eventually demonstrate the correct behavior. The development of legible handwriting is a good example of a situation in which teachers should and do reinforce closer approximations to a standard form. Shaping is also often used when a student is asked to read. A teacher may at first reinforce any attempt at a new word that begins with the appropriate initial consonant. Later, more complex word analysis will be required to gain reinforcement.

Of course, the goal for any teacher is that students eventually become sufficiently conditioned to exhibit desired behaviors without any form of prompting. This is generally accomplished by the gradual withdrawal of teacher intervention. This reduction of prompts from more to least intrusive, and ultimately to no teacher assistance, is known as fading. Figure 3–2 shows the sequence of prompts in the order of teacher involvement for developing a behavior and for fading teacher assistance.

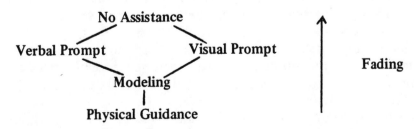

Figure 3–2 *Sequence of Prompts*

Practice Activity 3-5

Label each instructional example according to the technique the teacher is using, either *F* (fading) or *S* (shaping).

1. The lesson is on object words to be included in a sight vocabulary. The teacher places each word within an outline of the object. Slowly she begins to remove the outline, leaving only the word to be read.

2. Katie is learning to write complex sentences. The teacher reinforces each attempt, which builds on a previous, less complex sentence.

3. Ms. Owen has a fairly disruptive class this year. Upon realizing this, she began with a very structured program in which she repeated three class rules at the beginning of each lesson and repeated them once during the lesson. Gradually she has been reducing the emphasis upon rules. Her intent is only to have to remind the students occasionally about the rules by Thanksgiving.

Responses to Practice Activity 3-5

1. fading
2. shaping
3. fading

Self-Management

If getting students to take responsibility for their own behaviors is a primary goal of all education, then teachers should keep this in mind as they develop instructional plans. One fairly recent technique, but one that has been researched and shown effective, is cognitive behavior modification (CBM). CBM involves the manipulation of thoughts as a means of effecting behavior change. CBM basically consists of two steps: (1) directly instructing or demonstrating a strategy for correct performance, and (2) teaching a set of verbalized self-instructions to carry out the behavior (Meichenbaum, 1977). Examples of CBM in classroom settings include having a student verbalize internally a set of "teacher-pleasing behaviors," such as remembering to be on time, stay in seat, raise his or her hand, and be prepared. These silent reminders along with a cognitive image of getting a positive reaction from the teacher will help the child gradually change his or her behavior.

Another self-management technique is self-control, in which the child takes increasing responsibility for personal behaviors (both academic and social). As defined by Bandura and Perloff (1967), self-control requires that the individual do the following:

- Perform a self-assessment to determine how well the target behavior was performed;
- Self-record the frequency of the target behavior;
- Determine the type and amount of reinforcement to be given, contingent upon the demonstration of the target behavior.

Teachers will want to plan for students to be increasingly responsible for their own behaviors. Alberto and Troutman (1982) recommend several techniques for helping students achieve this goal:

1. *Explain reinforcement:* As reinforcement is given, the teacher explains what behavior resulted in reinforcement ("Jeff, you did an excellent job editing your paper before handing it in").

2. *Relate contingency:* The teacher asks the student to state what the contingent response is to a target behavior ("Carol, what is going to happen to your recess time if you continue to leave your seat instead of completing your work?").

3. *Self-reinforcement:* The teacher invites student participation in selecting reinforcement and determining the reinforcement value ("How many problems do you think you can complete today, and what would you like to do if you reach your goal?").

Self-management procedures have the decided advantage of prompting positive behaviors without dependence upon external stimuli, such as a certain teacher, a set classroom routine, or a single situation. Therefore, self-management techniques enable students to generalize appropriate behaviors across time and setting.

Practice Activity 3-6

Match each self-management technique with the appropriate example.

1.	cognitive behavior modification	(a)	"Elise, you did four sentences correctly. You get two points for each sentence."
2.	self-reinforcement	(b)	John repeats to himself the rules for editing a composition and then reviews his essay.
3.	self-control	(c)	"Elliot, these are the possible reinforcers. Which one would you like, and how many problems do you think you should complete before getting reinforcement?"

4. explaining the reinforcement
5. relating the contingency

(d) "Julie, what did you do? How many stars do you get?"
(e) Marty is responsible for checking his work, giving himself a grade, and recording his progress.

Responses to Practice Activity 3-6

1. b
2. c
3. e
4. a
5. d

Delivering Reinforcement

The delivery or timing of reinforcement is readily adaptable to specific individuals and situations. Known as the reinforcement schedule, the rate of delivery influences the effect of the reinforcement. Several types of reinforcement schedules exist. The most common is

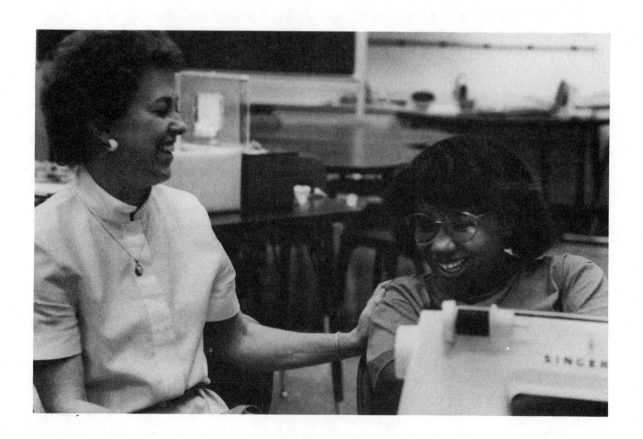

continuous reinforcement, in which the student is reinforced for each performance of the target response. For example, every time Tim answers in a complete sentence the teacher praises his response. In contrast, intermittent reinforcement is given for some, but not all, occurrences of the behavior. When grading papers, Ms. Dorry writes "good" next to certain passages but not next to all acceptable passages; she is using an intermittent schedule. Because of the number of responses made in the typical classroom during the course of a day, let alone over the years, it is impossible to reinforce each behavior. In fact, continuous reinforcement is desirable only during the initial stages of learning a skill or concept, when the student needs constant feedback as to the appropriateness of the response. Once the concept is learned (when it is within the child's repertoire), intermittent reinforcement is preferable. Skill maintenance and long-term retention of learning is increased through intermittent reinforcement. Teachers should plan on using continuous reinforcement when beginning either an academic or behavioral program and on reducing or "thinning" the schedule to occasional reinforcement as the child progresses.

Collecting and Recording Data

An effective method exists for gathering information concerning student progress toward a target behavior. The level of behavior displayed before a reinforcement or any intervention program begins is referred to as baseline performance. Specific information related to the student's performance (that is, data) should be collected on a regular basis. It is helpful to graph performance during baseline and intervention in order to achieve a pictorial representation of the program's effects. Such graphs understandably make a student's progress or lack of progress easier to demonstrate than do purely verbal descriptions. There are several ways to record data, including frequency, duration, latency, time sampling, and interval recording:

- Frequency is a simple count of how often a response occurs: "The child read ten words."
- Duration refers to the length of time any response lasts: "John spoke for three minutes."
- Latency measures the time between a given stimulus and a response: "After the teacher said, 'Be quiet,' it took two minutes for the group to come to order."
- Interval recording allows the teacher to sample a behavior during equal intervals of time. Rather than count the number of times a behavior occurs, the teacher counts the number of intervals in which the behavior was observed to occur at least once: "Within five out of ten of the two-minute intervals the teacher observed, Denise was on-task."

- Time sampling is a variation on interval recording in which the student is observed and the presence or absence of the behavior is noted only at the end of the interval: "At the end of eight intervals the teacher looked at Dan and saw that he was out of his seat."

For the purpose of graphing recorded data, time—stated in increments that apply to the situation—is generally used as the independent variable appearing on the horizontal axis of the graph. The dependent variable, of course, is the particular behavior being targeted for change and is graphed on the vertical axis. Figure 3–3 is a sample graph of "correct responses" during eleven reading sessions for one child. During the last seven sessions, the teacher tried a new way to teach reading. This was the "intervention." The student's progress is effectively noted through the graphic display.

Practice Activity 3-7

Do you ever collect data on student progress in your classroom? The answer should be yes. Even if you are only recording grades, you are collecting data. As you apply more reinforcement techniques, it will be useful to gather information more frequently.

Select a behavior to observe. Decide on a recording technique and record baseline information for three to five days. Be sure to analyze what you record.

Reducing Inappropriate Behavior

Most people think that punishment means the introduction of an aversive consequence following an inappropriate behavior. However, any intervention that is presented following a particular behavior and that reduces or eliminates that behavior is, technically, a punishment. Some punishment techniques involve the removal of positive reinforcers when inappropriate behavior occurs. Two such "positive punishment" techniques are extinction and response cost. Following are brief descriptions of these techniques, along with a discussion of the more well-known "negative punishment."

(It is important to emphasize the difference between negative reinforcement and punishment. As stated earlier, negative reinforcement involves the removal of an unpleasant stimulus and results in an *increased* likelihood of the behavior occurring; punishment is designed to *decrease* the probability that a particular behavior will occur.)

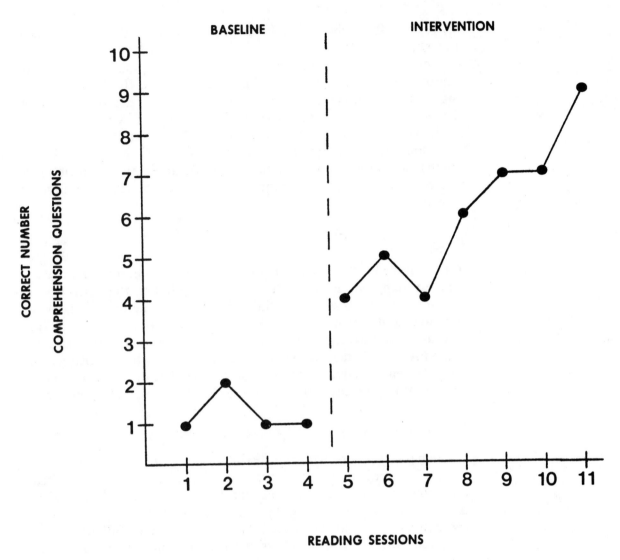

Figure 3–3 *Graphing an Academic Behavior*

Extinction

Extinction refers to the elimination of a behavior by withholding reinforcement. In many instances, this can be accomplished by removing teacher attention. For example, whenever Susan jumps out of her seat the teacher is certain to say something to her, but no matter what is said, Susan keeps popping up. In this case, it is possible that Susan continues to leave her seat as a means of getting her teacher to notice her. When the teacher first stops reacting in a typical manner to Susan, the student's out-of-seat behavior gets much worse. But the teacher continues to ignore Susan and eventually the behavior decreases. (The initial increase in the undesirable behavior is a frequent occurrence whenever an attempt is made to extinguish a behavior, so all teachers should anticipate a "tough" period before things get better.)

Another note of warning: Be sure you have pinpointed what is reinforcing the behavior. If you remove what you think is the reinforcer and the behavior continues over time, check again. Something else is working to reinforce the behavior. A good illustration of this is when one child acts as the class clown. Most often it is not teacher attention but peer reaction that is reinforcing this behavior. Unless the teacher can control each class member and assure that no reinforcement will be given, extinction should not be the technique of choice.

Response Cost

In this procedure the teacher removes units of reinforcement each time an inappropriate behavior occurs. Implicit in the definition is the fact that response cost is only effective if some level of positive reinforcement already exists. Taking away points or units of free time is a good example of a response cost technique. For instance, when Elisa continued to swear in class, even after being reminded of the rule against such behavior, the teacher began to reduce recess time by three minutes for each subsequent instance of swearing.

Negative Punishment

The behavior reduction procedure that teachers are most familiar with is negative punishment. This type of punishment involves the introduction of an aversive stimulus such as spanking or scolding following an undesirable behavior. If, after the aversive stimulus is applied, the behavior has not decreased, by definition punishment has not occurred. Nevertheless, teachers often label a consequence as punishing even without the resultant decrease in behavior.

Negative punishment should only be used as a consequence of an extremely undesirable behavior and then only as a last resort. The common use of punishment as a means of controlling behavior within classrooms probably is a by-product of punishment being used so commonly as a child-rearing practice. However, there is little to support the use of any sort of punishment as a technique to motivate learning. The application of punishment does (1) stop the immediate occurrence of an inappropriate response, (2) provide a discrimination between an acceptable and a nonacceptable behavior, and (3) demonstrate a clear behavioral consequence to other students watching the presentation of the punishment. Although the application of punishment can be reinforcing to a teacher, since it puts an immediate end to the annoying behavior, it has not proven as effective as other procedures over the long term.

If a teacher feels it is necessary to manage behavior by applying punishing consequences, it is important to realize that the most effective strategy is to pair punishment of an undesirable behavior with reinforcement of a desired behavior. In this way, a student not only learns what not to do but also what is an appropriate form of responding. Rather than being put down, the student has an avenue by which to achieve success.

Practice Activity 3-8

1. Examine your procedures for reducing inappropriate behaviors in your classroom. List each situation and the reducing consequence you apply. Note the type of punishers you use and analyze the result of the punishment. Is it working? If not, stop what you are doing and find another way.
2. Based on your understanding of behavior-reduction procedures, rate each of the following statements as either true or false.
   a. An effective means of encouraging student learning attempts is to criticize any incorrect response.
   b. Negative reinforcement and punishment have the same effect on behavior.
   c. A teacher whose attention has been reinforcing a student and who now ignores a student who shouts out during a class discussion is using extinction.
   d. Whenever any reinforcer is withheld, extinction will occur.
   e. Jeff never comes to school prepared. The teacher begins to take points off the assignment grade each time Jeff is unprepared. This is an example of a response cost procedure.

Responses to Practice Activity 3-8

2. a. F
   b. F
   c. T
   d. F
   e. T

Conclusion

Reinforcement is a powerful tool that can increase student academic and behavioral gains. Teachers who are adept at providing reinforcement are also successful at motivating students to learn. The array of techniques available to the teacher offers options suitable for almost any teaching style and/or classroom problem. The more the teacher knows about reinforcement and the related behavioral strategies, the more exciting the learning environment will be. Each beginning teacher will need to "experiment" at times. However, the wealth of available information related to reinforcement strategies should be used as a resource. Many of the problems experienced in your classroom have presented themselves in other classrooms before. Read about behavior-management principles. Observe how respected teachers (or parents and employers) apply reinforcement to increase or decrease behavior. Then make modifications to suit your situation. Understanding and applying reinforcement is central to successful teaching.

References

Alberto, P. A., & Troutman, A. C. (1982). *Applied behavior analysis for teachers.* Columbus, Ohio: Merrill.

Ayllon, T., & Azrin, N. (1968). *The token economy: A motivated system for therapy and rehabilitation.* New York: Appleton-Century-Crofts.

Bandura, A., & Perloff, B. (1967). Relative efficacy of self-monitored and externally imposed reinforcement systems. *Journal of Personality and Social Psychology, 7,* 111–16.

Brophy, J. (1983). Classroom organization and management. *Elementary School Journal, 83,* 265–85.

Craig, R. (1967). *The psychology of learning in the classroom.* New York: Macmillan.

Meichenbaum, D. H. (1977). *Cognitive behavior modification: An integrative approach.* New York: Plenum Press.

Skinner, B. F. (1953). *Science and human behavior.* New York: Macmillan.

Skinner, B. F. (1971). The technology of teaching. In C. E. Pitts (Ed.), *Operant conditioning in the classroom.* New York: Crowell.

Thorndike, E. L. (1905). *The elements of psychology.* New York: Seiler.

Chapter Four

Consistent Rules

Ruth Anne McLaughlin

Virginia Polytechnic Institute and State University

Definition

The competent teacher knows rules for classroom behavior must be clear so that learners understand and accept the rules and the consequences of violating them. When rules are unclear or applied inconsistently, teachers will have difficulty managing classrooms.

Purpose

The purpose of this chapter is to help you understand the importance of establishing and maintaining a system of rules for your classroom to facilitate a well-organized and well-managed learning environment. Teachers who are successful classroom managers set rules that are known and understood by all learners. These teachers also monitor rule adherence of their students throughout the school year. Once a rules system has been made a routine part of classroom activities, effective classroom managers demonstrate techniques that tend to prevent many infractions of the rules.

Background Knowledge

"Don't smile until Christmas!" "Give them an inch, they will take a mile!" "Be firm, fair, and friendly!" Do these bromides sound familiar? They should, because almost every teacher has been advised on how to run a classroom and avoid discipline problems. Many of the "gems of wisdom" focus on ways to set up rules and regulations, not only for control but for organizational purposes as well.

It may comfort you to know that others also perceive classroom management issues as a major problem in U.S. schools today. The Phi Delta Kappan annual Gallup Poll (Gallup, 1984) reported that the American public's number-one concern about public education during the past year was discipline. In fact, discipline has been listed as a top problem in U.S. schools for fifteen of the past sixteen years. This chapter examines research efforts related to establishing and maintaining a rules system that may alleviate classroom management concerns.

You want to set up an effective learning climate in your classroom, but you have many questions: How does an organized, well-managed class operate? What rules do you need to implement and enforce? What guidelines are now available to help you? In the past, classroom management issues have been synonymous with discipline; however, "management" is typically interpreted in broader terms today. Emmer and Evertson (1981) defined classroom management as "teacher behaviors that produce high levels of student involvement, minimal amounts of student behaviors that interfere with the teacher's or other students' work, and efficient use of class time" (p. 342).

According to Brophy (1984), a well-managed classroom reflects the results of teacher organization and planning. The room is set up for efficient use of time and space; teachers have clear goals for learning activities and quickly move students from one activity to another. Arlin (1979) observed that students in this type of environment seem to know what to do, how to do it, and what materials they need. To an untrained eye these classrooms seem to operate automatically, with the teacher serving as active facilitator in the learning process and not being burdened with management concerns. Brophy suggests this classroom atmosphere occurs when the teacher has systematically and consistently planned and implemented rules and procedures to govern all activities.

How do teachers make management plans appear to implement themselves automatically? Let's turn to research studies that have focused on observations of classrooms to determine what teacher behaviors or actions distinguish effective classroom managers from those who are less successful. First, we will review the research findings of Kounin (1970), which have been used as the basis for the study of classroom management in the past two decades. Specifically, we will examine teacher behaviors that tend to alleviate student deviancy in classrooms. Next, we will review recent research studies that have investigated how ineffective and effective classroom managers plan, implement, and monitor classroom rules systems.

Kounin's work has been influential in helping unravel classroom management problems. In his initial work he proposed to determine the difference between effective teachers (those who had high rates of student work involvement and low rates of student deviant behav-

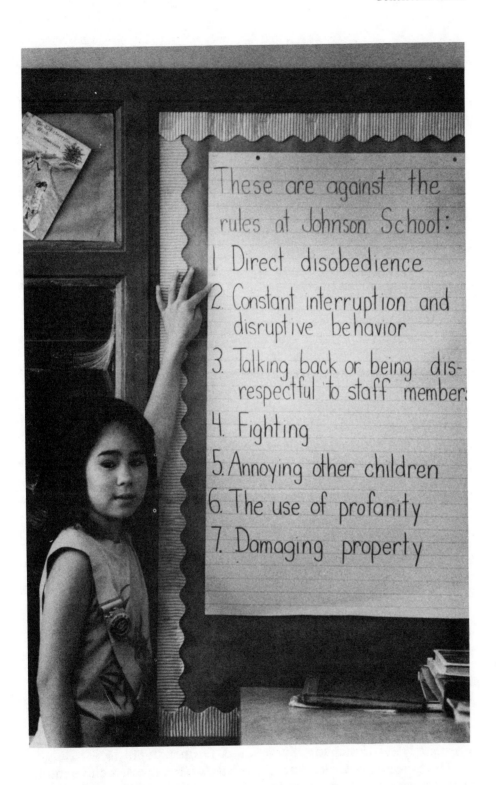

These are against the
rules at Johnson School:
1 Direct disobedience
2. Constant interruption and
disruptive behavior
3. Talking back or being dis-
respectful to staff member
4. Fighting
5. Annoying other children
6. The use of profanity
7. Damaging property

iors) from ineffective teachers (those who struggled to manage their classrooms). He analyzed videotapes of teachers in seventy-nine urban and suburban classrooms. These classrooms were divided into two groups: (1) those that were well-ordered and managed with students exhibiting on-task behavior, and (2) those that showed low student work involvement and many student misbehaviors. Kounin expected effective teachers to handle student disruption differently from ineffective teachers, but this was not the case. Instead he found that what distinguished the two groups were teacher behaviors that *prevented* the types of disruptions that happened frequently in the poorly managed classrooms.

Two of the concepts derived from Kounin's research are pertinent to our discussion of consistent rules. These are important because they facilitate the implementation of classroom management rules. Kounin found that effective teachers demonstrated what he identified as "withitness," which is like having "eyes in the back of the head." According to Kounin, a "withit" teacher knows what is going on in the classroom at all times and is sensitive to potential disruptive situations, moving to halt deviant behaviors before they increase in severity or spread to other students. The teacher displaying withitness is also able to identify the appropriate student target, the one who is the initiator of the potential or beginning misbehavior. Further, an effective teacher can easily recognize differences between serious and minor problems in the classroom and can take immediate steps to eliminate serious misbehaviors while ignoring the trivial.

The ability to "overlap" is also important for enforcing classroom rules. A teacher is often involved in performing several classroom tasks simultaneously. The better a teacher can attend to more than one task, the more overlap he or she is said to demonstrate. For example, an elementary teacher may be working with a reading group and asked to respond to another student's question. The degree to which a teacher can handle two or more events smoothly and without seriously ignoring any one student or group of students, the less likely it is that disruption or deviant student behavior will occur.

Texas researchers Emmer and Evertson (1981) conducted a study in elementary classrooms throughout the school year with the goal of trying to distinguish between teachers who consistently had students who were high achievers and teachers who had low achievers. Their findings, based on standardized test scores, confirmed the earlier observations of Kounin: Student achievement was higher in classes that had few student misbehaviors and had a teacher who was well organized and quickly moved students through scheduled academic activities. Additionally, the effective teachers rarely blamed the wrong student for a deviant behavior. *Relatively few rules were needed to guide the class, but those that were in place were clear, well explained, and consistently monitored* (Emmer & Evertson, 1981; Anderson, Evertson, & Emmer, 1980).

On closer observation the University of Texas researchers found that effective teachers spent more time *teaching* their students the rules, much as they would any academic subject, during the first few weeks of school. These teachers presented their students with the rules and the reasons for them on the first day and focused on the use of these rules in the first few weeks. Teachers explained the rules, gave examples, answered questions, allowed for practice, and provided student and teacher modeling of correct practices and procedures. The consequences for inappropriate behavior were clearly stated and applied quickly and consistently. When a student did not follow correct procedures, the teacher reminded the student of the rule or requested that the student state the rule and its consequence. As a result, effective classroom managers spent a lot of time implementing and monitoring a rules system at the beginning of the year, but once the rules were installed these classes tended to have the "automatic" quality described earlier. Moreover, during the year these teachers spent less time on management issues than did ineffective teachers (Evertson & Anderson, 1979; Anderson, Evertson, & Emmer, 1980). Moskowitz and Hayman (1976) also found that "best" teachers organized routines that established rules and expectations on the first day of school.

Effective teachers also differed in the ways they prevented and reacted to student misbehaviors. As was the case in Kounin's research, the Texas team found that once an infraction of a rule occurred, there was little difference between the way both groups of teachers (effective and ineffective) dealt with the misbehavior. By maintaining active involvement with students, effective managers were aware of problems before they began. Anderson, Evertson, and Emmer (1980) observed that effective teachers tended to do one of three things when they perceived a deviant behavior developing: signal the appropriate behavior by using a prearranged sign that alerts students they are not on task, establish eye contact with the student, or use a variety of rewards to reinforce those students who stay on task and observe classroom rules.

Regardless of how well rules are made an integral part of classroom learning environment, some students will misbehave. When it occurs, effective teachers act immediately to stop misbehavior. Effective teachers also clearly identify the student responsible and often cite the specific rule being violated. When effective teachers deal with inappropriate behavior, they do not use sarcasm or punishment, nor do they threaten or warn students. In applying consequences, these teachers use milder, more informative types of punishment, such as explaining why a behavior is inappropriate.

Emmer and his colleagues (1984) cautioned that inconsistency in rule monitoring conveys to your students "an arbitrary use of authority . . . resented by those whom the teacher chose to punish; it would teach those who were let off that they had a special privilege and confuse all of the students" (p. 99). Students want structure and predictability and will test the limits of the rules to determine how they will be enforced. The Texas research team claims that inappropriate behavior will increase if rules are not consistently applied to all students. Consistency in enforcing rule violations may be modified under two conditions. First, if a student has a legitimate excuse for breaking a rule, you may wish to examine the extenuating circumstance. If the class is aware of the rule violation, you should offer an explanation as to why an exception was permitted. Second, don't be afraid to change rules. After you plan and implement your rules, don't hesitate to evaluate the practicality or need for each rule and to discard or change those rules that do not accomplish your objective.

Follow-up research at the secondary level tends to support the conclusions drawn in the elementary studies (Evertson & Emmer, 1982; Sanford & Evertson, 1981). Although teachers at the secondary level need less time to teach rules, Good (1984) reported that Emmer and Evertson (1981) found effective classroom managers "set clearer expectations for behavior, academic work, and classroom procedures during the first several class meetings than did less effective managers" (p. 61). These same effective managers were actively involved with students and stopped inappropriate behavior quickly. Sanford and Evertson (1981) emphasized that secondary teachers not only needed to teach rules at the beginning of the year but also to monitor consistently their compliance throughout the year. Their year-long study revealed that in the classroom of ineffective managers the rate of inappropriate behavior increased by 50 percent by the middle of the year. In contrast, in the classrooms of teachers who spent time introducing rules and procedures at the beginning of the year and who consistently followed through on monitoring the rule system, inappropriate behaviors decreased.

What classroom rules are going to help you have a well-organized room and ensure the efficient use of time? It would be inappropriate to delineate a list of rules because each of you has unique needs and concerns that should be addressed by your own rules system. Emmer and his colleagues (1984) noted that rules differed among effective classroom managers, but that all effective teachers had some set of rules for classroom procedures. Emmer and his colleagues have developed an organizational framework that may be useful to you as you formulate the rules and procedures that would be most appropriate for your classroom. The following practice activity is adapted from two manuals developed by the Research and Development Center for Teacher Education at the University of Texas at Austin (Emmer et al., 1982; Evertson et al., 1981).

Practice Activity 4-1

Answer the following questions about instructional and noninstructional activities as they apply to your own classroom.

1. During your classroom instructional activities:
   a. How will students inform you if they have questions or need help? Where will you work with individual students who need extra help?
   b. Under what conditions may students leave their seats?
   c. Under what conditions will you allow students to leave the room to go to the bathroom or other locations?

What procedure will you follow for allowing students to leave the room?

d. What signal will you use to get the students' attention?

e. Will you allow students to talk to one another and/or to work together during seatwork or learning center activities?

f. What will students do if they complete seatwork or a learning center assignment early?

g. What kinds of equipment or materials will require special instructions or a demonstration?

h. What procedures will you need for laboratory work or student group projects?

i. How will you pass out and collect materials and supplies?

2. During your noninstructional activities:

a. If a student was absent on the previous day, what should she or he do?

b. If a student will be leaving during the school day, what should she or he do?

c. What is the procedure for students who are tardy?

d. What standards of neatness do you require before dismissing the class or a group from one activity to another?

e. What procedure will you use to dismiss the class at the end of the period, for recess, lunch, and so forth?

f. If PA announcements come on, what is expected of the students?

g. What materials are students expected to bring to class or group each day? If these vary from day to day, how will you let them know?

h. What responsibilities do you want students to have in passing out and taking care of materials or equipment?

Responses to Practice Activity 4-1

1. a. Most effective managers *require* students to raise their hands in order to be called on. When students are working at their seats and need help, you should have them raise their hands so that you may go to them or they may come to you.

b. To eliminate unnecessary wandering around the room, you should indicate when students are allowed to leave their seats.

c. This procedure must be established early in the year and consistently followed. Students should not be allowed to leave the room except in emergencies, as determined by the teacher.

    d. Some of the techniques used by teachers include ringing a timer bell, turning on the lights, sitting down by the overhead projector, standing by the chalkboard, or using a particular phrase, such as, "Let me have your attention."

    e. If this will be allowed, you will need to establish specific limitations. For example, you may say that during certain activities you will allow quiet talking, but if the talking gets too loud, then the privilege will be lost.

    f. If you have enrichment activities for students who work more quickly, you will need to specify rules for using materials.

    g. Instructions are usefully displayed whenever any material or equipment is used.

    h. If you are sharing facilities with other teachers, you will want to cooperate with them in standardizing rules for these procedures for all classes.

    i. To avoid traffic jams, plan distribution stations carefully. Use more than one station. When possible, save time by placing some or all necessary materials or supplies on students' desks or work tables before class starts. Be alert to possibilities for using student helpers.

2. a. If you have a particular location for roll call, you can have the student leave the absence excuse slip there for you to sign or bring it to you to sign while you are checking roll.

    b. First find out what your school requires. Follow generally accepted procedures.

    c. Find out the school policy and follow it. If there is no specific school policy, you will need to have a procedure of your own.

    d. You should expect students to leave the room or learning center as clean as it was when they entered.

    e. Most effective teachers require all students to be in their seats and quiet before they dismiss them.

    f. Tell the students specifically what their expected behavior is during announcements (for example, no talking; stop, or continue, working).

    g. Most effective managers expect students to have all their materials ready to use when the bell rings. You might help students prepare a list of materials expected for each day.

    h. If there are specific instructions for the care and use of equipment or materials, the instructions should be given and demonstrated, if appropriate, before passing them out.

Once you have thought through a workable rules system that addresses the procedures needed for your classroom, you should think

about how to maintain them and what the consequences will be for violating them. As you read in Chapter 3, effective classroom managers use appropriate reinforcement techniques. They reinforce appropriate behaviors and allow "reasonable," logical consequences to serve as sanctions when rules are broken by students (Evertson et al., 1984; Emmer et al., 1984). For example, if you have a class rule that hands should be raised before speaking, and students talk out, as a logical consequence they should be ignored while those who raise their hands are called on. This approach should reinforce hand-raising behavior. Another logical technique is reminding students of the rule. As another example, if you have a rule prohibiting inappropriate use of gum, a student blowing bubbles would have to get rid of the gum and perhaps lose gum-chewing privileges for a period of time. An unreasonable consequence in this instance would be the requirement that all students cease chewing gum, thereby extending to students who were obeying the rule a consequence intended only to those who were violating it. Evertson et al. (1984) and Emmer et al. (1984) maintain that if students understand the logical connection between what they do and what will happen to them, they may be more likely to choose acceptable behavior.

Allowing every rule violation to follow its course to its logical consequence is unwise because the consequence may be "dangerous, costly or occur too far in the future" (Emmer et al., 1984, p. 65). For instance, if a student forgets his or her necessary materials, you would not want him or her to miss the planned academic activities; therefore, you may allow the student to obtain the material from his or her locker or book tray, for example, or have another student lend the material. You might impose a penalty for not having the required material in class, such as points from a daily grade or demerits that can accumulate for time in from recess or for detention. These penalties should be explained carefully to the students when you are presenting the rules system to them. Keep in mind, however, that punishment can be demoralizing and that positive reinforcement for rule compliance can be a much more effective and preventative tool.

Practice Activity 4-2

Complete the checklists in Table 4–1. You may want to address some of the questions below concerning the rules systems for your class.

1. Have I clearly communicated the rules, procedures, and consequences for compliance and noncompliance to my students?
2. Am I having any particular management problem in my classroom in any of the procedural areas? (If the answer is yes, you should revise the rules for that area and spend some time actively teaching them.)
3. Am I consistently enforcing the rules for all students all of the time? (Students are very much aware of and sensitive to inconsistency in rule monitoring.)

Establishing and maintaining a well-managed classroom with sufficient rules necessitates that teachers take a leadership role and clearly identify expectations for student behavior. Although certain guidelines have been offered by researchers, you will have to decide how to apply them in your own classroom.

Despite the research findings that suggest that the same type of management techniques may work for both elementary and secondary classrooms, students' intellectual and social development needs should be considered when devising rules for your classroom. Brophy and Evertson (1978) identified four general student age levels that have implications for classroom management concerns (see Box 4–1).

It seems clear that a systematic approach to organizing your classroom may prevent many problems from arising. You should begin early to think about what rules will help students accomplish their goals, how best to teach these rules, and how to enforce them fairly

Table 4–1 *Checklist for Rules, Procedures, and Consequences*

Subject	Rules or Procedures for Students	Consequences

I. Instructional Activities
 	
  A. Teacher-student contacts
  B. Student movement within the room
  C. Student movement in and out of the room
  D. Signal for student attention
  E. Headings for papers
 	
II. Noninstructional Activities
 	
  A. Roll call, absentees, students who will be leaving early
  B. Tardy students
  C. Behavior during PA announcements
  D. Warm-ups or routines
  E. Distributing supplies and materials
  F. Putting away supplies and equipment
  G. Organizing different classes' materials
  H. Dismissing the class
  I. Student contact with teacher's desk, storage
  J. Other		

Note: Adapted from Evertson et al., 1981, and Emmer et al., 1982.

Box 4–1 *Stages of Student Orientation and Classroom Behaviors*

Stage one (kindergarten through grade 2 or 3). Most children are compliant and oriented toward conforming to and pleasing their teachers, but they must be socialized into the student role. They require a great deal of formal instruction, not only in rules and expectations, but also in classroom procedures and routines.

Stage two (grades 2-3 through grades 5-6). Students have learned most of what they need to know about school rules and routines and most remain oriented toward obeying and pleasing their teachers. Consequently, less time needs to be devoted to classroom management at the beginning of the year; less cuing, reminding, and instructing is required thereafter.

Stage three (grades 5-6 through grades 9-10). Students enter adolescence and become less eager to please teachers and more eager to please peers. Many become resentful or at least questioning of authority; disruptions due to attention seeking, humorous remarks, and adolescent horseplay become common. Classroom management again becomes more time consuming, but, in contrast to stage one, the task facing teachers is not so much one of instructing willing but ignorant students about what to do as it is one of motivating or controlling students who know what to do but will not always do it. Also, individual counseling becomes more prominent, as the relative stability of most students in the middle grades gives way to the adjustment problems of adolescence.

Stage four (after grades 9-10). Most students become more settled and oriented toward academic learning again. As in stage two, classroom management requires less time and trouble; classrooms take on a more businesslike, academic focus.

Note: From Brophy & Evertson, 1978, p. 34. Reprinted by permission from the *Educational Psychologist*. Copyright 1978, Division of Educational Psychology of the American Psychological Association.

and consistently. There is good reason to believe that those who must live with and by rules will do so with greatest productivity and goodwill when they participate in the development of those rules.

References

Anderson, L., Evertson, C., & Emmer, E. (1980). Dimensions in classroom management derived from recent research. *Journal of Curriculum Studies, 12,* 343–62.

Arlin, M. (1979). Teacher transitions can disrupt timeflow in classrooms. *American Educational Research Journal, 11,* 42–56.

Brophy, J. (1984). Classroom organization and management. In D. Smith (Ed.), *Essential knowledge for beginning educators* (pp. 23–37). Washington, D.C.: American Association of Colleges for Teacher Education.

Brophy, J., & Evertson, C. (1978). Context variables in teaching. *Educational Psychologist, 12,* 310–16.

Emmer, E., & Evertson, C. (1981). Synthesis of research on classroom management. *Educational Leadership, 38,* 342–47.

Emmer, E., Evertson, C., & Anderson, L. (1980). Effective classroom managers at the beginning of the school year. *Elementary School Journal, 80,* 219–31.

Emmer, E., Evertson, C., Sanford, J., Clements, B., & Worsham, M. (1984). *Classroom management for secondary teachers.* Englewood Cliffs, N.J.: Prentice-Hall.

Evertson, C., & Anderson, L. (1979). Beginning school. *Educational Horizons, 56,* 164–68.

Evertson, C. M., & Emmer, E. (1982). Effective management at the beginning of the year in junior high classes. *Journal of Educational Psychology, 74,* 485–98.

Evertson, C. M., Emmer, E., Clements, B., Sanford, J., Worsham, M., & Williams, E. (1984). *Classroom management for elementary teachers.* Englewood Cliffs, N.J.: Prentice-Hall.

Gallup, G. A. (1984). The 16th Annual Poll of the public's attitudes toward the public schools. *Phi Delta Kappan, 66,* 23–38.

Good, T. (1984). Recent classroom research: Implications for teacher education. In D. Smith (Ed.), *Essential knowledge for beginning educators.* Washington, D.C.: American Association of Colleges for Teacher Education.

Kounin, J. S. (1970). *Discipline and group management in the classroom.* New York: Holt, Rinehart & Winston.

Moskowitz, G., & Hayman, M. (1976). Success strategies of inner-city teachers: A year-long study. *Journal of Educational Research, 69,* 283–389.

Sanford, J., & Evertson, C. (1981). Classroom management in a low SES junior high: Three case studies. *Journal of Teacher Education, 32,* 34–38.

Chapter Five

Academic Learning Time

Ruth Anne McLaughlin

Virginia Polytechnic Institute and State University

Definition

The competent teacher knows that learning is directly related to the amount of time learners are actively engaged in planned learning activities. The one relationship most clearly established by process–product research is the relationship between academic engaged time and learners' achievement gains.

Purpose

The purpose of this chapter is to help you understand the concept of academic learning time (ALT) and to assist you in developing strategies to use time effectively and efficiently in your classroom. Specifically, we will address issues associated with time and learning over which you can exercise some control as you plan, implement, and evaluate your classroom activities. We will discuss ways you can plan for efficient use of class time by minimizing the amount of time spent on various procedural matters, such as transitions from one activity to another. We will also suggest ways to maximize use of ALT in the classroom through learner involvement in assigned tasks: maintaining continuous class focus on lesson topics, matching the pace of instruction to learners' abilities, and avoiding classroom disruptions.

Background Knowledge

On April 26, 1983, *A Nation at Risk: The Imperative for Educational Reform* by the National Commission on Excellence in Education was released. This report outlined our purported educational failures and challenged Americans to generate fundamental reform of our educational systems. Suddenly, it seemed, education had become front-page news. One major recommendation made by the authors of *A Nation at Risk* related to time. They called for a longer school day and a longer school year. This single, highly publicized recommendation is but the tip of the iceberg of concern about use of time in schools.

Research suggests a strong, consistent, positive relationship between the time students spend in learning activities and their achievement. This link between time and learning has guided many research efforts over the past few years. During the 1970s David Berliner and Charles Fisher identified various concepts of time usage and learning. Berliner, Fisher, and their colleagues examined factors associated with student learning by observing student behavior (see Fisher et al., 1980). They found that the amount of time a student spends engaged in an academic task that he or she can perform with high success is related to learning. High student success occurs when the learning task is clearly understood by the student and he or she can complete it with no more than a few careless errors. The more time a student spends in an activity aimed at increasing a specified knowledge or skill, the more learning that will result.

Fisher and his colleagues (1980) identified several concepts of time usage in the classroom that are important for teachers to understand:

Allocated Time	The amount of time assigned to each discipline area within the curriculum. This quantity of time may vary from teacher to teacher in the elementary school because individual teachers may have the responsibility for establishing time frames for individual subjects in their classroom. Most secondary teachers will not have this flexibility but will have to adhere to the structure of class time as designated by individual schools.
Engaged Time	The amount of time a student is actively involved in learning the subject matter. Engaged time can be expressed as a proportion of allocated time.
Academic Learning Time	Adds one more criterion to engaged time by stipulating that time spent in the classroom actively involved in learning also must be at an appropriate level of difficulty. Most studies have shown students learn best when interacting with learning experiences they can complete with a high rate of success.

This line of research associating time and learning is often traced to a model of school learning proposed by John Carroll in the early 1960s (cited in Karweit, 1983). Carroll showed how the relationship between time and achievement could be empirically tested by using a mathematical formula. His work is important because it suggests how an individual's aptitude in learning situations can be expressed as a function of time spent on an academic topic.

One of the first researchers to examine the connections between time and learning via Carroll's model was David Wiley. While reviewing the data from the *Report on Equality of Educational Opportunity* (Coleman et al., 1966), Wiley (1976) found that longer school years were associated positively with student achievement. By examining absenteeism he found that students with the lowest number of absences were higher achievers than those with more frequent absences.

Harnischfeger and Wiley (1978) observed classrooms to determine the amount of time teachers spend on various subjects. They found that teachers spent varying amounts of time on different subjects and that the more time teachers assigned to a subject, the higher the students scored on tests. Harnischfeger and Wiley expanded Carroll's original work on time and learning by specifying teacher activities that influence both the quality and quantity of time used by teachers in their classrooms. It is important to remember, however, that more time does not always yield more learning. In some cases, spending too much time on activities actually results in decreases in learning (see Chapter 7, "Close Supervision," especially Figure 7–1).

One of the best-known studies of time and learning is the Beginning Teacher Evaluation Study (BTES) (see Fisher et al., 1980). Initially the BTES was designed to identify teaching competencies that could assist educators in the evaluation of beginning teachers. During the planning phase of the BTES, the focus of the study moved more toward the need to identify research links between teacher behavior and student achievement. Further, while subjects selected for the initial phase of the study were beginning teachers, those selected for subsequent phases were experienced teachers.

The project was conducted in four phases over six years. The data from the final phase are the most important for us to examine. The BTES authors are the first to define and distinguish among allocated time, engaged time, and success rate and to formulate the concept of ALT. The major findings of Phase IV underscore the importance of the time and learning relationship. These findings are as follows:

- The amount of time that teachers allocate to instruction in a particular content area is positively associated with student learning in that content area.
- The proportion of allocated time that students are engaged in is positively associated with learning.
- The proportion of time in which reading or mathematics tasks are performed with high success is positively associated with student learning. (Fisher et al., 1980, p. 15)

Other researchers have also been concerned about the use of time in classrooms. Stallings and Kaskowitz (1974) evaluated seven elementary program models that ranged from very structured teaching models to flexible approaches that emphasized individualized self-learning objectives. The most persistent pattern in their data was a positive link between achievement and opportunity to learn, that is, the time students spent engaged in academic activities. In a later study Stallings and her colleagues evaluated reading instruction at the secondary level and again found that among those variables examined, quantity of instruction was the highest correlate of achievement (Stallings, 1984).

Brophy and Good (1986) have reviewed research from 1973 to 1983 examining teacher behavior and student achievement in typical elementary and secondary classrooms. They report that "academic learning is influenced by the amount of time the students spend engaged in appropriate academic tasks" (p. 121). This is one of the most consistent results found across all studies reviewed.

The findings of recent research imply that you can positively affect student achievement by effectively planning, implementing, and evaluating classroom activities that foster the most ALT for your students. While you might exercise virtually no control over class schedules, you can manage time in your own classroom. Let's take a closer look at the classroom time you have at your disposal.

Allocated time for classrooms is determined by many factors. First, the number of days a student spends in a classroom is established by state law and is fairly constant across the United States, ranging from 175 to 184 days and averaging 179 days. These numbered days may be reduced by student absenteeism, teacher strikes, school closings due to fuel shortages, financial problems, inclement weather, and so forth.

The minimum length of the school day is also set forth in state law. Recent estimates indicate that students spend an average of six hours a day in an elementary classroom and close to seven for secondary classes.

Given that students are attending school an average of six to seven hours a day for 174 days, how is their allocated time used for individual disciplines? According to Karweit (1983), Smith claims that in the elementary school, time spent on each subject matter varies substantially from place to place "dependent on [the] individual teacher's perception of what is important" (p. 31). At the high school level allocated time is more stable and is usually divided into fifty- to sixty-minute units devoted to individual class disciplines. The number of true units spent on individual topics is decided by student course selection.

Allocated time in the classroom is used for both instructional and noninstructional activities. Some instances of noninstructional time are:

- Changes from one activity to another;
- Administrative tasks, such as taking attendance or collecting money;
- Interruptions caused by announcements over the intercom or messages from the office;
- Monitoring of behavior, especially between classes.

Activities 1 through 3, are, of course, time consuming and rob teachers of valuable instructional time.

Studies of time use at the elementary level found that noninstructional time varies from 10 to 50 percent of allocated time. The most allocated time lost has been identified as transitional time, that is, time devoted, for example, to moving students from one activity to another or to getting students on task after recess, lunch, and bathroom breaks. A typical six-hour elementary classroom in the BTES study had four hours targeted for instruction and the remaining time allocated to noninstructional activities. After careful observation, the Austin, Texas, school system found that more than one-fifth of the school day was involved in these noninstructional activities.

Stallings (1984) observed that secondary reading classes with ineffective teachers spent 38 percent of the time on noninteractive academic activities with their students. These teachers attended to off-task behavior 12 percent of the time and spent more than one-fourth of class time managing and organizing activities. Conversely, effective teachers were off task only 3 percent of the time and spent only 12 percent of their time administering classroom routines.

According to Berliner (cited in Brandt, 1982), approximately half the teachers could reduce their noninstructional minutes in the classroom. Of this 50 percent, half "are probably badly under-allocating time in some areas of the curriculum" (Brandt, p. 13). In other words, allocated time in the classroom can be lost to noninstructional activities.

What factors facilitate the use of instructional, or engaged, time? Recent research shows that student level of engaged time is decreased when the student is not interacting with or being closely supervised by a teacher. In a teacher-directed environment, the pacing of instruction can be done at a level that allows students to accomplish tasks with moderate to high success. The effective teacher is able to move quickly through each activity and is well prepared. Thus, there are few interruptions resulting from the teacher's having to locate instructional aids or stop and consult a teacher's manual or lesson plans for direction.

The effective teacher is also aware of student interactions in the classroom that may interrupt class lessons and can move to stop inappropriate behavior when it begins. Such prevention can be accomplished by alerting the disrupting student with eye contact, moving toward the disrupter, putting a hand on the disrupter's shoulder, and involving the disrupter in the class activity to assure that instructional time will be maximized. These types of techniques will keep the class on task and avoid interruptions that cause the teacher to stop a group lesson because of misbehavior. If the class is involved in seatwork, the teacher must also show the same type of active involvement with students. The effective teacher moves about the room and actively gives task-oriented feedback to students.

When considering any behavioral control technique, it is imperative to recognize the importance of respecting students' self-esteem and maintaining a positive affective bond with students. As Robert Spaulding (personal communication, July 26, 1985) has noted:

Without such a bond, many of the control moves suggested [above] will work in a reverse fashion. When a student has been alienated from the teacher, her [or his] attempts to control (by glance, touch, or call to participate) will be interpreted by the student as threats to his or her independence and desire for autonomy and self-direction.

How much time do your students spend engaged in academic activities? From our reading we've learned that generally the more time students spend involved in academic tasks, the more they will learn. It would be very difficult to observe every student's actions during any specified time period, but viewing a few students may give you some clues to how task oriented your students are.

Although the influence of time on learning seems to be well established, certain concerns about research findings bear noting. Karweit (1983) reviewed the studies of time and learning and claimed that the evidence has not produced overwhelming support for the contention that more time produces more learning. Another review conducted by Frederick and Walberg (1980) suggests that learning is produced in school amid a mélange of variables that affect success. They argue that time devoted to academic tasks can be used only as a "modest predictor of achievement" (p. 194).

Further cautions are issued by others about generalizing from research results, as well as the methods used to obtain them. Goss

(1983) suggested the most important limitation of the research is that it has focused on elementary studies of the second and fifth grades and has involved only mathematics and reading classes. Generalization of the results of time and learning research to all disciplines and other age groups should be done only with caution. Furthermore, academic success has been almost exclusively defined by scores on standardized tests. Goss (1983) reported, however, that as much as 30 to 40 percent of the items on standardized tests is not covered by major commercial textbooks.

In summary, to get the most out of your allocated time you need to be actively involved in and in control of instruction in your classroom. Research suggests that teachers who dominate the classroom through lecturing, demonstration, discussion, reviewing, practice, or recitation and who closely monitor independent seatwork will have higher-achieving students. But you must remember that common sense dictates that quality of instruction plays an important role in helping students achieve. More time is not the only criterion for success, especially if it is more *bad* time. Soar (1977) reported that beyond a certain level, teacher direction may actually negate learning and that time might be more appropriately used by moving to new objectives.

It is also important to bear in mind that when teachers dominate classrooms "with a heavy hand," students' feelings of self-efficacy and of control over their own lives may suffer. Research on what is often called "cognitive style" suggests that students can and should make the decisions they are capable of making. When students do so, their chances for developing internal standards and values are greatly enhanced. Children who learn to make reasoned decisions in the classroom are more likely to do the same in other situations than are children who have always been told what to do.

You do have control over making decisions about the use of allocated time in your classroom, and there is a strong indication that the more time students spend on a subject, the more they will learn, up to a point. It is therefore imperative for you to examine your classroom to become aware of the noninstructional time that can be minimized and to familiarize yourself with techniques that encourage more engaged time and ALT for your students. Such techniques include making expectations for performance clear to students, providing task-oriented feedback, holding students accountable for their work, minimizing disruptive behavior, giving appropriately challenging assignments, and capitalizing on the intrinsic motivation of students.

There are many ways you make use of your allocated classroom time. Your activities can be divided into two major areas, noninstructional and instructional. To examine how allocated time is used in your teaching situation, choose an allocated time period from your normal classroom schedule. (Secondary teachers may want to use one or more of their allocated class periods. Elementary teachers might select a portion of their morning or afternoon academic schedule.) In the following activity, fill in your allocated time slot and read down the list of descriptors. Check off those descriptors you anticipate you will demonstrate during your allocated time slot and estimate the amount of time spent for each checked item. If you need to add other anticipated descriptors, list them in the appropriate place. Finally, total the minutes from each function and express classroom noninstructional time and instructional time as percentages.

1. Choose an allocated time frame for a specific subject from your daily class schedule and record. Express in terms of minutes:

	Subject Taught	*Amount of Time*
Elementary	_____	_____
Secondary	_____	_____

2. Next, review the following list of activities that will be occurring in your classroom during the allocated time listed in step 1. Check off those activities you anticipate you will do and estimate the amount of time needed to complete each task:

a. *Noninstructional Activities*	*Will Do*	*Estimate of Time*
Taking roll	_____	_____
Making announcements	_____	_____
Passing out material	_____	_____
Collecting material	_____	_____
Making transitions from one activity to another	_____	_____
Other:		
_____	_____	_____
_____	_____	_____

Total Number of Minutes _____

b. *Instructional Activities*		
Reviewing and discussing previous material	_____	_____
Presenting new information	_____	_____
Giving direction	_____	_____
Providing practice	_____	_____
Reteaching small groups	_____	_____
Monitoring individual student work (clarify activity _____)	_____	_____

Total Number of Minutes _____

3. Let's calculate the percentage of your allocated time that you anticipate will involve noninstructional and instructional activities.

    a. Record the total number of minutes calculated in step 2a; divide this total by the number of minutes in your allocated time frame recorded in step 1, and multiply by 100.

$$\frac{(Step\ 2a\ total)}{(Step\ 1\ total)} \times 100 = \underline{\quad}\% \quad \text{Estimate of time spent on } \textit{noninstructional} \text{ activities}$$

    b. Record the total number of minutes calculated for step 2b; divide this by the number of minutes in your allocated time frame recorded in step 1, and multiply by 100:

$$\frac{(Step\ 2b\ total)}{(Step\ 1\ total)} \times 100 = \underline{\quad}\% \quad \text{Estimate of time spent on } \textit{instructional} \text{ activities}$$

4. Now that you have estimated your times for noninstructional and instructional activities, let's examine your allocated time in a real classroom situation to check the accuracy of your estimates. You may either videotape your time period or ask another teacher to observe. Either you or the teacher will observe the allocated time frame following these directives:

    a. You will need a clock or watch with a second hand, a copy of the time chart in Figure 5–1, and the list of expected noninstructional and instructional behaviors from steps 2a and 2b.

    b. At the end of every thirty-second interval, code the teacher's behavior with either a plus sign (+) or a minus sign (−), according to how the teacher spent *most* of the time during each interval, as explained on the time chart.

    c. When the allocated time frame is completed, calculate the percentage of time the teacher was involved in instructional and noninstructional activities:

        ____% Allocated time actually involved in instructional activities

        ____% Allocated time actually involved in noninstructional activities

5. After gathering the data in step 4c, compare the figures to those generated in steps 2a and 2b:

	Estimated Time	Actual Time	Differences
Instructional Time	_____%	_____%	_____%
Noninstructional Time	_____%	_____%	_____%

	10 min.
	20 min.
	30 min.
	40 min.
	50 min.
	60 min.

+ = teacher involved in Instructional Activity listed in Step 2b.
- = teacher involved in Noninstructional Activity listed in Step 2a.

Figure 5-1 *30-Second-Interval Time Chart for Recording Schedule of Allocated Time*

6. If you find discrepancies between estimated and actual time, you might want to consider the following questions:

    a. Where are the differences?
    b. How important are the differences?
    c. Are you pleased with the percentage of time you spend on instructional and noninstructional activities?
    d. Should you gather data on this allocated time frame again or maybe even examine another time period?
    e. If you want to increase your percentage of instructional time, what plan of action should you take?

As you reflect on the five questions in the preceding practice activity, paragraph 6, you may want to keep these points in mind from the research on ALT:

INSTRUCTIONAL TIME INCREASES LEARNING!
The most consistent findings across elementary and secondary classrooms suggest that academic learning is linked to the amount of time students spend engaged in appropriate academic tasks. *Eliminate as much noninstructional time as you can.*

YOU CAN BE THE LEADER OF THE PACK!
Teachers who are in control of the instructional process are businesslike but friendly and task oriented. They adopt a "can-do" attitude for their students and tend to enhance learning. Students learn more when they are taught or supervised by teachers than when they work entirely on their own. *Be an active teacher.*

HIGH SUCCESS RATE MEANS HIGH ACHIEVEMENT!
Academic content needs to be divided into small units so that students can progress through materials briskly but with a high rate of success and minimal frustration and confusion. Students should be able to answer questions with success approximately 75 percent of the time during teacher-led instructional time, and students working independently should be able to complete the work with a 95 to 100 percent success rate. Students will achieve more if they are given the opportunity to interact with material that is familiar and easily enables them to assimilate new information. *Divide and conquer.*

McNergney and Carrier (1981) explain a pupil-observation system developed by Kounin (1970) that allows you to calculate student academic involvement and deviant behavior. Student work involvement is divided into three categories and is defined as the amount of time pupils spend engaged in academic work. The following explains each category:

Definitely In   Student exhibits expected academic behaviors, such as taking notes, completing a written assignment, volunteering to recite or answer questions, and reading or visually attending.

Probably In   Student reviews written assignment or listens to teacher, but does not demonstrate clear signal that he or she is actively involved in current classroom activity.

Definitely Out   Student doesn't have written assignment on desk and demonstrates that he or she is not involved with classroom activity.

Another category of student behavior in this system is deviant behavior. The system specifies three types of deviant behavior that pupils can demonstrate:

No Misbehavior   Student is neither purposefully acting out against another student or teacher nor breaking classroom rules.

Mild Misbehavior   Student demonstrates behavior of which most teachers would disapprove, such as talking to another student, passing notes, reading other material (library book, comic book, and so on), drawing or doodling, or throwing spitballs.

Serious Misbehavior   Student demonstrates disruptive behavior that interferes with others, damaging property, threatening students or teachers, or violating school rules.

Practice Activity 5-1

To examine a segment of your classroom for student behavior using the approach described above, you may either tape a segment of your class and code it yourself or have a fellow teacher observe and code the behaviors of selected students. Regardless of who does the observations, the following steps to applying Kounin's system can be used to guide the observer's activities:

1. Construct a diagram of the classroom that includes locations of students' and teachers' desks.
2. Divide the room into four sections and randomly select one boy (*B*) and one girl (*G*) in each quadrant to be observed.
3. Observe selected pupils and code their behavior for ten-second intervals over a specified time period. For example, the observer will focus on B_1 and G_1 for ten seconds and then code how each pupil spent the majority of his or her

time during the ten-second interval. The observer then turns to B_2 and G_2 and repeats the procedure.

4. After the data have been recorded, you may want to organize and interpret these data in several ways. If you want to examine the percentage of work involvement, you can compare the number of intervals coded as "definitely in" to the number of intervals observed. The scores of individual students can be averaged to get a score for classroom work involvement. Kounin (1970) suggested that the rate of deviant behavior be calculated by determining the percentage of ten-second intervals in which no misbehavior occurred. Using such an approach, the rate is stated in a positive way: freedom from deviant behavior.

References

Brandt, R. (1982). On improving teacher effectiveness: A conversation with David Berliner. *Educational Leadership, 40,* 12–15.

Brophy, J., & Good, T. (1986). Teacher behavior and student achievement. In M. Wittrock (Ed.), *Handbook of research on teaching* (3rd ed.) (pp. 328–75). New York: Macmillan.

Coleman, J., Campbell, E., Hobson, C., McPartland, J., Mood, A., Weinfield, F., & York, R. (1966). *Equality of educational opportunity.* Washington, D.C.: Office of Health, Education and Welfare.

Fisher, C., Berliner, D., Filby, N., Marliave, R., Cohen, L., & Dishaw, M. (1980). Teaching behaviors, learning time, and student achievement: An overview. In C. Denham & A. Lieberman (Eds.), *Time to learn* (pp. 7–22). Washington, D.C.: National Institute of Education.

Frederick, W. C., & Walberg, H. J. (1980). Learning as a function of time. *The Journal of Educational Research, 73,* 183–94.

Goss, S. (1983). Keeping students on task. *Schools and Teaching, 1* (1), 1–4.

Griffin, G. (1983). *Changing teacher practice: An experimental study.* Research and Development Center for Teacher Education. The University of Texas at Austin.

Harnischfeger, A., & Wiley, D. (1978). Conceptual issues in models of school learning. *Curriculum studies, 10,* 215–31.

Karweit, N. L., (1983). *Time-on-task: A research review* (Report no. 332). Baltimore: Johns Hopkins University.

Kounin, S. J. (1970). *Discipline and group management in the classroom.* New York: Holt, Reinhart & Winston.

McNergney, R., & Carrier, C. A. (1981). *Teacher development.* New York: Macmillan.

National Commission on Excellence in Education (1983). *A nation at risk: The imperative for educational reform.* Washington, D.C.: U.S. Government Printing Office.

Soar, R. S. (1977). An integration of findings from four studies of teacher effectiveness. In G. D. Borich (Ed.), *The appraisal of teaching: Concepts and process.* Reading, Mass.: Addison-Wesley.

Stallings, J. (1984). *Effective use of time in secondary reading classrooms* (Report no. 143). Nashville: Vanderbilt University, Peabody College. (ERIC Document Reproduction Service no. 246 393)

Stallings, J., & Kaskowitz, D. (1974). Follow through classroom observation evaluation, 972–1973. SRI Project URU-7370. Menlo Park, Calif.: Stanford Research Institute.

Wiley, D. E. (1976). Another hour, another day, quantity of schooling, a potent path for policy. In W. J. Sewel, R. M. Hauser, & D. L. Featherman (Eds.), *Schooling and achievement in American society.* New York: Academic Press.

Chapter Six

Accountability

Martin Aylesworth
Radford University

Definition

The competent teacher knows the importance of holding learners responsible for completing assigned tasks. It is important for the teacher to make sure that all students actually undergo the learning experiences planned for them. Holding the learner personally responsible for completing assigned learning tasks is also important because it gives practice in assuming and discharging personal responsibilities.

Purpose

This chapter is designed to help you understand the importance of learner accountability and to provide some strategies for assisting you in making students accountable for their learning. We will look at ways to plan just what tasks each learner is supposed to complete. We will also examine strategies for making clear to students what they are expected to accomplish and for establishing the consequences of not completing an assigned task. Finally, we will address methods for checking to see whether students work on their tasks and for determining whether assigned tasks have indeed been completed.

Background Knowledge

Accountability is an extension of Academic Learning Time (ALT). The results of instruction are a function of both what the teacher

does and what the student does. By providing ALT, the teacher increases the efficiency of class time; by fostering student accountability, the teacher increases the effectiveness of instruction.

In a review of research on teacher behavior and student achievement, Brophy and Good (1986) cite numerous studies that indicate the importance of accountability. In the Texas Teacher Effectiveness Study, Brophy and Evertson (1976) found that the most effective teachers were those who matched their assignments to students' abilities, monitored students' work on assignments, provided reminders and even demands when necessary, and checked that students' work was completed carefully. Evertson, Anderson, and Brophy (1978), in their junior high study of achievement in English and mathematics, found that the most effective teachers thoroughly explained assignments before students began work and took care not to become so involved with some students that they ignored the work of others.

Research from the massive Beginning Teachers Evaluation Study (BTES) showed strong relationships between achievement and accountability factors including the appropriate assignment of tasks, student engagement in learning tasks, and student responsibility. In a study of Title I students in reading and mathematics, Crawford (1983) found that achievement was related to factors including teacher monitoring and other strategies that facilitated student engagement in learning tasks. Coker, Medley, and Soar (1980) also found similar relationships: Student achievement was related to such teacher behaviors as selecting appropriate learning activities for individual students and providing clear task directions.

Brophy and Good (1986), in summarizing correlational studies of teacher effects, note the important point that "the data indicate the need to consider the quality of academic activities, and not just the time spent on them. . . . [The] 'time on task' that is linked most closely to achievement is time spent in teacher directed lessons or in seatwork actively supervised by the teacher" (p. 360).

Practice Activity 6-1

Reflect on your usual teaching behaviors that relate to the research just summarized.

1. Do you usually assign the same task to all students in your class, or do you usually differentiate assignments?
2. Do you usually assume that students understand what they are to do after you have given an assignment, or do you check to determine whether they understand it?
3. Do you usually assume that students will do the task because you have assigned it, or do you monitor each student's work?
4. Do you believe that students should already be responsible, or do you plan actions to foster responsibility?

Assigning Tasks

As noted in the preface of this text, many of the competencies are interrelated. Accountability is related not only to ALT, but also to individual differences. Simply put, a learner is more easily accountable for tasks that are appropriate than for those that are not. Because differences among students are inevitable, the teacher must plan just what tasks each learner is supposed to complete. The failure to differentiate tasks can lead to a number of undesirable outcomes:

- Students will not become as actively engaged in tasks as is intended.
- Student responsibility for completing tasks will diminish.
- Students will develop poor work habits.
- The teacher will find that classroom management is made more difficult.

Differentiating assignments is one of the most difficult tasks for teachers. As Brophy and Good (1986) note, it not only involves additional preparation time in providing different assignments, but it also makes the task of assisting students more difficult as the teacher switches from one to another. Such differentiation, however, is made easier by using the following strategies.

Determining Who Needs Differentiated Assignments

It is unlikely that any teacher has different learning tasks for each student. Tasks are differentiated only when needed, as under the following circumstances.

1. The student needs more or less complex assignments than the majority of the class. For example, an assignment that is at an appropriate level for the majority of students may be far too complex for a slow learner. The same assignment may be so shallow for a gifted student that the learner can never really get involved in the task. It is difficult, if not impossible, to foster accountability if the task is too far above or below the level of the learner.

2. The student needs a different presentation format or response format than is typically used. The most common problems related to this need involve handicaps that students may have (and that may not be obvious) and the readability level of materials. An inability to comprehend the content or to respond as directed will, quite understandably, retard student engagement and preclude accountability.

3. The student requires a different rate of learning than is typically used. One implication of individual differences is that different students require different amounts of time to master the same objectives. In one illustrative study, Aylesworth and Noonkester (1984) found that one-third of a fourth-grade class had already mastered more than 50 percent of their school's grade-five objectives for math and language arts. Other students may require more time than is typically allocated for mastery. To provide the same learning activities for both groups of students would, as Brophy and Good (1986) note, "result in moving too slowly for the brightest students but too quickly for the slowest."

The following are examples of strategies you can use to determine which students may need differentiated assignments.

1. Look for indirect clues. Frequently, students will not verbalize their problems but will provide clues that problems exist. Comments like "I don't understand," frequent requests for help, and behaviors like daydreaming or carelessness may be indications that the tasks are inappropriate for the student.

2. Look for signs of lack of responsibility. Just as appropriate learning tasks are necessary to foster student accountability, the lack of responsibility may be a sign of inappropriate tasks. Students' failure to attend to tasks in school or failure to complete homework are common indications of inappropriate assignments.

3. Look for underachievers. Students whose work is not up to your estimate of their abilities and students whose work is not commensurate with their efforts may simply be showing signs of a need for you to differentiate activities. When a student's work is not up to his or her abilities, more complex tasks or a faster pace may be needed to make the tasks appropriate. When student learning is less than would be expected, given his or her efforts, it may mean that the material is too complex, the presentation format is beyond the student's comprehension, or the pace is too fast.

4. Listen to other teachers. Although a student's experiences with another teacher may not always be applicable in your classroom, you can learn much about your students' needs by listening judiciously to others. The commonly heard phrase, "I don't want to be biased by the impressions of others," is not valid if you use the information carefully. You should not conclude that another teacher's assessment is undoubtedly the case; however, information that a student may have a problem elsewhere could be useful in trying new approaches to foster student accountability.

One final factor relating to appropriateness of learning activities pertains more to the activities than to individual differences: the extent to which the activities are likely to be found interesting. Although educational research has clearly documented the importance of drill and practice for meeting many instructional objectives, this does not imply the usefulness of drill and practice activities that are inherently boring. A little creativity can turn a rote drill-and-practice activity into a game. Variety of activities can add to students' interest. Allowing students to select from options or to relate your objectives to their interests can greatly improve the appropriateness of learning activities.

Practice Activity 6-2

1. Use your lesson plans for one subject to list all the activities that you assigned students during any two weeks. Include in-class activities and homework, and remember that listening to your explaining is a student activity.
2. Evaluate your list by asking the following questions:
   a. Is there variety, or do the activities tend to be of the same type?
   b. Are the drill and practice activities mostly rote, or do you frequently use games that are appropriate to your students' age level?
   c. Is the content of most of your activities relevant to the interests of students of that age?
   d. Do you provide any opportunities for students to select from options or to apply their interests to your activities?
   e. If you were a student of that age, how interesting do you believe you would find these activities?
3. Use the following questions to identify two students who may need differentiated activities, one who may need greater challenge and one who may need less.
   a. Is there a student in your class who frequently needs your individual assistance?
   b. Is there a student in your class whose performance is not up to her or his effort?
   c. Is there a student whose performance is definitely not commensurate with her or his ability?
   d. Is there a student who frequently does not complete assignments?
   e. Is there a student who you have reason to believe may have a handicap?
4. For each of these two students:
   a. Discuss the problem with the student, other teachers, parents, and a counselor if available.
   b. Check the student's records for information on past achievement, reading level, and previous evidence of the problems you have identified. Make a line graph of the student's rate of reading improvement using standardized scores from her or his permanent records. Do the same for math achievement scores.
   c. Do not jump to conclusions. Compare the information

you obtain from discussions with others and from the student's records.

  d. Look for patterns in the information that suggest:

  - A need for more or less complexity in activities
  - A different presentation or response format
  - A different pace

5. If the information suggests that modifications may be appropriate, try them. Do not expect instant results, but monitor the problems you had noted previously to determine whether there are signs of improvement.

Making Expectations Clear

An assumption is all too commonly made that students understand expectations simply because they have been explained. Everything we know about communication points out the error of this assumption. That of course is not to say that explanations are unimportant; students need clearly explained teacher expectations. This, however, is just a beginning toward making expectations clear. The following strategies will be useful in improving communication.

1. Explain to students as clearly as possible what you expect them to do in any activity. In almost all cases it is helpful if you can explain why they are participating in the activity and what you expect them to learn from it. The explanation should include what resources they should (or may) use, when they should complete the activity, and if there is to be a product, what format they should use.

2. Particularly common with older students are questions like "How long should our reports be?" Students are generally just asking for a clarification of expectations. If length or number of hours spent are not appropriate descriptors of expectations, provide guidelines that do appropriately describe them.

3. If the learning activities involve response formats that students may not have used before, demonstrate how to respond, or, if possible, give them examples to use as models. Even for bright, older students, giving concrete examples is one of the best ways to communicate expectations.

4. Remember that the question, "Does everyone understand what to do?" is generally not helpful. At best, it usually only serves as a polite but not particularly clear way of asking, "Did everyone hear the explanation?" Students (and adults) generally do not know whether they understand until they attempt the activity; understanding directions and expectations is itself a learning activity and requires practice. For this reason, it is helpful if students can be given some time in class to begin homework so that they can be given help if they do not understand.

5.   As students begin an activity, check first that every student's work demonstrates understanding of the task. The sooner you can give students feedback regarding their understanding of your expectations, the less likely that students will become frustrated. Positive feedback is as important as negative feedback, if not more so.

6.   It is important that students understand from the very beginning of the year that your expectations are not that they merely do the activity, but that they do it successfully at the level you expect of them individually. All too often students view their work and your feedback in terms of "I got it right" versus "I got it wrong." Anything you can do, through words and actions, to get students to think instead in terms of growth and improvement will help them greatly. A student who always "gets it right" may not be working under sufficiently high expectations. Frequently, such students are devastated when they eventually get something wrong, and they all too often avoid challenges because they do not know how to cope with failure. Similarly, a student who consistently "gets it wrong" may develop or reinforce poor attitudes and poor self-concept as a learner. Students need to become aware that a first try is only that—an attempt at something in which one lacks experience—and should anticipate teacher expectations for revisions and improvements.

Practice Activity 6-3

1.   After giving an explanation for a new task to students, do you check that they understand it before they are well involved in the activity? Do you remember how frustrated you used to be when your teachers were not clear about their expectations?

2.   Do your actions foster a right-versus-wrong attitude among your students? Do you accept work that is below your expectations and call it "good enough"? Do your students expect that they will regularly be asked to revise and improve, or is the first try usually the only try?

Establishing Consequences

Students are human beings. This seemingly trite observation can take teachers a long way toward understanding students' behaviors. Two characteristics common to all human beings will affect any teacher's ability to make students accountable for their learning: (1) Whenever a student has any reason not to do an activity, he or she will consider the consequences of not being accountable, and (2) the same consequence may be viewed differently by different students.

Human growth and development are characterized not only by increasing knowledge, but also by increasing independence. Thus, in summarizing research on effective instruction, Brophy and Good (1986) note that in later grades it is especially important to make expectations clear and follow up on accountability demands. Even in the early grades, however, the consequences of not completing assigned activities need to be established. Two teacher behaviors are most important in effectively establishing such consequences. First, the teacher needs to inform students of the consequences both through words and actions. If students do not realize what the consequences will be, they will understandably test to determine the teacher's limits. This unfortunately leads to having to "establish rules in midgame" and exacerbates classroom management problems. Second, the teacher needs to be consistent in enforcing the consequences. Even very young students realize that it is not the verbalized rules but rather the enforced rules that are important. Older students, particularly as they develop more sophisticated moral reasoning and greater independence, will base much of their respect for a teacher and many of their behaviors on the consistency with which rules are applied.

As noted, another important element in establishing consequences is realizing that the same action may be viewed differently by different students. In establishing consequences of not completing an assigned task, the teacher is trying to create a deterrent to undesirable student behaviors. This will be effective only to the extent that the consequence will indeed influence the student's behaviors. For example, a failing grade is an effective consequence only if the student views a failing grade as undesirable—so undesirable that he or she will complete the task. If the consequence is not undesirable to the student, it will not serve the purpose the teacher intended. This problem is compounded by the phenomenon of acclimatization: After getting a few failing grades for not completing assignments, the student may feel used to getting such grades and the consequence seems no longer so undesirable. In such a situation, the consequence may again no longer serve the teacher's purpose. As the teacher finds that the consequences, even when clearly understood and consistently enforced, do not change behavior, the teacher must change the consequences to fit the student.

Although students need to understand that there are consequences for undesirable behavior, it is vitally important for teachers to capitalize in positive ways on the things students do well. Students will be more likely to hold themselves accountable when teachers reinforce positive behaviors in classrooms. The effective teacher is always on the lookout for those aspects of learning that are intrinsically motivating for students. The things that students like to do and do well can be used to reinforce learners to view school as rewarding and worthwhile.

A useful strategy for influencing student behavior involves collaborative problem solving with the student. In using this method the teacher must begin by trying to get the student to accept "ownership" of the problem. That is, you must change it from the teacher's problem to the student's problem, or at least to a mutual problem. In the course of such discussion other related problems frequently surface. Once the problems have been acknowledged, the teacher assumes the role of helping the student solve problems rather than the role of enforcing rules. This strategy is most helpful when a student's need to assert independence is related to the failure to complete work.

Practice Activity 6-4

Consider the consequences of a student's not completing assigned work in your class.

1. Do your students clearly understand the consequences?
2. Do you assign more work simply to keep them busy?
3. Do you give them choices of what to do?
4. Do you make them wait for others to finish?
5. Do you consistently enforce your rules?
6. Do some students persist in not completing work despite the consequences?
7. Are you trying to find work that interests students?

Monitoring Students

If you as a teacher expect students to come to school with an already developed sense of responsibility for completing their work, you will frequently be disappointed. Student accountability, like academic understanding, must be fostered by the teacher. The teacher can most effectively do this (without having to resort to enforcing consequences) by checking to see whether learners work on their tasks and whether assigned tasks are completed and by giving credit for those who are on task and who have completed tasks. As noted in the background information section of this chapter, the regular monitoring of students is one of the most important elements in effective teaching, provided that the monitoring is characterized by positive feedback strategies.

McNergney and Carrier (1981) note that actions to promote student accountability are closely related to the concept of "withitness," knowledgeability of student behavior and misbehavior (mentioned briefly in Chapter 4). They (p. 92) cite Kounin in providing the following examples of teacher behaviors that can foster student accountability during recitations:

- Teacher asks students to hold up their props, exposing performances or answers in such a manner as to be readily visible to the teacher.

- Teacher requires students to recite in unison while the teacher shows signs of actively attending to the recitation.
- Teacher brings other students into the performance of a student reciting. (Teacher says, "Jim, you watch John do that problem and then tell me what he did right or wrong.")
- Teacher asks for the raised hands of students who are prepared to demonstrate a performance and requires some of them to demonstrate.
- Teacher circulates and checks products of nonreciters during a student's performance.
- Teacher requires a student to demonstrate and checks his performance.

Other activities by which teachers can foster student accountability include calling on nonvolunteers, collecting seatwork regularly, returning marked homework papers, regularly moving around the room while students are doing seatwork, and making notes in a teacher's record book of each student's rate of progress (noting problems completed, pages read, and so forth) and attention to task. Such actions, when done consistently, create an environment in which students expect that they must engage in assigned activities. Such an environment, in turn, will foster students' personal sense of accountability.

Practice Activity 6-5

Consider your own behaviors related to monitoring students' work.

1. Do you call on nonvolunteers as well as volunteers?
2. Do you collect assignments to check that students have completed them?
3. Do you move around the classroom while students are working at their desks?
4. Do you engage other students when selected students are performing or reciting?
5. Do you find students who are on task and find a way to reinforce them (touch or smile at them, comment positively, sign your initials on their work pages, or record points in your record book)?

References

Aylesworth, M., & Noonkester, M. (1984). *Teaching what they already know.* Unpublished research report. Radford, Va.: Radford University.

Brophy, J., & Evertson, C. (1976). *Learning from teaching: A developmental perspective.* Boston: Allyn & Bacon.

Brophy, J., & Good, T. (1986). Teacher behavior and student achievement. In M. Wittrock (Ed.), *Handbook of research on teaching* (3rd ed.) (pp. 328–75). New York: Macmillan.

Coker, H., Medley, D., & Soar, R. (1980). How valid are expert opinions about effective teaching? *Phi Delta Kappan, 62,* 131–34, 149.

Crawford, J. (1983). A study of instructional processes in Title I classes: 1981–82. *Journal of Research and Evaluation of the Oklahoma City Public Schools, 13,* 1.

Evertson, C., Anderson, C., & Brophy, J. (1978). *Texas junior high school study: Final report of process–outcome relationships.* (Rep. no. 4061). Austin: University of Texas, Research and Development Center for Teacher Education.

McNergney, R., & Carrier, C. (1981). *Teacher development.* New York: Macmillan.

Chapter Seven

Close Supervision

Jeremy Burnham
George Mason University

Definition

The competent teacher knows that more is learned during individual, small, and whole group activities if the learners are monitored than if they are not. Research indicates that learning is facilitated during activities in which learners are monitored rather closely, presumably because this increases the amount of learner engagement. Close supervision also provides opportunities for the teacher to assist and encourage learners.

Purpose

The adage "A watched pot never boils" may hold true in the kitchen, but within your classroom the phrase is inoperative. When teachers supervise students—or monitor activities and offer help when needed—chances for student learning are enhanced. The primary objective of close supervision is to maximize student involvement with learning tasks so as to increase achievement.

Background Knowledge

No sooner had video technology been introduced into classrooms than people began asking, "Will TV replace the classroom teacher?" With the refinement and sophistication of modern computer capabilities, many people are exploring ways to utilize this technology to help children learn.

109

Although technology may facilitate learning, you can rest assured that there is no electronic robot educator blinking and beeping its way to take your job. The classroom teacher is still a powerful force in helping students by actively encouraging learning.

Brophy and Good (1986) reviewed research that focused on teaching behaviors related to student achievement. They concluded that "students achieve more in classes where they spend most of the time being taught or *supervised* by their teachers rather than working on their own." Good and Brophy have applied the term *active teaching* to describe teachers who are closely supervising their students.

Teachers engaged in active teaching often present information and develop concepts through teacher-led discussions. These teachers rely on student feedback through frequent questioning and recitation designed to check for student comprehension. Not until teachers are assured that students understand concepts will the students be released to practice newly learned material at their seats. During individual seatwork the teacher monitors progress of students working independently and assists those having difficulty, reteaching if necessary.

In this active-teaching or close-supervision model of teaching, the teacher takes major responsibility for conveying content to students rather than depending on curriculum materials (Brophy & Good, 1986). Teacher talk is prevalent during the learning situation, but it focuses on the academic subject matter. The teacher asks questions and provides feedback rather than lectures. Few teacher comments are made on procedural, managerial, socialization, or personal issues.

In some studies, teachers of students who made the greatest achievement gains (at least as measured by certain tests) demonstrated these types of active teacher behaviors at both the elementary and secondary level (Good & Grouws, 1977, 1979; Evertson et al., 1980; Good, Grouws & Ebmeier, 1983). Teachers of students who made less progress had their students work independently at their desks more often than did effective teachers. Also, these less-effective teachers gave inadequate instructions for seatwork and did not recognize signals from students who had either "procedural or substantive" misunderstandings about the assignments. In essence these teachers were not actively supervising their students.

Good and Grouws (1979) reviewed one hundred third- and fourth-grade students' math achievement scores and found marked differences among types of teaching in the students' classrooms. Despite the fact that teachers used the same curriculum materials and had students of comparable abilities, some teachers had higher-achieving students than did other teachers. After observing teachers in classrooms, the researchers found that more effective teachers demonstrated the behaviors characteristic of active teaching. (You must remember these were correlational studies, which do not prove that teachers actually cause learning.) These characteristics have been summarized by Good (1983). According to Good, effective teachers will do the following:

- Teach the class as a whole
- Present information actively and clearly
- Focus on tasks (for example, during a math lesson, they spend most of the period on math, not on socialization)
- Refrain from being evaluative, creating a relaxed learning environment with comparatively little praise or criticism
- Express higher achievement expectations (for example, they assign more homework, use a somewhat faster pace, and are more alerting than ineffective teachers)

Good and Grouws (1979) wrote a manual for teachers to encourage the use of active teaching. The key instructional and management strategies that served as the basis for the manual have been summarized by Gagne (1985) (see Box 7–1).

When mathematics teachers implemented this program, the performance of their students was considerably higher than the performance of students in a comparative control group. Good and Grouws (1979) concluded that teachers do affect student learning and that through inservice training, teachers can learn teaching strategies that facilitate student achievement.

Another finding among researchers has been the positive relationship between teacher control of learning time and student achievement. As teachers exert control over student time on task, achieve-

---

Box 7–1 *Instructional and Management Strategies*

1. *Daily review* (first 8 minutes except Mondays)
    a.   Review the concepts and skills associated with the homework.
    b.   Collect and deal with homework assignments.
    c.   Ask several mental computation exercises
            using process/product questions (active interaction)
            using controlled practice.
    d.   Repeat and elaborate on the meaning portion as necessary.

2. *Seatwork* (about 15 minutes)
    a.   Provide uninterrupted successful practice.
    b.   Momentum–keep the ball rolling–get everyone involved, then sustain involvement.
    c.   Alerting–let students know their work will be checked at end of period.
    d.   Accountability–check the students' work.

3. *Homework assignment*
    a.   Assign on a regular basis at the end of each math class except Fridays.
    b.   Should involve about 15 minutes of work to be done at home.
    c.   Should include one or two review problems.

4. *Special reviews*
    a.   Weekly review/maintenance
            conduct during the first 20 minutes each Monday
            focus on skills and concepts covered during the previous week.
    b.   Monthly review/maintenance
            conduct every fourth Monday
            focus on skills and concepts covered since last monthly review.

Note: Adapted from Good & Grouws by Gagne, 1985, p. 230.

ment levels rise, up to a point. Increases can be followed, however, by decreases (see Figure 7–1). This means that teachers can have students spend so much time on a task that their performance suffers.

Research by Brophy and Evertson (1976, 1978) also shows that the successful classroom teacher is a manager of academic learning time through close supervision. Moving about the classroom during instruction and during individual seatwork, reducing classroom interruptions, appropriately directing disciplinary action, and providing appropriate feedback to students are all teacher actions that can result in improved learning.

Another aspect of the Brophy and Evertson (1978) study serves as an excellent illustration of effective close supervision. Contrary to what one might think, greater student learning occurred in reading

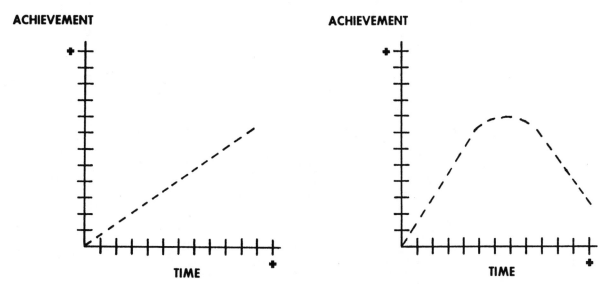

Figure 7–1   *Relationships Between Teacher Control of Learning Time and Student Achievement*

groups when students read aloud in an ordered rotation than when students read in random order. Use of ordered rotation reduced the distraction of hand raising and the typical "me next" comments from the students. This allowed for better concentration on the lesson in a stable environment. The teacher also was able to focus attention on all the students and provide equal assistance to each. These same principles can be utilized in total group instruction, provided the teacher has properly prepared for and explained the correct procedures and explained them to students.

Reading instruction was the focus of two studies by Stallings and colleagues (1977, 1978). The first study examined elementary students; the second was conducted at the high school level. Both sets of data indicated gains were realized when teachers effectively managed the academic learning time of their students through small group instruction, silent and oral reading, praise for success, and constructive feedback.

Some may think that teachers provide close supervision of students only through a model of whole group instruction, but Good points out that active teaching really "connotes a broader philosophical base." Teachers may closely supervise and demonstrate active-teaching behaviors while using small group instruction. In addition, the teaching presentation may be either inductive or deductive; that is, student learning may be either self-initiated or teacher-initiated. Instead of employing only one style of teaching, an active teacher may accomplish his or her learning objectives through a variety of techniques. The key factor is that teachers must be actively involved in the process, clearly setting expectations for student academic work and behaviors.

The term *close supervision* may conjure images of mechanistic teaching, but just the opposite is true. Spaulding (personal communication, June 26, 1985) said it well:

> Close supervision, to be maximally effective, must be preceded by a conscious effort to establish affective bonds with each of the students. Bonding is established gradually by distributing positive and negative reinforcers to each and every student from the very first day of class. The teacher should be near the entrance to the class as the students enter for the first time each day, greeting them with hellos, with questions about how they are feeling, or with comments about some topic of personal interest to them.
>
> By bell time, the students should be beginning to work on assignments built into their plans or listed on the board and the teacher should be moving about the room commenting on work underway and recording positive comments on worksheets and in a teacher record book. The marking on papers and the notes in the teacher's record book should contain no aversive or critical comments. Those students who do not deserve positive or negative reinforcers at this time (when the bell has rung and academic work is expected) should be passed by without comment. After a work period of 10 to 15 minutes, the teacher should call the attention of the class to a lesson she

has prepared. The information should be revealed on a prearranged overhead transparency or on a chart or chalkboard (which has been covered until this point). The lesson should proceed quickly and be interspersed with practice activities (these may be narrative, inductive, deductive, transductive, or rule governed).

When the lesson has been completed (after 5 to 10 minutes), a seatwork time should follow. Again the teacher should move about the room, pausing briefly at each desk or work station. Using a technique called "pause, praise, prompt, and leave" the teacher should identify an example or exercise done correctly, praise the student for working hard, prompt him or her to pay attention to some item on the worksheet, and leave. This brief visit should not be extended even when the student seeks to be given further instruction. By moving from student to student about the room, the teacher will provide close supervision to all students and not allow one or two students to dominate his or her time. When the teacher does not stay for an extended period with any one student, explaining in detail, the students soon learn to listen during the lesson rather than rely on personal instruction during seatwork.

When students are strongly bonded (after three or four weeks with a teacher who avoids criticism and makes liberal use of reinforcers), they will be very responsive to losses of teacher attention and his or her symbols of approval. They will strive to be on task in the presence of the teacher and will voluntarily initiate work soon after entry to the classroom. A glance or approach by the teacher will motivate, not by fear of disapproval, but by a desire to maintain or restore the strength of the relationship established with the teacher. Observers will not be able to see the bond itself but will be impressed by the manner in which the students go about their work without verbal reminders of rules and teacher expectations.

Practice Activity 7-1

The following narratives describe fictitious classroom situations. The first is about a secondary class; the second concerns an elementary class. After each stage in the narratives, analyze the events in terms of close supervision. What actions or strategies served to facilitate or inhibit the teacher's attempts at close supervision? What could have been done to prevent some of the problems that occurred?

1. a. Mr. Hoover's ninth-grade literature class has just begun. Before he says a word to the class he takes a few minutes to write on the board the three activities he has planned. He also includes that night's homework assignment. The first activity is to do oral reading from poems by Robert Frost. The first student is selected randomly to read from the podium at the front of the room. Mr. Hoover stands at the back of the room and

continues to call on students at random. The activity is taking longer than expected because students such as Eric, the class clown, are hamming it up as they travel to and from the podium.

b. In an effort to keep his time allocation on target, Mr. Hoover cuts short the readings and moves into a writing assignment. Each student is to write a paragraph or two about their emotional reactions while listening to the readings. Again, time is lost when several of the students walk about borrowing paper because they did not have their notebooks with them. Once the students have settled down, Mr. Hoover moves about the room. He concentrates on being near the students he knows have difficulty with creative writing. Beth and Joanna are beginning to talk about last night's game, and Mr. Hoover quickly moves to the board and writes their names on the board. The two girls return to the task at hand.

c. The time allocated for the second activity has elapsed, and all the students have completed the assignment. The students are asked to arrange their seats in a circle. When this is done, Mr. Hoover, who is seated with the students, leads a discussion of emotional imagery in writing. Maggie is called on to answer a question, but she asks instead to the bathroom. This results in many giggles and a break in the discussion. No sooner does Mr. Hoover get the class back on track than the bell sounds, ending the period.

2. a. Mrs. Taylor's fourth-graders are all in their seats reading the first four pages of chapter six in their science text while she is at her desk correcting papers. There is a sudden commotion in the back of the room, and Mrs. Taylor looks up to see Jennifer out of her seat picking up papers that are scattered on the floor. "That's it!" says Mrs. Taylor, "No recess for you." Jennifer starts to respond, but Mrs. Taylor cuts her off and reminds her that the instructions were to work quietly at their seats. She does not see little Regina giggling to herself because she was the one who knocked Jennifer's papers on the floor.

b. At this point Mrs. Taylor walks over to see how Leland, who has a reading problem, is doing. He appears to be doing well, but she also notices that Sherry has a puzzled look on her face. Mrs. Taylor eases over and looks at Sherry as if to say, "Is everything okay?"

c. "I just don't get it," says Sherry. While she is assisting Sherry, Mrs Taylor notices that Ed has his hand raised. She winks, holds up her hand, and Ed goes back to his reading. Before she checks back with Ed, Mrs. Taylor does a quick scan of the room and finds everyone has gone on to the problems at the end of the chapter as instructed.

d. Ed is having trouble with the first problem, so Mrs. Taylor writes out a few simpler ones for him on the back of his paper. He zips through the first two with high praise from his teacher. The third problem is tough. Ethel is playing with the knitting she has in her desk. Mrs. Taylor keeps waiting for Ed to work out the problem. Ethel keeps knitting. Finally Ed starts to cry because he cannot do the problem. Mrs. Taylor comforts Ed and tells him to go on to the next problem in the book because he really does know how to do it.

e. Mrs. Taylor returns to her desk and takes the papers she is grading with her as she circulates through the room. As the students raise their hands she responds to their questions. Ethel is still knitting and now Tom is more interested in that than his math. Noticing Tom's attention is not on his task, Mrs. Taylor sharply tells him to get back to work. Several students look up and try to see what is happening. Mrs. Taylor continues to glare at Tom while Ethel slips her knitting away undetected.

Responses to Practice Activity 7-1

Analysis 1a: Mr. Hoover might usefully have written the information on the board before the students arrived, but this is probably a case of "better late than never." Reading in order might have worked better than reading randomly, and time could have been saved by having the students read from their seats. Being at the back of the room provides a good vantage point from which to monitor the students.

Analysis 1b: Having the assignment on the board helps smooth transitions. Mr. Hoover should make more effort to have all students come to class prepared. He shows "withitness" by being near students he suspects might need help. Beth and Joanna obviously know what it means when their names are on the board, and this was handled very well with no disruption.

Analysis 1c: Having to rearrange the room is very disruptive. All the activities could have been conducted in the circle, which also enhances the teacher's visual contact with students. Maggie's exit could have been less disturbing if rules had been clearly set ahead of time.

Analysis 2a: Mrs. Taylor should not have been so involved with her desk work, since it led to accusing the wrong student. If she had been monitoring, this whole situation might have been avoided.

   Analysis 2b: Checking on Leland was appropriate; noticing Sherry's confusion also showed "withitness." By using a facial expression the teacher allowed the student to initiate the assistance activity.

   Analysis 2c: Using a nonverbal cue (the wink) was an excellent way to keep Ed on task in a quiet manner while working with Sherry.

   Analysis 2d: This shows how timing errors can be upsetting. Mrs. Taylor waited too long and Ed became totally frustrated. She was not aware of Ethel. If Ed really knew the work, Mrs. Taylor was actually working against him.

   Analysis 2e: Mrs. Taylor was "overlapping," or working on two things: grading her papers and monitoring the class. Unfortunately, she made an error by scolding Tom when it really was Ethel who created the diversion.

Practice Activity 7-2

   Arrange for the observation or videotaping of a lesson you know will include seatwork and during which you will be able to move about and provide student assistance. Prepare a chart similar to the sample in Figure 7–2. Include the locations of your own desk and those of your students. You or your observer can then complete the chart according to the coding system described.

   By interpreting the coded responses for each student, you will be able to determine the degree of success you had while closely supervising your students. Strive for as many positive attended situations (PAS) and as few negative attended situations (NAS) as possible. Unattended situations (US) and avoidable interruptions (AI) should be minimized. Unavoidable interruptions (UI $+/-$) should be handled positively.

References

Brophy, J., & Evertson, C. (1976). *Learning from teaching: A developmental perspective.* Boston: Allyn & Bacon.

Brophy, J., & Evertson, C. (1978). Context variables in teaching. *Educational Psychologist, 12,* 310–16.

Brophy, J., & Good, T. (1986). Teacher behavior and student achievement. In M. Wittlock (Ed.), *Handbook of research on teaching* (3rd ed.) (pp. 328–75). New York: Macmillan.

Evertson, C., Anderson, C., Anderson, L., & Brophy, J. (1980). Relationships between classroom behaviors and student outcomes in junior high

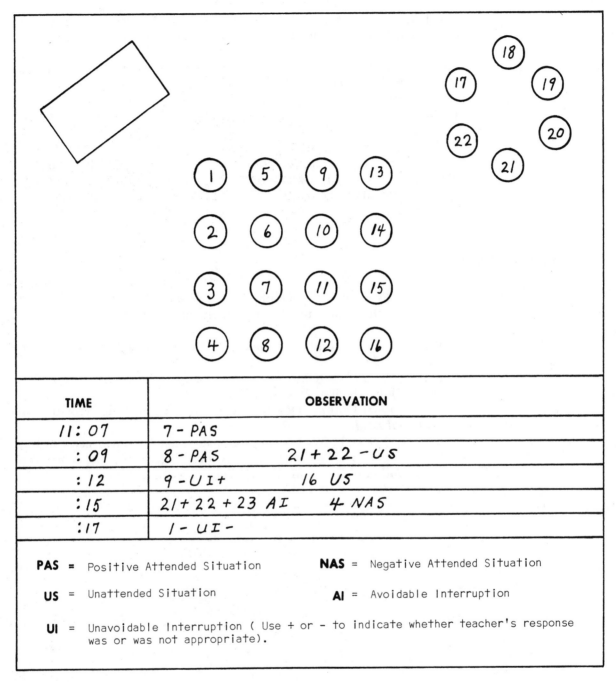

Figure 7–2 *Seating Arrangement Chart*

mathematics and English classes. *American Educational Research Journal, 17,* 43–60.

Gagne, E. (1985). *The cognitive psychology of school learning.* Boston: Little, Brown.

Good, T. (1983). Recent classroom research: Implications for teacher education. In D. C. Smith (Ed.), *Essential knowledge for beginning educators.* Washington, D.C.: American Association of Colleges for Teacher Education.

Good, T., & Grouws, D. (1977). Teaching effects: A process–product study in fourth grade mathematics classrooms. *Journal of Teacher Education, 28,* 49–54.

Good, T., & Grouws, D. (1979). The Missouri mathematics effectiveness project: An experimental study in fourth grade classrooms. *Journal of Educational Psychology, 71,* 355–62.

Good, T., Grouws, D., & Ebmeier, H. (1983). *Active mathematics teaching.* New York: Longman.

Stallings, J., Corry, R., Fairweather, J., & Needles, M. (1977). *Early childhood education classroom evaluation.* Menlo Park, Calif.: SRI International.

Stallings, J., Cory, R., Fairweather, J., & Needles, M. (1978). *A study of basic reading skills taught in secondary schools.* Menlo Park, Calif.: SRI International.

Additional Readings

Emmer, E., Evertson, C., & Brophy, J. (1979). Stability of teacher effects in junior high classrooms. *American Educational Research Journal, 16,* 71–75.

Flanders, N. (1970). *Analyzing teacher behavior.* Reading, Mass.: Addison-Wesley.

Kounin, J. (1970). *Discipline and group management in classrooms.* New York: Holt, Rinehart & Winston.

Soar, R. S. (1968). Optimum teacher–pupil interaction for pupil growth. *Educational Leadership, 26,* 275–80.

Soar, R. S., & Soar, R. M. (1979). Emotional climate and management. In P. Peterson and H. Walberg (Eds.), *Research on teaching: Concepts, findings, and implications.* Berkeley, Calif.: McCutchan.

Chapter Eight

Awareness

George M. Bass and **Roger R. Ries**
College of William and Mary

Definition

The competent teacher knows that effective classroom management depends on his or her knowing what is occurring in the classroom and in assuring as well that the learners perceive this awareness on the teacher's part.

Objective

Competent teachers know that effective instruction and good classroom management do not happen accidentally; they must be carefully planned and systematically implemented. Competent teachers also recognize that they must develop a comprehensive and well-conceptualized approach to instruction and classroom management that integrates both theory and research findings. A failure to do this will force teachers to rely on a stopgap approach, frequently emphasizing simplistic and gimmicky panaceas. The purpose of this chapter is to help you recognize the many verbal and nonverbal events that are going on in classrooms. We will suggest ways to increase your awareness of these events so you can increase learner participation and reduce classroom disruptions. Further, we will offer suggestions for making your students aware of your "teacher awareness."

Background Knowledge

Of what should a teacher be aware during a teaching lesson? Indeed, what happens in the classroom while you are teaching? Because the classroom is such a busy, complex place, it is impossible for you to notice everything occurring. Moreover, since you are engaged in the task of teaching, it is not always easy to observe all your students' behaviors, let alone to monitor your own actions. Yet it is important to observe key aspects of both your students' and your own behavior to guide your instructional and classroom management decisions.

You are constantly making decisions while you teach. One researcher has estimated that teachers make as many as thirteen hundred decisions each teaching day (Jackson, 1968). These decisions can be as varied as dealing with Frank's out-of-seat episodes, Sally's calling out answers, Terry's need for extra guidance, or Pat's ability to finish assignments before the rest of the class. In all these decisions you are considering many different kinds of information.

One important source of information for instructional decision making can be classified as Antecedent Conditions (Shavelson & Stern, 1981). While you are planning your instruction, you should consider the following:

1. Information about students (their past behaviors, present abilities, or general willingness to participate)
2. Aspects of the instructional task (the subject matter, lesson goals, or available materials)
3. Characteristics of the classroom or school environment (learning climate, group cohesiveness, or extracurricular pressures)

You should examine this information in relation to your teaching attitudes, values, and beliefs.

Another important source of instructional information can be classified as Classroom Interactions. While you are actively teaching the lesson you so carefully planned, you ought to consider (1) student involvement in the lesson, (2) student understanding of the lesson objectives, and (3) student readiness for more or different learning. To ascertain these outcomes you need to interpret the students' behaviors during your teaching. Yet because there are so many potential behavioral cues, you need to be aware which cues are most suggestive and what actions you can take to produce the desired student outcomes. In this section we will introduce you to important observational cues, interpretative strategies, and classroom actions you can take to remain instructionally "aware" and communicate that awareness to your students.

Antecedent Conditions

The knowledge teachers have about Antecedent Conditions influences both the preactive (planning) and interactive decisions they make about subject matter, content, instructional tasks, and classroom management.

Information about Students

No two students are identical. Each student comes to the classroom with a unique set of personal characteristics that plays an important part in what and how he or she learns. To plan and implement effective instruction and classroom management, you need to be aware of a variety of information about students. Intelligence, past achievement, self-concept, academic motivation, and level of development are just some of the many variables that have been identified and studied as precursors of learning. To the extent that you can become sensitive to these variables and assess their influence on student learning and behavior, you can function as an effective decision maker.

Cognitive development is one of the most important aspects of human development for you to understand. One of the first questions you need to ask yourself about students is "What is going on in the heads of the students I am teaching?'' In other words, what concepts are they capable of understanding, and what types of reasoning patterns are they using? By assessing the types and levels of reasoning patterns students use in approaching learning tasks, you can design effective instructional techniques and select materials that students are capable of understanding. According to Piaget (1970), the clinical interview (a method of critical exploration) offers teachers an assessment strategy that enables them to determine their students' present levels (or stages) of cognitive functioning. The clinical interview involves presenting different kinds of problems to students and questioning them about how they approach the problems and arrive at their answers. Through systematic questioning and probing, you can discover the reasoning pattern students are using to solve problems. Books that will help you understand the reasoning of your students include *Piaget for the Classroom Teacher* (Wadsworth, 1984) and *Understanding Piaget* (Pulaski, 1980).

By using the clinical interview with young children, you will become aware that they are busy interpreting the world in ways that are consistent with their cognitive stages of development. While their inferences may seem inaccurate and humorous to an adult, they are perfectly logical and reasonable to a child. Your assessment will reveal, not surprisingly, that children do not reason in the same fashion as adults.

If you are teaching adolescents, you will find many of them capable of thinking abstractly and logically, of reasoning hypothetically and deductively, of recognizing implicit assumptions, of mastering hypothesis testing, and of appraising their own reasoning. These adolescents have reached the most advanced stage of thinking. However, you need to remember that the onset of adolescence does not necessarily mean these reasoning capabilities will appear all at once. Individual variation in reasoning abilities exists, and the transition from one stage of reasoning to the next is gradual and overlapping. Many students may be in a transitional stage, showing inconsistencies in the reasoning patterns they use in solving the multitude of tasks presented in classrooms.

Knowing the cognitive level at which your students are functioning and the reasoning patterns of which each student is capable can be useful if you are to select and present tasks at an optimal level of complexity, neither too easy nor too hard. Cognitively challenging tasks are more likely to arouse interest and maintain the attention of your students than are unchallenging tasks.

Practice Activity 8-1

It is important to become aware of the developmental characteristics of your students. Visualize one of your classes and think about the variety of behaviors you have observed. Take a few moments to answer the following questions. You should write out your responses and try to clarify and evaluate your thoughts and feelings. Speculate about the implications these characteristics have for your teaching.

1. How do your students reason or think? How does their thinking differ from yours? Do they tend to operate at a concrete or abstract level? Are your students intellectually curious? Are they more interested in possibilities than realities?

2. Are your students egocentric in their thinking? Are they capable of understanding another person's perspective? Do they recognize when the other person understands their view? What are their perceptions of you as a teacher? How do they view your interactions with other students? What is their perception of other school personnel?

3. Are your students developing a sense of autonomy? Are they experiencing feelings of genuine accomplishment? Are they developing a sense of identity? Do they interact in positive ways with their peers? How do they express their individuality?

Social cognition.   Cognitive developmental theorists have begun to study social cognition. They have focused on what developmental changes take place in children and adolescents. As children mature, they develop abilities to reason about moral and ethical issues, to

take the perspectives of other persons, to understand themselves and others, to conceptualize interpersonal relationships with parents, friends, and authority figures, and to understand social conventions and social institutions. Becoming aware of these developmental changes will help prepare you for the wide range of reactions your students will display in your classroom.

Robert Selman (1980) has formulated a theory of social perspective taking that views role-taking skills as proceeding in a sequence of stages. During the early elementary years, children begin gradually to differentiate their own interpretations of a situation from those of others and to realize that a person's overt actions or words may not reflect inner feelings. They do not, however, realize that their perceptions may be influenced by how they think others view them. Toward the end of the elementary school years, children are capable of taking a more detached and analytical view of their own behavior as well as the behavior of others. They understand their expectations of themselves and those of others in a variety of interpersonal settings. It is at this time that students can conceptually "place themselves in the shoes of another" and view themselves from that vantage point. Although the sequence of these changes is always the same, the ages at which children go through the sequence vary widely.

Students' social perspective-taking abilities strongly influence their concepts of teachers and teacher behavior—what teachers are like and what they think, feel, or intend. Students actively interpret and draw inferences about what is happening in the classroom. Unfortunately, their view and your view may not correspond.

Nature of the Instructional Task

In planning instruction you need to be aware of the many elements in a classroom situation that can directly or indirectly affect both your behavior and the behavior of your students. Two factors that have been identified as influencing teacher and student behavior are the physical arrangement of the classroom and the structure and sequence of the lesson (Brophy, 1983).

Arranging the physical setting for lessons includes making decisions about classroom space, furniture, equipment, and supplies. In planning the instructional setting, you need to consider your instructional objectives and the characteristics of your students. The physical setting of your classroom should be designed to use your available space efficiently and to encourage orderly movement from one activity to the next with as few disruptions as possible. You need to be sure that the physical arrangement of your classroom is conducive to student involvement and allows you to monitor your students continually. It is important that students be able to see instructional presentations easily and that they can be easily seen by you. If there are not clear lines of sight between you and your students, it will be difficult for you to monitor attention and prevent disruptions.

The structure and sequence of a lesson refer to the specific organizational components and phases of the instructional activity. The structure of the lesson may involve whole class instruction, small group discussions, or independent seatwork. The sequence of the lesson involves the functions the teacher or students carry out from the beginning to the end of an activity. It is important to remember that variations in student involvement and disruptions are associated with different types of instructional activities and with different segments within these activities. For example, to maintain student attention and involvement during large group instruction, it is important that you focus your students' attention and explicitly structure the lesson, proceed in small steps but at a brisk pace, ask a great number of questions, and provide prompts and precise feedback. In managing seatwork, you can enhance involvement by making sure your students are capable of succeeding at the task, breaking the instruction into small segments, and actively circulating among the students, asking questions and giving explanations (Rosenshine, 1983).

Practice Activity 8-2

Have a colleague videotape a twenty- to thirty-minute lesson. View the tape and identify segments of the lesson in which you deliberately attempted to engage your students in the learning task; also identify points in the lesson at which you tried to increase the level of concern of your students. Select three or four students and view the tape with them. At the points of the lesson you have previously identified, stop the tape and try to assess whether the students were aware of what you were trying to do and why you were trying to do it. You may have to ask explicit questions, such as "Can you describe what I am doing now?" "Why did I do that?" "What do you suppose I want you to be doing (attending to, thinking about, remembering) now?" "Was it clear what you were supposed to be doing?" "How could I have made it clearer?" You will have to probe your students in order to assess the cognitive processes in which they were engaged at that point in the lesson. Do not be surprised if many of your instructional moves failed to promote the type of behavior or thinking you intended (see, for example, Peterson & Swing, 1982).

As you proceed through a lesson, your motivational tasks will change. During the initial phase of an instructional activity, you will need to stimulate student interest and focus attention. For example, to get students interested in Japan, you could begin the lesson with a class discussion of what first comes to mind when they think of Japan. Mistaken notions and common stereotypes about Japan could be explored. Asking students to develop a list of questions about what they want to know about Japan would enable you to assess their level of knowledge and identify their existing interests. Specifying clear and explicit instructional goals helps focus students on what is to be learned. Allowing student choices among learning activities is an excellent way of capitalizing on student interest and facilitating involvement.

After starting a lesson, you will need to make certain that students maintain their involvement. This can be accomplished more easily if, whenever possible, you allow students to control the pace and tempo of the instructional activity. You can vitalize your classroom presentations by planning your use of movement, body language, pauses, and auditory and visual aids. You should capitalize on the arousal value of suspense, doubt, uncertainty, bafflement, and contradiction. Creating learning situations that facilitate active participation by students helps to keep them involved. Designing a sequence of instruction so that your students experience initial success is critical in maintaining interest. It is also important to minimize aversive consequences of involvement.

Practice Activity 8-3

Student involvement can and should be positively reinforced. This can be accomplished by providing feedback that emphasizes the positive and by liberally using praise. Consult veteran teachers in your school and solicit suggestions for using praise effectively. (Chapters 3 and 13, "Reinforcement" and "Learner Self-Concept," respectively, provide additional guidelines for using praise.) Task involvement also can be increased by minimizing unpleasant consequences of involvement. Brainstorm with your students for classroom events or occurrences that led to aversive effects. Analyze your own behavior to determine whether it was a contributing factor.

The Classroom and School Environment

Every classroom exists in a psychosocial context that influences what happens within it. For our purposes, classroom environment (or climate) refers to the perceived atmosphere of the classroom that manifests itself in the attitudes and feelings teachers and students have toward each other and the learning tasks. (Chapter 14, "Affective Climate," explores this concept in depth.) Climate can be seen and heard in how students talk and act toward one another, how they approach learning tasks, and how they relate to the teacher. The classroom environment influences your judgments and decisions as a teacher and, in turn, is influenced by them. When interactions are characterized by defensiveness, fear, rejection, alienation, and hostility, learning and personal growth are inhibited. School environments that manifest the characteristics of openness, friendliness, acceptance, belonging, and trust facilitate learning and personal growth. There are several strategies you can use to assess your classroom environment and, if necessary, to develop a "sense of community."

Climate surveys are an excellent way of assessing your classroom atmosphere. Published instruments for the high school level include the Learning Environment Inventory (LEI) (Fraser, Anderson, & Walberg, 1982) and the Classroom Environment Scale (CES) (Moos & Trickett, 1974). Classroom dimensions that are assessed on the LEI include friction, satisfaction, speed, and goal direction. Items on the CES focus on affiliation, task orientation, rule clarity, and innovation. At the elementary school level a twenty-five-item version of *My Classroom Inventory* (Fraser & O'Brien, 1985) has been developed to measure class satisfaction, friction, competitiveness, difficulty, and cohesiveness. The survey form listed in Box 8–1 is one of many possible instruments that could be developed to solicit student feelings about your classroom atmosphere. Alternative procedures include open or structured interviews with your students or observations of your classroom by colleagues. Self-diagnostic inventories that focus on your behavior and how it influences the classroom atmosphere can be given to your students in order to determine their perceptions of your behavior. In implementing these strategies, it is important for you to seek honest feedback. An open discussion of the results may facilitate a more positive and cohesive classroom atmosphere.

Practice Activity 8-4

Administer the climate survey in Box 8–1 to assess your students' perceptions of your classroom environment. Feel free to add terms or change items to fit the survey to your particular grade level and classroom situation. You may want to administer the survey twice: once to assess the actual (or real) environment and once to assess your students' preferred environment. Do not be surprised if your perception of the environment is more favorable than your students'. If there are large discrepancies between your actual classroom environment and that preferred by your students, you may want to attempt to change the environment. Ideas for changing your environment can be developed by carefully analyzing the terms you used in your survey. For example, if your students feel that your classroom environment is too competitive, you can develop a more cooperative goal structure to facilitate involvement and group cohesiveness.

Box 8-1   *Sample Classroom Climate Survey*

Directions.   Please mark the appropriate space on the continuum which best describes our classroom.   The atmosphere of this classroom:

Encourages personal responsibility	1 2 3 4 5	Encourages conformity
Recognizes accomplishment	1 2 3 4 5	Ignores accomplishment
Is interesting	1 2 3 4 5	Is boring
Is cooperative	1 2 3 4 5	Is competitive
Is organized	1 2 3 4 5	Is chaotic
Accepts feelings	1 2 3 4 5	Ignores or rejects feelings
Sets high expectations	1 2 3 4 5	Expectations are low or nonexistent
Is satisfying	1 2 3 4 5	Is dissatisfying
Is safe	1 2 3 4 5	Is dangerous
Is relaxing	1 2 3 4 5	Is tense

Classroom Interactions

In an effort to differentiate successful classroom managers from unsuccessful ones, Kounin (1970) analyzed videotapes of teachers conducting their regular classroom lessons. However, Kounin's initial attempts failed because he and his associates could detect no significant differences in the ways these teachers dealt with student inattention, disobedience, and misbehavior. Fortunately, they did discern one important distinction between teachers who have generally smoothly running classrooms and those who have more or less chaotic ones. *Successful classroom managers were more successful because they reduced the frequency of trouble, not because they were more skilled in handling disciplinary problems when they did occur.* These teachers kept students involved with meaningful work so there was less opportunity or reason for them to cause disruptions.

As noted in earlier chapters, among the specific characteristics of these successful classroom managers was a quality Kounin called "withitness." Teachers who communicate to students they know at all times what is going on in the classroom have withitness. Teachers who are "withit" notice the first signals of deviant student behavior. They then initiate an identifiable action to deal with this misbehavior. These teachers made few errors either in the target of the deviant behavior or in the timing of their corrective intervention (Kounin, 1970). In other words, teachers having withitness dealt with the initiator of the misbehavior before the problem increased in seriousness or spread to other students in the classroom. ("Awareness" might better be substituted for the "withit," which attempts to describe the teacher who "has eyes in the back of his or her head.")

How can you become a "withit" teacher? The best strategy is to learn to observe student actions, interpret the likely meaning of these "messages," and react to these behaviors in clear, positive ways. One way to simplify the analysis of the many actions occurring in a classroom is to categorize behaviors as "input," "processing decisions," or "output." Input would be the student verbal and nonverbal cues that you observe; processing would be the interpretations you make of what you see in light of your own knowledge and attitudes; output would be the verbal and nonverbal action you take to send a message to your students.

Input: Student Cues

When you are conducting your lessons, students may respond in many varied ways. Paul stays attentive during your lesson, offering appropriate reactions and asking intriguing questions. Peter also stays alert throughout the lesson, but he typically only makes humorous or irrelevant comments and appears bored with the topic being studied. Ruth looks at you during the lesson, appears to understand what is going on, but never spontaneously offers any comments. Felix looks right through you while you talk as if he were watching a different program entirely. Rhonda does not even appear to be interested in what the class is doing. What are the clues that might allow you to determine the levels of attention, interest, and understanding of the students in your classes?

Students provide you with two main channels of information: verbal and nonverbal cues. The questions they ask, the comments they make, and the general noise level during class discussions or seatwork all provide you with helpful verbal cues to the effectiveness of your teaching activity. Hennings (1975) has suggested that students' verbal messages be observed according to a two-by-three category system like that shown in Figure 8–1. The following practice activity will help you examine the verbal messages of your students.

	TYPE	
PURPOSE	Contributing	Being
Response to Teacher		
Response to Other Students		
Initiation		

Figure 8–1 *Classifying Students' Verbal Messages.* From Hennings, 1975.

Practice Activity 8-5

Tape record a classroom discussion you are leading. Then perform the following simple analyses.

1. Count the number of comments, statements, or questions made by you and those made by students. Who is talking most, you or the students?
2. Now use a stopwatch to determine the amount of teacher, student, and multiparticipant talking, and the amount of silence. What percentage of time is spent on "teacher talk," on "student talk," and in silence or confusion? Is this percentage what you expected or desired?
3. Using the recording sheet in Figure 8–1, follow these steps to classify each student comment according to Hennings' six-category method:
   a. Classify each student's statements as "Contributing" or "Being" by placing checkmarks in the appropriate boxes. A Contributing statement is one that is related to the ongoing lesson or classwork ("I believe he was our only fourth-term president," "Would the Depression have really ended without World War II?"). A being statement is a non-learning-related statement ("I'm too

hot to work on this worksheet," "When are we going to finish this book?").

   b. Identify whether each statement is a Response to the Teacher, a Response to Other Students, or an Initiation Without Teacher Prompting.

   c. Tally the students' remarks in each box to determine the tone of your students' class participation. What is the most frequent kind of student statement? Again, is this what you wanted for this discussion?

4. Finally, identify each student who made a comment during the discussion by recording his or her contribution on a seating chart of your room. Do certain students tend to make the same category of remarks? Does their physical or social position in the room affect their participation in the lesson? How do these student participation patterns affect your learning goals for class discussions?

Students provide the aware teacher with more than just verbal messages during learning activities. Sara focuses her eyes on the speaker during class discussions, while Emily tends to stare into space. Kevin smiles and nods his head as he listens to a fellow student, while Fred grimaces and moves excitedly in his seat. Gary constantly fiddles with his pencil during class discussions, while Brenda glances expectantly at students seated around her. Even when students are not speaking they can be sending messages regarding their attentiveness, interest, and understanding.

In *Mastering Classroom Communication* Hennings (1975) has constructed a guide for analyzing student nonverbal language. She identifies three kinds of nonverbal messages: language of participation, language of being, and language of heightening.

There are two forms of nonverbal cues indicating participation. When students make motions that place them in the center of an activity and involve them directly with others, they are "contributing" (Hennings, 1975). Examples of nonverbal student behaviors that would fit this type of communication are raising or waving a hand, actively moving at desk, pointing, making exaggerated facial expressions, or vigorously shaking the head.

Hennings defines the second form of participation messages as "engaging." The purpose of these nonverbal gestures is to help the student be involved with the learning activity on an individual basis without contributing directly to the overall class learning environment. Examples of these engaging behaviors are orienting the body in the direction of the speaker, leaning forward toward the speaker, moving the head, smiling or frowning at another's comment, wrinkling the forehead, raising the eyebrows, squinting the eyes, pursing the lips, pointing a finger, or tracing on written materials. While these participation movements may vary among individual students, a teacher who actively observes and notes these nonverbal cues can better judge the typical reaction patterns of each student, as well as the overall level of class involvement and understanding.

The language of being involves body language that indicates a lack of attention or an attempt to distract or socialize, to adjust one's self, or to carry out other activities. Examples of these nonverbal cues include glancing continually out a window, not focusing attention on the speaker, staring vacantly into space, making faces at other students, making "irregular" hand gestures, poking other students, exchanging quick looks and knowing smiles with other students, moving close to another student, or making any habitual personal gesture. The aware teacher can often judge student restlessness, fatigue, anger, anxiety, confusion, or sociability through observation of these nonverbal behaviors.

The final type of nonverbal message fits the language of heightening category. This involves the gestures that accompany verbal communications and make the meaning more emphatic and/or explicit. Examples of this body language in students include making hand gestures while giving an oral report, changing body posture to indicate a change in topic or idea, pantomiming motions to express a particular emotion, altering facial expressions to reinforce the intensity of spoken words, lightly touching the arm of the person being addressed, pounding the desk to express frustration or anger, and even pausing, which can dramatically enhance the meaning of a communication. Naturally, you will find some students to be more expressive than others with their nonverbal communications, yet even these individual differences may allow you to understand better the "hidden meaning" of their verbal communication.

Practice Activity 8-6

1. Observe the nonverbal motions made by students in your classroom (or better yet, videotape the students during one of your lessons). Classify the behaviors you see as participation-contribution, participation-engaging, being, or heightening. When a lesson is going well, what kinds of nonverbal messages are being exhibited? When a lesson is not going well, what is the distribution of these nonverbal student behaviors?

2. Using a series of classroom observations or videotaped classroom interactions, try to develop a nonverbal behavior profile for each student in your class. Which students communicate the same message verbally and nonverbally? Which students often communicate a different message with their body language from that with their oral language? If there is a contradictory message, which channel do you emphasize in trying to interpret what the student is feeling or thinking? Looking at nonverbal cues alone, which students would you rate high on concentration, motivation, and perseverance? Which students suggest a low degree of these qualities based on the intensity of their nonverbal cues? Are there certain conditions under which identifiable, characteristic motions for each student tend to appear? Which students are better able to use nonverbal messages with their fellow students? Do some students appear more or less sensitive to the nonverbal messages of their classmates? As you selectively attend to the many student nonverbal cues in a typical classroom interaction, you will be better prepared to interpret the underlying message being sent.

Processing Decisions: Teacher Interpretations

Given all the verbal and nonverbal messages that students project in the classroom, do teachers actually attend to these cues and use them in their teaching decisions? Furthermore, even if some teachers seem to be aware of these messages, how can a new teacher learn to make sense of the enormous amount of student information in classroom interactions?

Woolfolk and Brooks (1983) examined the limited research on nonverbal communication in teaching and concluded that students' use of interpersonal distance, visual attention, voice quality, and smiles and frowns can influence teachers' impressions and expecta-

tions about students. They wrote "[It] seems that teachers form positive impressions about students who evidence the nonverbal behaviors usually associated with interest, involvement, approval, or liking" (p. 109).

Sometimes teachers interpret cues about students in such ways that their own nonverbal behaviors are influenced. Reviewing empirical studies of laboratory tutoring situations and live classroom interactions, Woolfolk and Brooks (1983) again concluded that the teacher's own interpersonal distance, body lean, voice tone, facial expressions, eye gaze, and affirmative or negative head nods can reveal their own attitudes toward students. A number of studies have shown that teachers use more positive nonverbal language (such as forward body lean and smiles) to students they assume to be bright, to students of their own race, and to students they like (Woolfolk & Brooks, 1983).

Knowing that all teachers do interpret the nonverbal and verbal messages of their students encourages each individual teacher to monitor consciously his or her reactions to particular students. This is especially important when a teacher is dealing with students from a cultural or racial group other than his or her own. A teacher should also be careful about making inferences about students' sensitivity to the teacher's own nonverbal cues unless these cues have the same meaning in the students' culture. In fact, cultural differences between teachers and students from different parts of the country may preclude the same interpretations of communication patterns.

Practice Activity 8-7

1. Examine your own interpretations of nonverbal language cues you observe in your students. Make two columns, one headed "Positive," the other "Negative." Place each of the following cues in a row under the two headings: eye movements, gestures, body stance, physical distance, touching behavior, speed of action, and vocal effects. Then list specific student behaviors that you interpret positively and negatively for each of these cues. After you have finished this list, analyze your interpretations to see whether there is any cultural, racial, or gender bias in your preferences.

2. Another exercise you can do is to list each student you teach and develop a "dictionary" of their nonverbal "vocabulary." How does each student communicate enthusiasm, receptiveness, inattention, boredom, disapproval, understanding, and confusion? Try to pinpoint at least one nonverbal cue for each student attitude or thought that sends this message to you.

Of course, the verbal responses of students are also important features in the classroom interaction process. It can be very helpful to the beginning teacher to be able to interpret two aspects of students' "talk": thinking level and covert meaning. First, aware teachers should be able to evaluate the thinking level exhibited by their students' statements. Hennings (1975) suggests a six-category system for analyzing student utterances according to thinking level:

1. Recalling—thinking that requires retrieving information already in the student's memory
2. Reflecting—thinking that requires translating ideas or concepts into the student's own words
3. Relating—thinking that identifies interconnections between ideas or concepts
4. Projecting—thinking that goes beyond what is given to hypothesize new relationships or systems
5. Inventing—thinking that is imaginative and creative
6. Valuing—thinking that represents a personal judgment or opinion supported by communicable reasons.

Other educators have created similar taxonomies to classify student responses. Bloom's taxonomy, for instance, is discussed in Chapters 9 and 15, "Questioning Skill" and "Evaluation," respectively. The key similarity among these classification schemes is the distinction between recall of fundamental knowledge and those higher-level activities more associated with human understanding. While it is important for a teacher to stress the memorization of basic information at all levels of a student's schooling, it is also important not to neglect other cognitive operations like reflecting, relating, projecting, inventing, and valuing. Overemphasis of any one type of thinking restricts students' educational experiences and their intellectual growth.

Practice Activity 8-8

Tape record a classroom discussion and classify each student's statements according to Hennings' six levels of thinking. (If you find making discriminations that fine to be too difficult, just categorize the statements as either "recalling" or "more than recalling.") How does the context of student comments affect your analysis? What did you think of your students' statements during the actual discussion? Upon this further analysis do you have different interpretations? Do you believe the percentage of recalling statements is too high, too low, or just about right? What is your justification for your interpretation? What kinds of higher-level statements should your students be offering? What kinds of teaching actions would tend to increase these types of comments?

The second kind of "student talk" analysis involves your interpretation of a student's overt (evident) and covert (hidden) message.
Thomas Gordon (1974) stresses the technique of "active listening."
Gordon argues that most listening is relatively passive and seldom
reveals whether the listener has actually understood the speaker's
message. He suggests that teachers check their interpretation of a
student's oral message by sharing their decoded interpretation of the
original message. By providing the sender with feedback of your
interpretation, you can get confirmation of the correctness or incor-
rectness of your decoding. For example, if a student complains, "This
new chapter doesn't make any sense; it's too hard for me to understand," you might interpret the underlying message to represent that
student's inability to spend enough time to complete that assignment. Your active listening response might be "You're afraid you
won't have time to finish our next assignment." If you are wrong,
the student will most likely correct you by continuing, "No, I could
spend the time on it if you would just show me how these problems
relate to the ones we did last week." The point of active listening is
that you keep the communication channels open rather than closing
them by responding prematurely to student messages with orders,
warnings, criticisms, advice, praise, or even sympathy.

Practice Activity 8-9

To experience the many uses of active listening you need to try it
with your own students. Commit yourself to try active listening
with at least one student comment each hour of the school day. As
you listen to the student's words, think of the most likely message
he or she is trying to communicate. Mirror your interpretation back
to the student. Continue this type of active listening until the student has solved his or her own problem or until it is clear you need
to provide more help in the problem solution. Gradually increase
the number of times you use active listening each day until you
feel comfortable in using this interpretation and feedback strategy
whenever open and straightforward communication is required.

Output: Teacher Actions

Once you have observed a student behavior and interpreted its meaning, it is time to communicate your own message to that student or
to the class as a whole. Such communication can be made verbally
and nonverbally.

Obviously, many of the classroom verbal messages sent by a
teacher relate to instruction. You gain the attention of your students
by adopting a standard method to signal the formal start of the lesson. (Perhaps you are comfortable just saying, "Okay, class, it's time

to begin today's lesson." Or you may prefer a more directive opening, "Everyone please turn to page 229 in your text." Regardless of your personal preference, you should develop a predictable, standard way to mark the start of a new activity or the transition to a new topic.) You introduce new concepts by presenting new information and new ideas. You encourage student thinking and involvement by asking them different types of questions. You react to their answers by giving them corrective feedback, praise, criticism, or further questions. In all of these verbal messages your objective is to strengthen the instructional interaction.

Sometimes, however, you want to send verbal messages to deal with student misbehavior and influence overall classroom management. Gordon (1974) argues that typical discipline "solution" messages, "put-down" messages, or "indirect" messages are doomed to fail more often than they succeed. When teachers order ("Stop that talking right now!"), threaten ("If you don't spit that gum out this instant, you can wear it on your nose the rest of the class"), moralize ("I expect sixth-graders to set the example for the rest of the school to follow"), lecture ("Class assignments won't get done unless you start on them"), or advise ("Talk to each other on your own time, not during our lesson time"), they are using familiar, but ineffective kinds of communication. According to Gordon these solution messages often fail because they portray the teacher as the Authority who makes all the decisions. Even when the teacher gets compliance, Gordon believes it is often accompanied by student resentment.

He sees teacher put-down messages ("You're acting like first graders"; "You never remember to bring enough paper to class"; "You could be a good student if you applied yourself"; "And where do you think you're going?") as even more destructive of students' self-images. Indirect messages using sarcasm, oblique humor, and vague digressions ("When you finally know it all, then we will be glad to listen to your spontaneous outbursts"; "So when did you become the teacher?"; "Sometimes I dream that you'll become a teacher and have a class full of students just like you") also seldom work because they are either not understood or too easily ignored. Such indirect comments may also lead the students to characterize the teacher as unwilling or unable to confront the problem directly.

Gordon's solution to these ineffective communication techniques is to recommend the use of "I-messages." These are teacher statements in which the focus is on the teacher's point of view and feelings rather than on a student's failure to meet expectations. Instead of saying, "You'd better quiet down, or else!" Gordon suggests the teacher would solve his or her problem better by saying, "When I hear lots of people talking without permission, I get really frustrated because there's too much noise to permit concentration on the lesson."

Generally an I-message has three parts: a nonjudgmental description of what is unacceptable ("When I hear lots of people talking without permission"), the feelings generated within the teacher ("I really get frustrated"), and the tangible effect of that behavior ("because there's too much noise to permit concentration on the lesson"). Gordon believes this type of communication is more effective because it contains minimal negative evaluation of the student, does not injure the student–teacher relationship, and encourages the students' willingness to change.

Of course these I-messages are more risky than sending blaming, guilt-producing "You-messages" because they involve disclosing inner feelings and needs, not always a comfortable thing to do. I-messages allow the teacher to take responsibility for his or her inner feelings about a problem while at the same time sharing the assessment with the student. Ideally, the student receiving the I-message will realize the concrete effects on others of his or her behavior and take responsibility for changing this undesirable behavior. However, there is always the risk that the student will fail to initiate this self-modification.

Practice Activity 8-10

1. Monitor the kinds of statements you make to students who are disobeying class rules. Do you send solution, put-down, or indirect messages? Do these messages usually result in the positive behavioral change that you seek? Are these messages as effective now as they were earlier in the school year? Do you feel comfortable relying on these kinds of comments?

2. The next time you find yourself in a class situation in which you are tempted to rely on one of Gordon's ineffective messages, try an I-message. What was the student's immediate reaction to your I-message? What was the effect on the student's later behavior? How did you feel about using the I-message? Because any new communication technique takes time to master, commit yourself to practice using I-messages. Try to increase the number of I-messages each day until you regularly respond with them even without consciously trying.

In addition to offering verbal messages, a teacher can also communicate using nonverbal behavior. Grant and Hennings (1971) studied videotapes of classroom teachers to identify nonverbal behaviors in teaching. They wanted to understand more clearly the role of nonverbal "teacher moves" in communicating meaning to students. They were able to classify nonverbal instructional behavior into three distinct, reliably observable categories: conducting, acting, and wielding. While teacher moves in all three categories can be used for instruction, conducting moves, in which the teacher controls participation and obtains attending behavior, are most important in communicating teacher awareness. (Acting moves involve the teacher's using bodily motion to amplify or clarify meaning. Wielding moves involve the teacher's interacting with objects or materials in the room.)

Grant and Hennings suggest the following behavioral moves as options in your nonverbal teaching style. To indicate which students are to participate during the lesson, you can choose among the following nonverbal options: smiling at the designated student, focusing your eyes on the student, nodding at the student, turning your body toward the student, pointing at the student, walking toward the student, or touching the student. To communicate different nonverbal reactions to a student's participation, you can use facial expressions, shake your head, shrug your shoulders, or make a hand gesture like the "okay" sign. To obtain student attention, you can choose among the following options: Walk to the front of room, stand at

---

Box 8-2 *Nonverbal Deterrents to Student Misbehavior*

1. Orient your body toward and focus your eyes on the inattentive student.

2. Frown at the child.

3. Raise your eyebrows.

4. Wave your hand at the child.

5. Shake your head in the direction of the child.

6. Point your finger at misbehaving child.

7. Raise your hand and arm in the direction of the child.

8. Snap your fingers at the child.

9. Walk toward the misbehaving child.

10. Put your hand on desk of misbehaving child.

11. Sit down near child.

12. Touch the child.

13. Touch the object the child is touching.

Note: Reprinted by permission of the publisher from Grant & Hennings, *The Teacher Moves: An Analysis of Nonverbal Activity* (New York: Teachers College Press, © 1971 by Teachers College, Columbia University. All rights reserved.), pp. 98–99.

attention, survey the class by making eye contact, hold up your hand, pick up a textbook or lesson plan book, tap a desk bell, or flick the lights.

When you must deal with a misbehaving student, these nonverbal motions can be very effective because they make less of an issue of a minor infraction than a verbal statement might and because they do not interfere with your ongoing teaching actions. Grant and Hennings (1971) suggest several ways a teacher can signal the student to stop the disapproved action (see Box 8–2).

The use of these nonverbal teacher behaviors in conjunction with appropriate verbal comments can be an effective deterrent to student misbehavior. Furthermore, the use of consistent verbal and nonverbal communications provides a clear message to students that the teacher is in charge of the class and aware of the students' activities in that class.

Practice Activity 8-11

Ask a fellow teacher (or even one of your students) to videotape you while you teach a typical lesson. Review the tape, paying special attention to your nonverbal body language. (Sometimes it is helpful to turn down the sound as you view the tape.) Use the following categories to observe your nonverbal behaviors: gestures, eye movements, body stance, distance from students, touch, and speed of motion. How frequently do you use these nonverbal behaviors? What kinds of nonverbal cues do you seem to prefer? Do you use different kinds of body language with different students? Why, or why not? Were you conscious of the motions you used while teaching? Do you tend to have a particular nonverbal orientation? How can you communicate your nonverbal messages more effectively?

Conclusions

Because you must make so many quick decisions in dealing with students, it is important to think about possible teaching problems before they occur. As you plan your instructional and management activities, be aware of available information about your students, the nature of the instructional task you are presenting, and the classroom/school environment in which you teach. These antecedent conditions should be considered before you enter the classroom to teach the lesson. With careful planning you can provide meaningful activities directed toward important curricular goals that capture your students' interest and involvement. Maximize the productive work of your students and you will minimize their misbehavior.

When you are conducting a classroom lesson, you should remain aware of the many communication cues occurring between you and your students. When you are actively involved in classroom interaction, you need to follow set teaching routines. Get students' attention before you start a lesson. Keep their attention by reducing redundancy and dead time during the lesson. Monitor the many verbal and nonverbal cues they are sending during class activities. Regularly scan the classroom to discover signals of inattention, disinterest, or confusion. When you spot a potential trouble situation, interpret the seriousness of that incident. If it is a minor misbehavior that is likely to disappear on its own, ignore it. If it is a misbehavior that might spread to other students or disrupt the meaningful work of the class, stop it immediately. You can send a clear message to your students with nonverbal behaviors, such as eye contact, head and body gestures, physical closeness, or touch. Sometimes, however, verbal messages become necessary when the nonverbal fail to solve the problem. As you decide how to intervene, remember the guideline to "eliminate the problem as quickly as possible and with as little distraction of other students as possible" (Good & Brophy, 1978, p. 196). As you master this overall classroom awareness, you will find yourself more in control of the teaching situation and more satisfied with your students' learning accomplishments.

References

Brophy, J. (1983). Classroom organization and management. *The Elementary School Journal, 83,* 265–85.

Fraser, B. J., Anderson, G. L., & Walberg, H. J. (1982). *Assessment of learning environments: Manual for Learning Environment Inventory (LEI) and My Classroom Inventory (MCI).* Perth, Australia: Western Australian Institute of Technology.

Fraser, B. J., & O'Brien, P. (1985). Student and teacher perceptions of the environment of elementary school classrooms. *The Elementary School Journal, 85,* 567–80.

Good, T. L., & Brophy, J. F. (1978). *Looking in classrooms* (2nd ed.). New York: Harper & Row.

Gordon, T. (1974). *T. E. T.: Teacher effectiveness training.* New York: Wyden.

Grant, B. M., & Hennings, D. G. (1971). *The teacher moves: An analysis of nonverbal activity.* New York: Teachers College.

Hennings, D. G. (1975). *Mastering classroom communication: What interaction analysis tells the teacher.* Pacific Palisades, Calif.: Goodyear.

Jackson, P. W. (1968). *Life in classrooms.* New York: Holt, Rinehart & Winston.

Kounin, J. C. (1970). *Discipline and group management in classrooms.* New York: Holt, Rinehart & Winston.

Moos, R. H., & Trickett, E. J. (1974). *Classroom environment scale manual.* Palo Alto, Calif.: Consulting Psychologists Press.

Peterson, P. L., & Swing, S. R. (1982). Beyond time on task: Students' reports of their thought processes during classroom instruction. *Elementary School Journal, 82,* 481–518.

Piaget, J. (1970). *Science of education and the psychology of the child.* New York: Viking.

Pulaski, M. A. (1980). *Understanding Piaget: An introduction to children's cognitive development* (2nd ed.). New York: Harper & Row.

Rosenshine, B. S. (1983). Teaching functions in instructional programs. *Elementary School Journal, 83,* 335–51.

Selman, R. L. (1980). *The growth of interpersonal understanding: Development and clinical analysis.* New York: Academic Press.

Shavelson, R. J., & Stern, P. (1981). Research on teachers' pedagogical thoughts, judgement, decisions, and behavior. *Review of Educational Research, 51,* 455–98.

Wadsworth, B. J. (1984). *Piaget for the classroom teacher* (2nd ed.). New York: Longman.

Woolfolk, A. E., & Brooks, D. M. (1983). Nonverbal communication in teaching. *Review of Research in Education, 10,* 103–50.

Chapter Nine

Questioning Skill

James Mackey
University of Minnesota

Deborah Appleman
Carleton College

Definition

The competent teacher knows how to phrase questions and to use them to develop learners' academic knowledge. Asking questions is a major teaching tool, and the skillful use of questions has been extensively studied.

Purpose

The purpose of this chapter is to present the notion of questioning as an integral element of any teacher's repertoire of instructional strategies. A primary goal of the chapter is to enable you to incorporate questioning effectively into your teaching by describing the elements of questioning skills as well as specific strategies for employing those skills in the classroom. We begin by discussing the importance of questions and reviewing the pertinent educational research in questioning skills. Then we explicate different levels and types of questions in some detail. We continue by examining the component parts of the interaction skills that questioning requires, and we explore several common problems of teacher questions to help you avoid them in your own teaching. Finally, we present several exercises that illustrate the major principles of questioning.

Background Knowledge

Questioning plays a curious role in our ideas about teaching. On the one hand, the effective teacher is viewed as an explainer. A series of images is etched in our minds—from Ichabod Crane, his tattered coat waving in the breeze of his gyrating lecture, to the cool smoothness of Lucas Tanner, able to field all adolescent problems on the first bounce with common-sense explanations. On the other hand, we admire the skillful discussion leader who unfolds complex situations through the application of an adroit questioning style.

While questioning skills often appear to be magical and mysterious (TV talk-show hosts, for example, are paid large salaries primarily because of their ability to ask questions that elicit an interesting response), there is, behind the apparently seamless flow of questions and responses, a systematic strategy that most teachers can incorporate into their classroom technique. The consensus among teachers about the centrality of questioning skill is indicated by the response to a recent survey that asked teachers to identify the most important skills of good instruction: Various aspects of questioning occupied first, third, and fourth place in the list of responses (Davies, 1981).

The use of questions provides the teacher with an opportunity to accomplish many things that an expository lesson simply cannot do. In its simplest conception a question serves a dual purpose: "[It] prods the respondent to think so as to supply a response, and it directs that respondent to think about a particular topic" (Hyman, 1979, p. 1). More specifically, teachers should use questions to accomplish at least four major educational objectives, described by Davies (1981):

1. Provide motivation for the students by gaining their interest and attention
2. Promote the thinking and mental activity of the students
3. Involve more students in the process of instruction
4. Obtain feedback on the students' progress.

The use of questioning techniques has several advantages. The questioner is able seriously to consider students not as blank slates but as the repositories of knowledge and analytical ability, capable of contributing to a conceptual and substantive dialogue. Questioning encourages students to try to contribute new notions and issues for the class to examine. Questions provide practice for students in using new concepts for analyzing and categorizing various elements of their surroundings. Questions also help students translate knowledge into their own ways of thinking. Many cognitive psychologists, especially those who examine the acquisition of reading skills, stress the importance of prior knowledge (schemata). These observers of the learning process claim that students are likely to make greater cognitive gains when the material presented can be easily subsumed under preexisting mental constructs (Anderson & Pearson, 1984). While helping students translate knowledge into their own mental constructs, the use of questions also motivates students to search for knowledge. In that search they often come face-to-face with the validity or inadequacy of their own ideas. Question-asking approaches to teaching, along with the confusion that follows in the wake of the process, subject students' ideas to a vigorous examination that "will scatter their ideas like chaff or if they have any real substance, root them more strongly" (Wain, 1981, p. 251).

Although there is an enormous amount of positive discourse about the utility of questions, there is a paucity of material for the teacher interested in incorporating questions into his or her teaching.

Much of the research findings on questioning skills are actually refined common sense. Clear questions, for example, are more productive than ambiguous ones. If teachers wait after raising questions, giving students time to think rather than rushing to answer their own questions, the quality of students' answers is generally better. (Educators refer to this phenomenon as "wait time.") In the same vein the research suggests that while teachers should acknowledge correct student answers, too much teacher enthusiasm is dysfunctional because it tends to embarrass students and inhibit their future responses. Empirical research confirms further that it is important to train students not to shout out their answers, but to wait until they are called upon.

How Teachers Use Questions

The most important fact about teaching, the root fact necessary to penetrate to its essence, is that it is an intellectual enterprise. But because teaching is a dynamic occupation in which events unfold with lightning rapidity, teachers can seldom afford the luxury of reflection characterizing most intellectual enterprises. Thus, teachers are unlikely to have premeditated reasons for most of the questions they pose.

Because this unit seeks to develop skill in question-asking, we will first examine the functions of questions. Teachers use questions in the following four distinctive ways. Figure 9–1 illustrates the different uses of questioning.

1. To elicit student responses. The questioner attempts to draw out of students information they know but which has remained unarticulated. It is as if pulling out the information—perhaps writing it on the chalkboard or on an overhead projector—can make the material more easily examinable. If information can be seen metaphorically as a light bulb, in these instances it is dull. It is shaded by the overwhelming amount of other information in the student's mind. Eliciting the student's ideas allows the bulb to shine more brightly and to offer greater illumination.

2. To establish student responses. The purpose of this use of questioning is to impart new ideas. By providing a new concept, the questioner figuratively installs a light bulb into the student's thinking apparatus as a means of illumination. In the light of this new knowledge the student sees preexisting ideas more clearly.

3. To expand student responses. This use of questioning assumes that the student's responses need to expand in range, to illuminate a larger compass. No new knowledge is introduced; preexisting knowledge is simply intensified, and light is shed upon a greater area.

4. To extinguish student responses. While the previous functions have argued for greater, clearer, and more extensive illumination, the present use concerns the questioner's desire to extinguish what she or he believes to be poorly formed or generally incorrect notions. The teacher seeks to turn off a light that distorts, favoring another light, perhaps at a different angle.

Practice Activity 9-1

Label the following questions according to the categories that have been discussed.

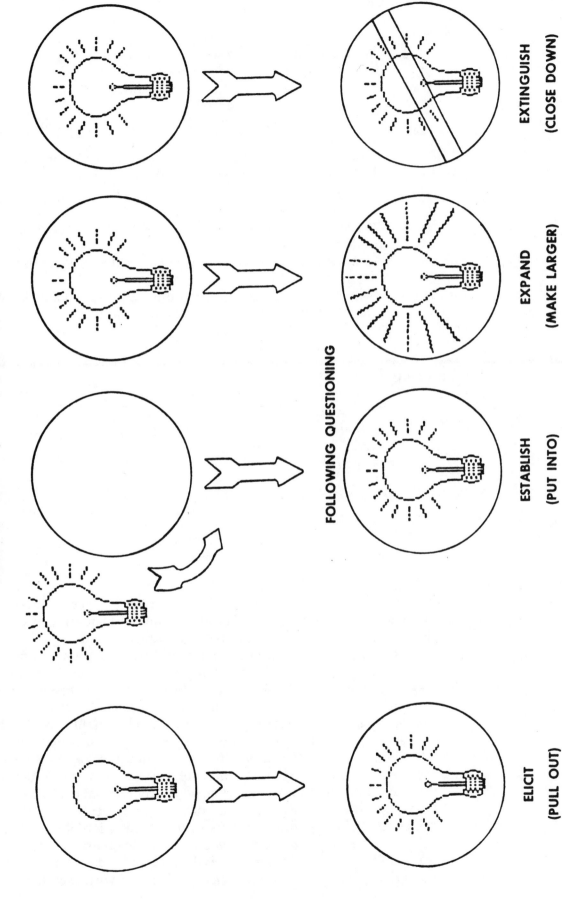

Figure 9–1 *How Teachers Use Questions*

1. "What kind of evidence would convince you that the statement you just made is erroneous?"
2. "If students are required to attend school, what subjects do you think should be required?"
3. "Why do you think Walter Mondale was defeated for the presidency?"
4. "How would you feel if you were a white person in an all-black society and someone said all white people are ignorant?"
5. "For what does social security pay?"
6. "If you were a newly freed slave in Alabama, what problems would you face?"
7. "Can you list the reasons why there seems to be no human life on other planets?"
8. "Why have Northern European immigrants been able to fit into U.S. society so quickly and successfully?"

Responses to Practice Activity 9-1

1. Extinguish
2. Expand
3. Elicit
4. Extinguish
5. Elicit
6. Establish
7. Expand
8. Establish

Levels and Types of Questions

As every skilled teacher knows, there is a different type of question for every instructional goal. This section presents an array of question types from which you can make informed choices.

Although good questioning technique has been important to teachers at least since the time of Socrates, it wasn't until the mid-1950s—when a team of researchers led by Benjamin Bloom developed a taxonomy, or classification system, of educational objectives—that the systematic organization of question-asking began. Bloom and his colleagues (1956) devised a six-level scheme that classified educational objectives, making it possible to raise questions appropriate to each of these six objectives. This system of hierarchically ordering thinking skills from lower to higher, popularly referred to as Bloom's taxonomy, has been widely used both for formulating educational objectives and for guiding teachers in the formulation of questions. Table 9–1 lists the basic components of the taxonomy. In Box 9–1 we include a brief explanation of each level, with examples of questions that demand the thinking skills associated with each level.

Table 9-1　*Basic Components of Bloom's Taxonomy*

Questioning Category	Bloom's Category	Student Activity	Typical Stem Words
LOWER LEVEL	Knowledge	Remembering: facts, terms, definitions, concepts, principles.	What? List, name, define, describe.
	Comprehension	Understanding the meaning of material.	Explain, interpret, summarize, give examples . . . , predict, translate.
	Application	Selecting a concept or skill and using it to solve a problem	Compute, solve, apply, modify, construct.
HIGHER LEVEL	Analysis	Breaking material down into its parts and explaining the hierarchical relations.	How does . . . apply? Why does . . . work? How does . . . relate to . . . ? What distinctions can be made about . . . and . . . ?
	Synthesis	Producing something original after having broken the material down into its component parts.	How does the data support . . . ? How would you design an experiment which investigates . . . ? What predictions can you make based upon the data?
	Evaluation	Making a judgment based upon a pre-established set of criteria.	What judgments can you make about . . . ? Compare and contrast . . . criteria for . . . ?

Note:　From Goodwin et al, 1981, p. 5.

Box 9–1   *Question Classification According to Bloom's Taxonomy*

Remembering and Understanding Information

I.   *Knowledge:* remembering previously learned material.

    A.   *Identifying Characteristics*
1. Only recall or recognition of information from past experience is required.
2. Little or possibly no understanding of the information is required.
3. The learner is not asked to compare, relate, or make any inductive or deductive leap on his own.

    B.   *Examples*
1. Who is President of the United States?
2. What is produced in the city of Richmond?
3. When did the state of Virginia join the Union?

    C.   *Verbs to Use in Question Formulation*

       repeat   recite   recall   define   record   name   list

II.   *Comprehension:* understanding the meaning of remembered material, usually demonstrated by explaining in one's own words or citing examples.

    A.   *Identifying Characteristics*
1. The emphasis is on change in form.
2. Some extension beyond what is given in the original may be required.
3. Relationships are stressed.
4. The learner looks for the denoted meaning of a communication.

    B.   *Examples*
1. What information can we obtain from this diagram?
2. What concept does the cartoon illustrate?
3. How does the Emancipation Proclamation relate to the attitudes of people in both the North and the South?

    C.   *Verbs to Use in Question Formulation*

       restate   recognize   identify   discuss   explain   describe

Using Knowledge

III.   *Application:* using information in a new context to solve a problem, to answer a question, or to perform another task.

    A.   *Identifying Characteristics*
1. Deals with usable knowledge and emphasizes use of information or skill.
2. The whole of ideas and skills are dealt with rather than just the parts.
3. Contains a minimum of directions or instructions because the questions are based on previous learning and the student is expected to know what to do. He selects what information is appropriate for use in the new situation.

    B.   *Examples*
1. Draw a picture that shows how families interact in a different situation.
2. How would our country be different if the flow of settlement had been from west to east instead of east to west?

Box 9–1 *(continued)*

    C.   *Verbs to Use in Question Formulation*

        employ   dramatize   interpret   apply   demonstrate   illustrate

IV. *Analysis:* breaking a piece of material into its parts and explaining the relationship between the parts.

    A.   *Identifying Characteristics*
       1.   Student needs prior knowledge or rules and reasoning.
       2.   Question deals with both form and content.
       3.   Process begins by breaking a communication into constituent parts (premise, assumptions, hypothesis, supporting data, conclusions, etc.).

    B.   *Examples*
       1.   Why do these historical accounts differ?
       2.   Why did a city grow in this place?

    C.   *Verbs to Use in Question Formulation*

        distinguish   contrast   debate   analyze   criticize
           examine   compare   relate

V. *Synthesis:* putting parts together to form a new whole, patterns, or structure.

    A.   *Identifying Characteristics*
       1.   Emphasis on creation of an original product (combining parts of past experience to create a new whole).
       2.   Involves divergent thinking and many possible answers.

    B.   *Examples*
       1.   After reading and discussing a problem about laws and rules, what kind of law would you make that would solve this problem?
       2.   On the basis of your study about the problems of a city, propose a solution to the transportation problem.

    C.   *Verbs to Use in Question Formulation*

        compose   formulate   plan   arrange   create   propose
           design   prepare

VI. *Evaluation:* using a set of criteria established by the student or specified by the instructor to arrive at a reasoned judgment.

    A.   *Identifying Characteristics*
       1.   Emphasis on judgment.
       2.   Only those evaluations that are or can be made with distinct criteria in mind are considered. It is not merely an opinion based on a snap decision.

    B.   *Examples*
       1.   Do you think the Eighteenth Amendment is a good law? Why? What criteria did you use to help you decide?
       2.   Assess the reasons given by the citizens for the Boston Tea Party. Were they valid or not? On what basis?

    C.   *Verbs to Use in Question Formulation*

        judge   evaluate   assess   appraise

Practice Activity 9-2

This exercise will help set in your mind the basic order of Bloom's taxonomy. Read the brief newspaper article in Box 9–2 and the series of questions that follows. Then identify the level of Bloom's taxonomy each question represents.

1. Why are parents discouraged from positive involvement?
2. Speculate as to the identity of the person who wrote the editorial.
3. Restate in one sentence what the author thinks has happened to our schools in the past fifteen years.
4. Can you devise a strategy to increase parental involvement in the lives of their children?

Box 9–2

WHERE HAVE ALL THE PARENTS BEEN?

Sometime in the past 10 to 15 years parents have lost interest in what is taught and how it is taught. Many have come to regard the school as a baby-sitter, disciplinarian and trainer of social graces, but they don't bother to find out exactly how the surrogate is raising their children.

The parents send unrespectful, undisciplined children to school, anticipating that they will become intelligent, civilized adults after 13 years. But heaven help the teacher or counselor who calls the parent because their child is using drugs or has behavior problems. Then the school is at fault for failing the child. Then the indignant footsteps of the parent shake the walls of the administrative offices.

But where are these parents when a band-parent is needed? Why don't school concerts and plays overflow the auditoriums? Why aren't there hundreds of parents at PTA meetings, instead of handfuls?

It appears that parents have just been too busy fulfilling their own needs, be they financial or otherwise, to care much about the educational progress of their children.

This pursuit of fulfillment often interferes with adequate communication between the parent and child. It certainly prevents even minimun communication between parents and the school.

Schools, on the other hand, must not give the impression that parents' opinions and questions lack substance and validity. Teachers and superintendents sometimes are defensive when a parent does inquire about a curriculum or a method of study. This attitude discourages the parents from positive involvement.

Note: From *Minneapolis Star and Tribune,* Mon., Sept. 5, 1983.

5. Does the author present enough evidence to support what he or she said?
6. What kinds of children have American parents been sending to our schools?
7. Why did the gap between parents and the school grow?
8. Prepare a brief response to the writer of the editorial.
9. How do you feel about the parents described in the selection?
10. Can the decline in parental involvement explain the increased adolescent retreat from school?
11. Tell why the reasoning in the following quotation from the article is sound or unsound: "This pursuit of fulfillment often interferes with adequate communication between parent and child. It certainly prevents even minimum communication between parents and the schools."

Responses to Practice Activity 9-2

1. Knowledge
2. Application
3. Comprehension
4. Synthesis
5. Evaluation
6. Knowledge
7. Analysis
8. Synthesis
9. Evaluation
10. Application
11. Analysis

Open and Closed Questions

Another way of categorizing questions is to refer to them as either open or closed. A closed question is one to which there is a limited number of answers, most of them known by the instructor (Davies, 1981). There are two types of closed question:

1. Questions that ask for confirmation or denial. These questions are answered with "yes" or "no."

   - Can you boogie?
   - Did you do the assignment?
   - Do you know which presidents are on Mount Rushmore?

2. Questions that ask for a specific piece of information. These can be answered simply in most cases.

- What is the largest city in Western Washington?
- How long is a football field?
- Where is Karl Marx buried?

As is apparent from these examples, closed questions are somewhat limited in their usefulness. They tend to rely entirely upon recall and do not take discussions very far.

Open questions are more creative, less restrictive, and give students more opportunity to give creative responses. In addition, they nudge students up to the higher levels of the cognitive ladder. Some examples of open classroom questions include:

- How would the story have been different if Ted had been a strong dog able to pull George out of the surf?
- What would Chicago be like if it hadn't been situated on Lake Michigan?
- Under what conditions could world peace prevail?

In sum, closed questions serve to check students' comprehension and recall on a low level of comprehension. Open questions, on the other hand, encourage students to practice higher-order skills, such as synthesis and analysis. Both are necessary to the teacher's repertoire of questioning.

Strategies for Employing Questions in the Classroom

Just as there are many different types of questions, there are also many different ways of organizing questions for classroom use. In this section we describe different formats that should be considered when you plan to use questioning as an instructional technique: written questions, small group questions, individualized questions, tutorial questions, student questions, and full class discussions.

Written Questions

Written questions are most frequently encountered in the form of study guides or as comprehension checks at the end of assigned reading. When using written questions for either one of these purposes, several considerations should be kept in mind. First, present the questions as a means to greater comprehension, rather than as an end in themselves. Too often students who are inundated with worksheets and study guides view questions as "busy work" and not as facilitators to understanding. Vary your mode of evaluating answers to written questions; you might collect and grade them sometimes, use a simple check-off system at other times, or alternatively ask students to read their responses aloud in class. In other words, avoid the tedium of assigning and grading questions after every reading. In this way, written questions can retain their purpose and vitality and not become drudgery.

Vary the level of written questions, from lower- to higher-order cognitive skills. Do not use written questions merely for recall. If most of your written questions start with "what", "where", "when", or "describe," you are limiting your students to the lower-levels of cognitive skills. Use the range of the hierarchy, including speculative questions for which there is no single correct answer.

Finally, do not rely solely on the prepared questions that often accompany texts. While many of these questions are well constructed, they have not been prepared for the specific instructional needs of your individual students. Teacher-constructed materials are often significantly more effective than "ready-made" materials because they are truer to the aims of the class.

Small Group Discussions

To add variety to your teaching and to give your students the benefits inherent in cooperative learning settings, you might consider employing questions in a small group setting. Each group receives either the same set of written questions or a different aspect of the same general topic. The latter, for example, is an efficient way to cover several short chapters of a novel or an assigned text. Pick a recorder, who will be responsible for writing out the group's responses, and a reporter, who will share these responses with the whole class. As the groups discuss the questions, circulate around the room to make certain that the students stay on task; after a designated period of time, reconvene the entire class and have each reporter present the group's answers.

Individualized Questions

Individualized questions are designed to provide an in-depth account of a single student's attitudes, beliefs, or understanding. They are also generally intended to provide the student with increased self-awareness about a particular topic. If you have ever taken a rate-your-self quiz in a popular magazine, then you are already familiar with this particular questioning format. Individualized questions can also take the form of checklists or self-assessments. Box 9–3 shows an example of an individualized questionnaire for parents to complete

---

Box 9–3   *Sample Individualized Questionnaire: Alienation*

1.   My child is not much interested in the TV programs, movies or magazines that most people seem to like.
     Agree   Disagree

2.   My child thinks that a job is the most important thing in a person's life.
     Agree   Disagree

3.   More and more, my teenager feels helpless in the face of what is happening in the world today.
     Agree   Disagree

4.   My teenager likes to participate in school activities (sports, clubs, dances, etc.).
     Agree   Disagree

5.   My child thinks that most people know what to do with their lives.
     Agree   Disagree

6.   Sometimes my teenager acts as if she/he could just as easily   live in another country or another time.
     Agree   Disagree

7.   My child believes that people will be honest with you as long as you are honest with them.
     Agree   Disagree

8.   My teenager usually tells his/her teachers what they really want to hear.
     Agree   Disagree

9.   For my child, school is most important as a place to make friends.
     Agree   Disagree

10.   My teenager believes that the problems of life are sometimes too big for her/him to handle.
     Agree   Disagree

about the alienation of their children; Box 9–4 provides directions for scoring the questionnaire.

Tutorial Questions

Tutorial questions are asked by a teacher in a one-to-one interaction with a student to facilitate comprehension or help improve a skill. These encounters should be carefully planned. Formulate specific objectives for the session and write out questions and follow-up probes. Keep a record of your questions and the student's responses to keep track of progress.

Student Questions

The value of student-generated questions is all too often overlooked in lesson planning. With some guidance, students can learn to formulate meaningful questions that are often closer than those of a teacher to the class's level of understanding. Student questions can be used to open discussions, clarify misunderstandings, or review. Rather than simply asking whether there are any questions, have students jot down questions and then ask them to read them aloud or exchange them. Another effective technique following an assigned reading or a lecture is to have students bring in two questions, one to which they know the answer, the other for which they have no answer. Learning is, after all, an interactive process. Students should be encouraged to question as much as the teacher does.

Full Class Discussions

Leading an effective discussion with an entire class is one of the most difficult skills a teacher must master. Because it is such a complex and important task, we have created a step-by-step strategy to help you plan and implement class discussions. While most of the following considerations have been written with the full class discussion in mind, you will also find them useful for the other questioning formulas that have been discussed.

People most commonly fail to respond to a question because they do not understand what they are being asked. Generally, the question is vague, tricky, elliptical, loaded, poorly phrased, or uninteresting to the intended respondent. Some reasons why questions misfire are illustrated by the following anecdote from Fraenkel (1973):

> Max Lerner once described his passing the front of a small pawn shop whence a sign in the window asked: "If you're so smart why aren't you rich?" Admittedly fascinated by the sign, he returned to it again and again. "I couldn't answer the question," he remarked, "and what's more, I didn't know why I couldn't! Then it came to me. It was the wrong question!" (p. 179).

Box 9–4 *Directions for Scoring Alienation Questionnaire*

What does this test show about your child's level of alienation? To determine his/her alienation score follow these directions:

1. Give your self one point for agreeing with 1, 3, 6, 8, and 10.
2. Place this subtotal number of points in Square 1 on the ''Score Card'' below.
3. Give yourself one point for disagreeing with items 2, 4, 5, 7, and 9.
4. Place this subtotal number of points in Square 2 on the ''Score Card'' below.
5. Add the subtotals, the numbers in Square 1 and Square 2, and place the sum in Square 3.

The score in Square 3 is your teenager's ''alienation score.''

SCORE CARD

Point System		Possible Score	Your Teenager's Score
You receive one point for agreeing with items 1, 3, 6 8, 10.		5	Square 1
You receive one point for disagreeing with items 2, 4, 5, 7, 9.		5	Square 2
			Square 3
TOTAL		10	

To interpret your teenager's score, see the alienation indicator below. Scores of 7-10 show high alienation; scores of 4-6 moderate alienation; and scores of 0-3 indicate low alienation.

What is your child's alienation score? Check his/her score on the Alienation Indicator.

ALIENATION INDICATOR

10	H
9	I
8	G
7	H
6	
5	MODERATE
4	
3	L
2	O
1	W

What is the result of the inventory you took? How do you feel about your child's score? Does it surprise you? What does it mean if your child scored fairly high on the inventory? Should you worry about his/her alienation?

Practice Activity 9-3

Let us provide some illustrations of how poorly constructed questions can confuse us. Your task is to examine the questions and determine why the questions confuse you or are difficult to answer. Then attempt to rephrase each question, making it more interpretable. Good luck!

1. How, when, where, and why did the War of Independence begin?
2. How long do you think man has been on earth?*
3. Isn't it true that abortion laws should be liberalized?
4. Why did boiling the water without the balloon and placing the flask in a cool place make the air pressure in the flask different from the pressure of the first experiment?'*

Designing Appropriate Questions

Poorly formed questions confuse the intended audience and make answering nearly impossible. The teacher's task then is to present questions to students in the clearest fashion possible.

Become Familiar with the Material

Good question askers are very familiar with the subject under discussion. If it is written material, they have carefully read it, forming initial impressions, spotting confusion, locating words and sentences that are likely to confuse their students. The material under scrutiny, then, has become a part of the intellectual property of the question asker, acquired through discipline and careful reading. Even if the focus of the discussion is not textual material, the teacher still has to prepare him- or herself similarly by carefully examining the material, searching through other sources of information on the subject, and in general absorbing the material in greater depth and breadth than any possible audience.

Formulate Your Objectives

In *Rabbit Run*, John Updike's protagonist is told by a service station attendant that "the only way to get somewhere, you know, is to figure out where you are going before you go there" (1960, p. 27). This

*From Weigand, 1971.

is sage advice for teachers interested in developing a sound question-asking strategy.

Properly conducted, the process of questioning is similar to that of planning a journey in which the well-prepared traveler is advised to ask three questions before proceeding: Where am I going? How will I get there? How will I know I have arrived?

Carefully devised objectives make it possible to ask questions of the appropriate level and type and to know when you have arrived at your destination. The teacher without an appropriate objective risks either crashing his questioning strategy into some barrier or swerving off the road. Simply put, teachers must avoid questioning students beyond the answer they desire and should anticipate the answers they want before asking their questions.

Anticipation is especially important in questioning. In many ways maintaining one's head during a questioning sequence is nearly as difficult as hitting a fastball. But in an important way the situation is different. There is seldom an opportunity for questioning practice, and a person nearly always ventures into the classroom unrehearsed. Therefore, the only reliable method of successful questioning is to have a carefully formulated objective.

Develop a Strategy for Question Construction

While it is true that a good discussion depends to a great extent on one's ability to react spontaneously to the often unpredictable responses of the students, it is equally important to prepare questions in advance. One possible strategy is to think of the discussion as having distinct sections, each with a particular purpose. This can prevent a discussion from becoming mired in redundancy.

All question-asking scripts should begin at the same place. Before it is possible to raise discussion questions about a subject, the "five W's and H" questions must be answered. The five W's are "Who?" "What?" "Where?" "When?" and sometimes "Why?" "H" is "How?" If we raise questions of this sort first, all members of the audience will begin the discussion with a clear map showing the lay of the land. (This tactic serves to eliminate much of the confusion that characterizes many question-asking situations.)

After these questions have been answered, it is possible to move to the more substantive aspects of question asking. Box 9–5 shows an example of such a strategy, designed for a discussion of a poem or a short piece of fiction.

Handle Effectively All Ranges of Student Responses

When a teacher asks a question, several things can occur: Students can respond correctly, give an incorrect response, ask a question or give no response. The following are techniques to deal with each type of occurrence.

Box 9–5 *Sample Strategy for Planning Questions for a Teacher-led Discussion of Literature*

I. *Skimming the surface*
Initial impressions, confusions; attempts to find out what's going on, who's involved, where they are, etc.

II. *Checking the form*
Divisions in the work; opening, closing; unusual style.

III. *Getting inside*

   A. *The work itself*
   Words, images, contrasts, repetitions, patterns, connections, figurative language.

   B. *The reader*
   Feelings, understanding, confusion, identification.

IV. *Moving beyond*

   A. *Abstraction:* theme(s)
   What was the writer trying to communicate about life?

   B. *Abstraction:* application to own life
   What does this work lead me to question about myself? My world?
   My life?

V. *Looking back*
What was the writer trying to do with this work? Did he/she succeed? What was the best line? The best part? The best image? Why? What could have made the work better? Why? How does it compare with/contrast with/stack up against other works you've read?

Correct responses.   It is critical that a teacher employ a variety of positive reinforcements when a student offers a correct response, in order to encourage future participation. Reinforcement can be provided nonverbally through smiling, nodding, winking, moving toward the student, and so forth, or it may be provided verbally by praise or by testing the student's answer. Having students clarify or elaborate their responses is also a positive way of recognizing what they've already said and encouraging them to go farther. The following are examples of this treatment of student responses:

- "What you've said is fine, but can you further develop your ideas?"
- "Can you provide an example of that concept?"

Incorrect responses.   Incorrect answers require diplomatic handling because the teacher must respond to the student and appear accepting of all attempts to answer while at the same time redirect thinking toward the correct answer. After an incorrect response has been given, the teacher can try to reword the question to make it clearer, provide some information to help students come up with an answer, or break the question down into more manageable parts (Goodwin et al., 1981). In addition to these techniques, adjusting or refocusing a student's incorrect response can also be employed to get the discussion back on track.

It is important to keep in mind that an instructor's reaction to incorrect responses may influence future participation. Teachers should never respond to incorrect answers by using the following:

- *Sarcasm.* Most children cannot fully appreciate the substance and feel only the barbs.
- *Reprimand* (for example, "Write the correct answer one hundred times"). The negative carryover to the subject matter being studied can be quite damaging.
- *Personal attack* (for example, "Boy, are you stupid!"). Students tend to function on the level the teacher sets for them.
- *Accusation* (for example, "You didn't study that, did you?"). You may be inaccurate in your accusation.
- *No response at all.* At least say, "I enjoyed your thinking," or something similarly positive. Not responding to a student's answer is not only rude, it has a negative connotation. It also tends to make the student feel that his or her contribution is worthless (West, 1975).

Student questions.   Only when students feel free to ask questions can real learning take place. Teachers can encourage the frequency of student questions by listening carefully to the questions and responding nonjudgmentally to them. Rather than immediately answering the question yourself, help the student answer his or her own question through prompting or breaking down the question, or redirect the question to the class. If a student's question is off the topic or applies only to a personal situation, ask the student to stop by before or after class to discuss it. Only as a last resort or when time is of the essence, answer the question yourself (Goodwin, et al., 1982).

If you cannot answer a student's question, be honest and say so. Never fake an answer. Encourage the class to try answering the question or work together to obtain the answer.

No response.   Creating a classroom climate that is accepting of student responses is perhaps the most critical factor in dealing with a lack of student response to teacher questions. We hope the suggestions outlined above will help you do just that. Even the most skillful of teachers, however, are sometimes faced with a sea of apathetic faces.

Having students jot down their answers facilitates responses because it makes students more accountable than does a simple request for an oral response. The teacher can collect and read a range of responses, or students can read each other's response.

From time to time, a graded discussion might spur participation. Students can be given a specific number of points for appropriate responses. On the whole, however, establishing a risk-free environment and asking questions that are interesting and not beyond the students' ken are the best ways to prevent the problem of no response.

References

Anderson, R. C., & Pearson, P. D. (1984). A schema-theoretic view of basic processes in reading comprehension. In R. C. Anderson & P. D. Pearson (Eds.), *Handbook of reading research*. New York: Longman.

Bloom, B. S., Englehart, M. B., Furst, E. J., Hill, W. H., & Krathwohl, D. R. (1956). *Taxonomy of educational objectives: The classification of educational goals. Handbook I: Cognitive domain*. New York: Longmans Green.

Davies, I. K. (1981). *Instructional techniques*. New York: McGraw-Hill.

Fraenkel, J. R. (1973). *Helping students think and value: Strategies for teaching the social studies*. Englewood Cliffs, N.J.: Prentice-Hall.

Goodwin, S. S., Sharp, G. W., Cloutier, E. F., & Diamond, N. A. (1981). *Effective classroom questioning*. University of Illinois at Urbana-Champaign.

Hyman, Ronald T. (1979). *Strategic questioning*. Englewood Cliffs, N.J.: Prentice-Hall.

Updike, John (1960). *Rabbit run*. New York: Fawcett Crest Books.

Wain, John (1981). C. S. Lewis, as a teacher. In J. Epstein (Ed.), *Masters: Portraits of great teachers*. New York: Basic Books.

Weigand, James E. (1971). *Developing teacher competencies*. Englewood Cliffs, N.J.: Prentice-Hall.

West, E. (1975). *Leading discussions*. Unpublished. Minneapolis: University of Minnesota.

Chapter Ten

Clarity of Structure

Pauline Pagliocca
University of Virginia

Definition

The competent teacher knows that learning is facilitated if the lesson is presented in a clear, systematic sequence consistent with the objectives of instruction. Learning is a conscious activity of the learner that proceeds (according to research in human learning) most efficiently when the learner is aware of the relationship of each part of the activity to the other parts and to the whole.

Purpose

The purpose of this chapter is twofold: to acquaint you with the research literature related to the clarity of the structure of a lesson and to assist you in performing a number of activities typically associated with structuring the presentation of a lesson so that it can be followed by your students.

Specifically, this chapter will address four approaches that can be used in clarifying the structure of your lesson:

1. Preparing outlines, reviews, and summaries
2. Beginning the lesson or unit with an overview that relates the new material to the more general subject under study and to previously learned material
3. Making interrelationships among parts of the lesson clear to learners
4. Using reviews and summaries to aid retention.

You will be asked to complete a number of activities designed to provide practice in these four skills.

Developing the structure of a unit or lesson is obviously related to the more general area of instructional planning. However, planning activities not directly related to the structure of presentation are addressed in Chapter 2. Meaningfulness, which is discussed in detail in Chapter 11, will be referred to here only as it relates to presenting the framework of a lesson.

Background Knowledge

Students learn best when the structure of a presentation is clear to them. The teacher who knows this states objectives and gives overviews, alerts learners to important points, and summarizes frequently. Such strategies seek to increase learning and retention of subject matter by illustrating relationships between new information and information already familiar to students. Like most of the successful techniques that you have begun to include in your teaching repertoire, they work best with planning and with a knowledge of your students.

No doubt, in your undergraduate courses in education you spent much time and energy learning about effective teaching methods. It is likely that your professors stressed the importance of organizing and structuring your lessons. According to Brophy and Good (1986):

> Achievement is maximized when teachers not only actively present material, but structure it by: beginning with overviews, advance organizers, or review of objectives; outlining the content and signaling transitions between lesson parts; calling attention to main ideas; summarizing subparts of the lesson as it proceeds; and reviewing main ideas at the end (p. 362).

Brophy and Good explained how such structuring is consistent with the goals of effective teaching: "Taken together, these structuring elements not only facilitate memory for the information but allow for its apprehension as an integrated whole with recognition of the relationships between parts."

Most of us would probably agree that structure is important to any classroom activity. We can understand why it is necessary for us, as teachers, to have a clear idea of what we want our students to learn and how we can help them learn it. Lesson planning helps us clarify our objectives and strategies for ourselves (and for our supervisors!). But what about our students? How well do they understand the direction in which they are headed? And how well can they gauge their understanding of material as it is presented?

It is likely that as students we have all had the unfortunate experience of sitting through a class, assuming we were the only ones in the class who did not understand the lecture, or even if we understood the lecture, having no idea why it was important or how it fit into the course as a whole. Somehow, the teacher had failed to clue us in as to the material's relevance to the particular discipline. Perhaps three lectures later the relevance became apparent, but we had already forgotten the content of the lecture. Not having a map, a structure, a direction left us at a loss for organizing our own thinking as we sat through the class, passively confused.

To illustrate the flip side of such an experience, I once had the opportunity to work as a teaching assistant for a psychology professor who seemed to have grasped the importance of making his students aware of the structure of the material (as he had developed it). He taught a course in introductory psychology in a continuing education program to a large group of students with a wide range of academic and personal backgrounds—heterogeneous grouping carried to an extreme! Prior to each class, he wrote an outline on the board that alerted students to the content of the presentation and illustrated relationships among the concepts to be presented. As he lectured, he occasionally referred to his outline, usually to show how examples or issues raised by the students fit into the overall scheme. While he did not always manage his time so as to present a nicely prepared summary of the evening's lecture, he usually referred back to his outline to show the class where they were and where they would be headed in their reading and in the next class. If questioned, that professor might say that the outline was really designed to keep *him* focused and on-task, but that certainly did not prevent his students from benefiting by being able to anticipate the content and to begin to see how the bits of information presented were related.

So, we are really talking about giving students access to our thinking through our outlines and our objectives, that is, to the structure we have developed for our teaching and, consequently, for their learning. Although lesson planning and preparing help us organize our thinking and our teaching, making that plan more "public" may help our students better organize their own thinking and learning.

How might you apply such ideas? The remainder of this chapter is designed to demonstrate just that: to discuss some practical applications of structuring and to give you an opportunity to experiment with the suggested strategies.

Structuring can take place at the beginning, during, and at the close of a lesson. Various strategies can be used at each stage. Where appropriate, a strategy can be used in more than one way. It should be understood that all of the strategies discussed below require some prior preparation by the teacher.

Structuring Strategies

Hartley and Davies (1976) cite three advantages to using "preinstructional strategies" in establishing the structure of a lesson. They note that a well-organized "bird's-eye view" of the task does the following:

1. It supplies the student with a useful perspective of what lies ahead.

2. It serves as a framework on which subsequent learning can be arranged and related.
3. It provides means of enhancing motivation and perseverance.

It would be difficult for any teacher to pass up the opportunity to employ teaching strategies that promise to accomplish such goals.

Preinstructional strategies include advance organizers, overviews, outlines, and reviews. Regardless of the technique, the intent is to set the stage for instruction by providing a purpose and direction. As Dewey (1938) noted:

> It is part of the educator's responsibility to see equally to two things: first, that the problem grows out of the conditions of the experience being had in the present, and that it is within the range of the capacity of students; and secondly, that it is such that it arouses in the learner an active quest for information and for production of new ideas (p. 378).

Advance Organizers

A method for introducing academic material that has received a great deal of attention is the "Advance Organizer Model" developed by David Ausubel (1967). This method is based on Ausubel's theory of meaningful verbal learning, which addresses how knowledge is organized, how the mind processes information, and how teachers present new material to students. His theory of learning is unusual in that it translates directly to teaching methodology. Ausubel believed that each student carries a cognitive structure of a particular subject matter. He described the cognitive structure as "the substantive content of the learner's knowledge in a particular subject-matter area or sub-area at any given time, and its organization, stability, and clarity" (p. 21).

Cognitive-developmental psychology has stressed the importance of the role of cognitive structures in learning new information (Bruner, 1966; Charlesworth, 1969; Flavell, 1977; Keil, 1984; Piaget, 1967). The child is actively involved in using his or her existing cognitive structures to assimilate new material whether it is presented formally or occurs naturally in the environment.

Frank Smith (1975) also supported Ausubel's ideas about students' needs to organize the information they possess. He, too, used the term *cognitive structure* because it implies knowledge that is organized rather than a simple collection of unrelated facts and figures. In support of the importance of the cognitive structure, Smith declared, "What makes the difference between good and poor learners at school may be less the sheer amount of knowledge they possess than the degree to which they have it integrated and available for use" (p. 11).

To make new information meaningful, and more easily learned

and retained, the teacher must assist students in their active attempts to link it to their existing cognitive structures. Trying to do that for thirty different students (and thirty different cognitive structures!) would be an impossible task. So, our job is to *strengthen* the existing cognitive structures, so that our students are ready to absorb new information in a meaningful way. Ausubel (1967) likened the cognitive structure to a "mental scaffolding," the framework for integrating new information with existing knowledge, so that it can be more easily understood.

Ausubel's advance organizers are intended to provide broad conceptual frameworks that will help clarify the content to be presented. These frameworks serve as the context for understanding new information. The organizer is developed at a higher level of abstraction, generality, and inclusiveness than the actual subject matter. Thus, the details and specific ideas presented in the lesson are subsumed under the broader structure of the discipline as provided by the organizer.

Ausubel (1967) described two general types of advance organizers: expository and comparative. Expository organizers are used when new material is *completely unfamiliar.* Ausubel recommended presenting the organizer in terms already familiar to the learner. Joyce and Weil (1980) cited the Anthropology Curriculum Project of the University of Georgia (Clauson & Rice, 1972) as a curriculum based on Ausubel's meaningful verbal learning theory. Prior to a unit addressing acculturation in Kenya, which will probably be an unfamiliar topic for students, the following written expository organizer is presented:

> Acculturation takes place when the people of one culture acquire the traits of another culture as a result of contact over a long period of time. The British governed Kenya for about 80 years. During this period, the direction of cultural change was largely one way (p. 56).

This short, broad, conceptual scaffolding sets the stage, in this particular example, for the written material that follows it. The specific details contained in the learning material can be fitted to this conceptual framework of acculturation. You can see that the description of acculturation here could be used (with only minor modifications) before reading about other cultures as well, provided that the overriding concept of acculturation remains the focus.

The comparative organizer is the second type of advance organizer described by Ausubel. According to Joyce and Weil (1980), the comparative organizer is designed to integrate new concepts with similar concepts that are already present in the students' cognitive structures yet also to discriminate between the old and new concepts in order. The example in Box 10–1 might be used during the same acculturation unit.

In developing the advance organizer, Ausubel relied primarily on a continuous prose passage, as presented earlier in the example in-

---

Box 10–1 *Example of Comparative Organizer: Changes Resulting from Acculturation*

Cultural Universal	African Trait	European Trait
Social organization	Tribe and smaller kin groups	National government
Family	Extended; husband has more than one wife	Nuclear; husband has only one wife
Work	For self or in exchange for work	Day laborers for wages

Note: Adapted from Clauson & Rice, 1972; cited in Joyce & Weil, 1980.

volving acculturation in Kenya. Most of the research has also focused on this method. However, some authors (for example, Earle, 1969; Santeusanio, 1983) have complained that Ausubel's strategy is difficult to implement in the classroom. This, however, has not prevented teachers and researchers from applying Ausubel's notion of strengthening students' existing cognitive structures by using modifications of the advance organizer or adapting the advance organizer for students with varying abilities. A few variations will be described here.

Steinbrink (1971) reported the effective use of advance organizers in teaching geography to rural black, economically disadvantaged elementary students. He presented a conceptual advance organizer preceding the unit and daily advance organizers throughout the six-week instructional period. Jerrolds (1967) focused on memory for specific facts in constructing a modified advance organizer for use with ninth-graders. His modifications were constructed around main ideas and concepts and were used only with average to above-average readers with average to above-average intelligence. Neisworth (1968) constructed written advance organizers for use with educable mentally retarded adolescents who were studying about accidental poisoning.

The examples given above were selected not because they describe statistically significant research, but because they illustrate attempts to apply Ausubel's ideas in classroom settings. The teachers and researchers involved considered their specific students, subject matter, and teaching objectives in developing strategies designed to help students relate what they already knew to what they needed to learn. Lawton and Wanska (1977), in their review of the relevant research, suggested that the learners' age, expected competency, and naiveté regarding subject-matter and/or "process" concepts should determine the type of advance organizer to use and the number of concrete props needed to exemplify subject conceptual process concepts and strategies. With their suggestions in mind, it is now time for you to try your hand at constructing an advance organizer.

Practice Activity 10-1

For the purposes of this assignment, imagine yourself a high school social studies teacher. You are teaching a year-long psychology/ sociology course to eleventh- and twelfth-graders of average to above-average academic ability, some of whom expect to attend college. You are preparing a psychology unit on "personality." You plan to use a secondary-level psychology text, filmstrips, lectures, and class discussions. You also plan to assign students to observe at least two people and compare their personalities. You are fairly certain that the topic of personality has not been discussed formally in any other courses at your high school. Construct an advance organizer to use in introducing this new unit to your class.

Although you do not have access to the actual instructional materials, you can probably recall your own introductory psychology course (with any luck your professor made use of structuring strategies that aided your recall). Think of your reasons for teaching your students about personality. What information and concepts do you want them to understand when they complete this portion of the course? Keep in mind Ausubel's description of the advance organizer as *brief*, presenting *general* concepts, and constructed at a *higher level* of abstraction than the actual material (this does not mean that it should be more difficult to understand, however).

When you have finished your advance organizer, read the sample advance organizer in Box 10–2.

Perhaps yours is similar to the sample in the box. Or maybe yours is more content-specific. Perhaps you developed a vignette or role play that touched upon similar concepts. Or it is possible that you organized your class into triads to discuss the elements of "good" and "bad" personality and used their ideas to make a general introduction to the class. How you approached this assignment depends in part on your teaching style, your beliefs about how students learn, and the particular class you envisioned. Regardless of the specifc details of your strategy, to be effective your advance organizer should be tuned to address the age, competency, concept familiarity, and subject familiarity of your students. Remember, you are building on their existing "cognitive structure."

Structured Overviews

Another strategy that is meant to relate unfamiliar material to previously learned concepts and to provide a framework for organizing information is the structured overview. It has been described as a "visual and verbal representation of the key vocabulary of a learning task in relation to a more inclusive or subsuming vocabulary or concepts that have previously been learned by the student" (Estes, Mills, & Barron, 1969, p. 41). The key vocabulary of a particular unit of

Box 10-2 *Example of Advanced Organizer for Unit on Personality*

At one time or another you and a friend probably got together and discussed other friends. No doubt you identified those who "have a good personality," those who "have a bad personality," and some who simply "don't seem to have any personality at all." Such discussions make you realize that people behave in different ways. Each person in each category (good, bad, no personality) has his or her own unique personality. Do you know anybody who is exactly like you? Probably not. We all prefer different foods, types of entertainment, and school subjects.

Once you know people, you begin to see that while they have unique personalities, they are also consistent in the way they act. When you go to a party with friends, you probably can predict how each one will act. You come to expect these friends to behave in ways that are consistent with your past observations of them.

Note: Adapted from Santeusanio, 1983. *A practical approach to content area reading.* Menlo Park, CA: Addison-Wesley.

reading or instruction is arranged, either by the teacher or by the students, to show the relationships of the terms to each other and to the structure of the subject (Earle, 1969). Thus, the emphasis is on using important vocabulary as a means to introduce students to new subject matter. Barron and Earle, two of the primary developers of this technique, described two purposes of the structured overview: (a) to clarify the teacher's instructional objectives and (b) to provide students with a framework for organizing information meaningfully (Barron & Earle, 1973). You may recognize both of these aims from our earlier discussion of the importance and goals of structuring instruction—for ourselves, as teachers, as well as for our students.

Figure 10–1 is an example of a structured overview that was developed for a social studies unit on foreign affairs and Eastern Europe. You may wish to refer to it as you read through the following instructions for constructing and using a structured overview. It will be clear that this technique, like the advance organizer, requires preparation time.

You would take the following steps in constructing a structured overview.

1. Analyze the vocabulary of the unit or chapter you intend to present. Select and list every word you believe necessary for the students to understand the major concepts.
2. Take your word list and arrange and rearrange the words until you have a diagram (a schema) that shows the interrelationships among the ideas particular to that unit.
3. In order to depict relationships between this unit and the discipline as a whole, add to that diagram any vocabulary concepts (general and/or specific) you believe are already understood by the students.
4. Evaluate your overview. Have you clearly depicted the major relationships? Can the overview be simplified and still effectively communicate the relationships you consider to be most important?
5. On the first day of the unit, draw the diagram on the chalkboard or overhead projector. While doing this, explain briefly why you arranged the terms as you did. Encourage the students to contribute as much information as they can.
6. During the unit, relate new information to the structured overview as it seems appropriate. It may be useful to sketch portions of it on the chalkboard (or to keep the overhead projector available). The object here is to aid the students in their attempts to organize the information in a meaningful way.*

---

*Adapted from Barron & Earle, 1973; Earle, 1969; Robinson, 1978.

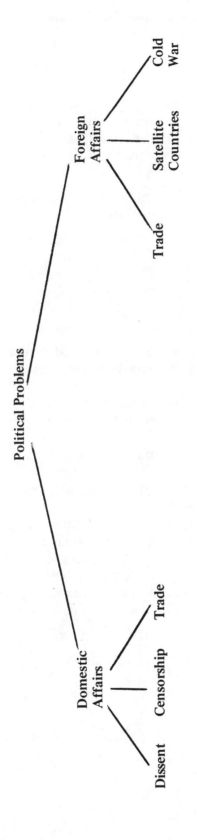

Note: Adapted from Robinson, 1978, p. 81.

Figure 10–1 *Sample Structured Overview*

Practice Activity 10-2

As you work through these exercises refer back to the directions presented above.

1. Assume you are an elementary teacher introducing the topic of vertebrate animals (at a later date you will introduce invertebrates) in your science class. Let us work through each step together.

a. Select the vocabulary you want to use to introduce the unit on vertebrates, such as:

animals
vertebrates
invertebrates
spinal column
mammals
birds

We have used a fairly short list. You will notice that not all of the terms would be considered "technical vocabulary." Some are common to the speaking vocabularies of most of your students; however, they are still important to the subject matter you want your students to understand.

b. Arrange and rearrange the words to show the relevant relationships. Writing the individual terms on index cards or slips of paper can really make your task much easier.

The terms used here seem to fall rather neatly into hierarchical relationships, such as those illustrated in Figure 10–2. You began with the very general class of "animals" and broke that down into two subcategories and then divided "vertebrates" further into "mammals" and "birds." Because you will be discussing inverte-

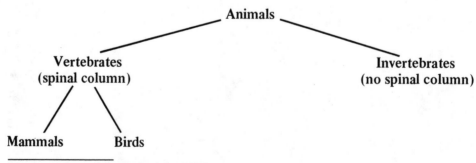

Note: Adapted from Smith, 1975.

Figure 10–2 *Constructing a Structured Overview: Sample, Step 2*

brates at a later date, you include the term here only to show the contrast. But you can build on this overview when you add that new information.

c. Add additional terms already understood by your students (concepts already in their cognitive structures) that will help them understand the new terms such as:

> backbone
> dogs
> cats
> whales
> canaries
> eagles
> pigeons

Our new structured overview might look like Figure 10–3. We have added some familiar examples to help students understand and remember some unfamiliar terms. Each lower level of the "tree" is an example of the higher levels to which it is connected. The levels should be as simple or as complex as is appropriate for the particular subject matter and students being taught.

d. Evaluate and simplify if necessary. We may want to delete either "spinal column" or "backbone," depending upon the knowledge of the students. Or we may want to arrange a longer list of animal examples into a column with a box drawn around it to show that they can be considered as a unit, as shown in Figure 10–4.

e. Present the overview to the class. You might draw the entire diagram on the board and then take students through each concept, explaining why terms are placed in particular locations. Or you might draw one level at a time, asking students to contribute their knowledge about what might be included on the next level. You

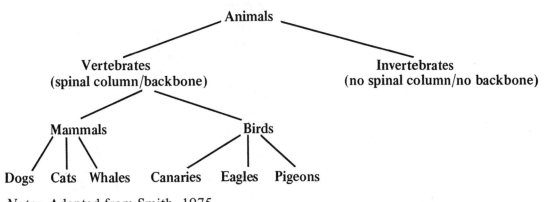

Note: Adapted from Smith, 1975.

Figure 10–3 *Constructing a Structured Overview: Sample, Step 3*

Figure 10–4 *Constructing a Structured Overview: Sample, Step 4*

can then incorporate their information into your predetermined structure, as appropriate. The important thing is that students understand why you arranged the terms as you did, even if it was as a circle or a hexagon.

f. Use the overview during the course of the instructional unit. For the example given, this will be especially helpful when you move on to study invertebrates.

Now that you have some understanding about how to develop a structured overview, the next activity will give you an opportunity to "play" student. Once your students are familiar with the rationale of the structured overview, you can try this approach with them. As the teacher, you will select pertinent vocabulary and ask your students to construct the overview.

2. You are a high school mathematics teacher about to begin a unit on rational numbers. From the students' text, you have selected the following technical vocabulary, representing the important concepts of the unit:

arithmetic

rational numbers

fractions

integers

nonintegers

positive

negative

common fractions

decimal

percent

members

numerator

denominator

ratio

comparison

proportion

Quite a lengthy list! Each term can be written on a separate card or slip of paper and arranged until the array makes sense to you, that is, until you could explain it if asked. Add any terms that you think would help your students understand the important relationships. When you finish, imagine yourself developing your class lessons from the diagram. Reposition any terms that cause a block in the flow of your presentation. Figure 10–5 illustrates one possible arrangement of the terms.

Compare the example in Figure 10–5 to your own. There were likely some similarities in the organizations, but perhaps you developed a different arrangement. Examine *your* example. How might you change it if you wanted to focus on integers? decimals? ratios? Just as your arrangement may have differed from that presented, your students' versions may differ from yours as well as from each other's. The test of the usefulness of the structure will be in your ability to present it so that your students understand and remember the content that follows it.

3. Select a unit or chapter that you will be starting in the coming week. Go through each of the steps for constructing a structured overview. Present and explain your diagram to a colleague or friend. Reconstruct it if necessary. Once you are satisfied, try it with your class. (*Hint:* When introducing a book or story—whether in a high school literature class or in a kindergarten storytime— you can use the names of key characters and perhaps some identifying personality traits or roles.)

Outlines

It is likely that you have more experience with outlining than with either of the structuring strategies discussed earlier. As a student you may have learned a particular form of outlining. As a teacher you might want to teach that same method to your students or you may prefer to develop outlines for yourself to use in teaching subject matter to your class. Like advance organizers and structured overviews, outlines can be used to organize information so that it can be learned and retained more easily by your students. So the question becomes, "How do you want to organize the material to be presented?"

Probably the most common pattern for outlining looks something like this:

    I. Major topic/main idea
        A. Main idea/important detail
            1. Related/supporting detail
            2. Related/supporting detail
   II. Major topic/main idea

This form would continue for all the main ideas to be covered. In constructing, as well as in presenting, the outline, you should focus on the important information and the important relationships. What-

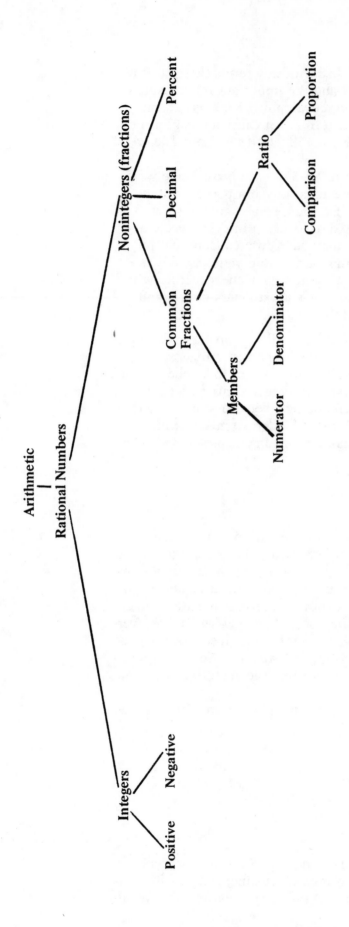

Note: Adapted from Earle, 1969.

Figure 10–5 *Sample Structured Overview*

ever form you choose should be a visual representation of those ideas and relationships. Following a specific format, which you explain to your students, will help them understand the relationships and understand the difference between main and supporting ideas.

In textbooks the organization for an outline is sometimes nearly accomplished for you. So why reinvent the wheel? Chapter headings, section headings, boldface print, words in italics—all of these are clues to the important ideas and terms. An advantage in using the text in this way is that when your students begin to read they will already be familiar with many of the ideas and vocabulary and already have some ideas about their relative importance.

Your class, however, may be reading texts that provide no such organization. Or you may not be using a text at all. Or you may be using a multitext approach. All of the work is then up to you. You may prefer outlining to other structuring techniques.

Practice Activity 10-3

1. The following is an excerpt from a middle school basal reader. As you read, begin to collect main ideas; you can attend to the details later. Consider that this selection is only the beginning of a social studies/science unit you are developing that will focus on the discovery, uses, and importance of fire in humankind's development.

Early [humans] found several very important uses for fire in [their] home[s]. The first was as heat. Not being equipped with protective fur, [humans] found fire extremely useful during the long, cold winter nights. Built under the shelter of a rock overhang or inside a cave, a fire gave a cozy warmth.

Fire also produced light, and light gave more meaning to the long, dark nights. It was probably by firelight that the first artists in history painted the wonderful pictures which have been found in prehistoric caves. This light also enabled the women to make clothes and the men to chip weapons.

Fire performed another valuable function, as well. All wild animals were deathly afraid of the blazing heat which singed fur and caused pain and death. So fire was perhaps [the] first defensive weapon. But there were other and more important uses of fire yet to come.

It seems quite natural today to use fire for heat to cook food, but it undoubtedly took a great many years before early [humans] learned to use fire in that way. Perhaps it came about accidentally when some raw meat fell into a fire. Or maybe hunters found the burned bodies of animals after a forest fire. However it was discovered, the use of fire for cooking was extremely important in the history of [humans].*

You probably concluded that the excerpt focused on early uses of fire. Following the outline structure presented earlier, this could serve as the first major topic:

I. Early uses of fire

The main uses of fire subsequently discussed were heat, light, defense, and cooking. Build the outline:

I. Early uses of fire
    A. Heat
    B. Light
    C. Defense against animals
    D. Cooking

Now reread the selection for important supporting details that might help your students understand and remember the information better. Remember that you will be explaining the outline to your students as you present it, so you will be guiding them in understanding key concepts and relationships. Your final outline might look like this:

I. Early uses of fire
    A. Heat
    B. Light
        1. painting
        2. making clothes
        3. making weapons
    C. Defense against animals
    D. Cooking

If you were planning to have the class read this selection or a similar chapter, you might present only the major topics and main ideas and ask them to fill in the details. This would serve as a study guide through the material and could be an introduction to outlining as well. It is just as possible to omit the main ideas but include the supporting details in your presentation and have the students read to find the main ideas. The outline could then be completed with input from the entire class. You can weave it into other motivating strategies designed to involve students more actively in their learning, as well as in your teaching.

---

*From Early, M., Canfield, R., Karlin, R., & Schottman, T. A. (1970). *Reading to learn* (2nd ed., pp. 202–3). New York: Harcourt Brace Jovanovich.

2. For the next activity assume you are a high school social studies teacher. In a unit on economics you will be discussing employer–employee relationships. Because of space limitations, we cannot review all the materials you might use in this unit. We will look only at a small section of a textbook; the topic selected is employee strikes. Your goal in this unit is to present as fair a picture as possible but also to encourage discussion and help students develop informed opinions. As you read the selection, be alert for main ideas; focus on details after you have your basic outline.

> Why do strikes start? What issues cause them? One major cause of nearly all strikes is the demand for general wage increases. The rising cost of living seems always to diminish the purchasing power of the worker's dollar. To offset this trend, workers periodically seek new contracts with significantly higher wages. Employers, on the other hand, oppose large-scale wage increases, since their own costs have been rising, too. These rising costs, coupled with a larger payroll, severely reduce profits. Workers and employer cannot come to terms, so a strike results.
>
> Job security is another root cause of strikes. Job security is protected in part by rules involving seniority and division of work. A worker who has held a job with a company for a long time is said to have *seniority*. . . .
>
> Recently, union workers have been *demanding job security in the form of a guaranteed annual wage.* *

Now develop a basic outline for use in introducing this new topic to the class. Try to work all the way through before comparing it to the sample (see Box 10–3). You can use individual terms, phrases, or complete sentences. (Do it now and return to text.)

Note: When developing an outline, bear in mind that you need not present it in complete detail in the introductory phase of the unit. Like the structured overview, the outline can be presented in stages, if that is more appropriate to your purposes. You can also refer to the outline, or to segments of it, as you progress through your learning materials. This approach is especially useful in showing how new concepts are related to those which the students have already learned. A few terms, such as "employee perspective," that have been added in this example may not be represented in yours. They were added primarily to assist in explaining the conflicts to the class. Your outline may have focused on the unfamiliar vocabulary included in the excerpt. Because of the importance of technical vocabulary in understanding economics, this may be a worthwhile approach. What is most important here is that your outline be structured so that your students become familiar with

---

*From Linder, B. (1971). *Economics for young adults* (pp. 166–67). New York: Sadlier.

Box 10–3 *Sample Outline: Employee Strikes*

I.   Causes of Employee Strikes

    A.   Demand for general wage increases leads to conflict between
        employer and employee

        1.   Employee perspective
          a.   Cost of living increases

        2.   Employer perspective
          a.   Rising costs
          b.   Larger payroll

    B.   Job security for employees

        1.   Seniority

        2.   Division of work

        3.   Guaranteed annual wage

---

key concepts and relationships and begin to understand the structure of this new information in view of the larger topic or the larger discipline.

3. For this exercise refer back to Activity 10-2, Exercise 1. Using the same vocabulary list (the complete one), develop an outline instead of an overview. Remember that you are focusing on vertebrate animals, but show where you would include invertebrates in your outline. An example of an appropriate outline for this topic is shown in Box 10–4.

Compare your outline with your overview. You may find one easier to develop than the other, or you may find one easier to present to your class than the other.

4. Again refer back to Activity 10-2, this time to Exercise 3. You presented an overview to a colleague and then to your class. How well were they able to follow your presentation? Try the following activity with the same class. In preparing your lessons for your next unit of study, develop an outline to be written on the chalkboard or presented with an overhead projector. You want your students to participate actively in your presentation. Make your outline as complete as you can (check it with a colleague), but be prepared to add appropriate student ideas. Before students begin reading or before they prepare for a test, give each of them a copy of the completed outline. Be sure to refer to the outline as

---

Box 10–4 *Sample Outline: Types of Animals*

I. Vertebrates

    A. Major feature: have a spinal column

    B. Classes of vertebrates

        1. Mammals
            a. Dogs
            b. Cats
            c. Whales

        2. Birds
            a. Canaries
            b. Eagles
            c. Pigeons

II. Invertebrates

    A. Major feature: no spinal column

    B. Classes of invertebrates

---

you progress through the unit or story so that students know how new concepts fit in with known ones.

Which was easier to develop, the outline or the overview? Which was easier to present? Which did a better job illustrating the important concepts? Which did your students follow more easily? Which had a more positive effect on their retention? These questions are easier to ask than to answer. Much depends upon your students, the materials, the key concepts, and which method appeals to you more—all important points to consider in selecting a strategy.

You have now learned about, or had a refresher course in, the importance of structuring lessons. We have discussed and experimented with advance organizers, structured overviews, and outlining. We will now move on to the final strategy, reviewing, which is discussed separately here but is certainly related to the other strategies presented in this chapter.

Review

In this last section on specific structuring strategies, we will discuss the importance of review and suggest some effective uses of this method. Hoover (1971) described review as "one of the oldest, most basic methods of teaching" but also one of the "most widely misunderstood and misused practices" in education (p. 491). He stressed that the goal of review is to "develop a new view relative to previous learnings" (p. 492). He cited two criteria essential for effective review: First, the students must have actually learned effectively, and second, the learning must involve critical thinking or problem solving. While the first criterion may be self-evident, the second is not.

Think back to a class—any grade level will do—in which you and your classmates were led in an oral recitation "review" by your teacher. All of you could recite whatever information was requested but probably did not have a clue as to its meaning. Perhaps you remembered something like "What were the three causes of World War II?" or "What is photosynthesis?" Similarly, a common experience for the pre–"Sesame Street" preschooler was the request, "Say your ABCs for your grandmother." If tested, you could list the causes of the war, give the glossary's definition of the process, or go through all twenty-six letters almost on cue, but did you understand what you were saying? Could you perform as well today? Only your knowledge of the alphabet seems to have been strengthened by such drill. Answers to the other two questions probably seem more complicated now.

Hoover cautioned against using drill in place of review. Drill and practice are effective for learning skills and habits; this is usually best accomplished when done individually—remember your French flashcards? Review is best used in a group setting where your goal is to extend what students know by affecting their attitudes and understandings. In the past several years the word *drill* seems to have become an educational dirty word, but instead of examining our use of the practice, we've simply replaced the term with *review* and continued to misuse it! So rather than abandon an effective technique altogether, it would seem more sensible to use it discriminately.

The placement of a section on review at the end of a chapter seems appropriate, but actually it might well have been placed near the beginning of the chapter or even tucked between structured overviews and outlines. While it may be traditional to end a lesson with a review or summary, we might begin a class with a review of yesterday's lesson before introducing new material, or we might review in the course of a class period as a way of making a transition from one topic to another, or one concept to another. Your purpose, rather than any absolute, should determine the placement of any reviewing or summarizing you do with your students.

There are two basic phases to a review lesson: recapitulation, or recall of what has already been learned, and extension of learning to related areas. You can see how this might be done at the end of a unit as a way to summarize and then encourage broader understanding and discussion of a topic. It might also be done between units to organize the information just learned and to begin to speculate upon what might be covered in the upcoming unit. Herber (1970) took a rather strong position on the importance of review:

> A student will experience learning difficulties if he or she does not have the benefit of review. If he [or she] does not go over previously learned information to speculate on its relative value and bearing on the new topic, his [or her] only recourse is to memorize isolated bits of information with little purpose or focus (p. 33).

As with the strategies discussed previously, "how to" becomes the question. Before you flip on the switch for the creative synopses to begin sparking, take a few minutes to review the activities in the previous sections. Advance organizers, structured overviews, and outlines can all be used in reviewing as well as in introducing a class or a whole unit.

Practice Activity 10-4

    1. For this activity, refer back to Activity 10-1. How could you modify your advance organizer to use it as a post organizer before moving on to a unit on child development and child rearing? Remember Hoover's two phases of review, recapitulation and extension. Stop here and develop a brief written review based on your advance organizer, focusing on the recall phase. (Remember the assignment you initially gave your students.) When you have finished, develop three or four discussion questions to set the stage for the next unit on child development.

    As part of the recall phase, you might have focused on how and why personalities differ, why we evaluate a personality as good or bad, or what consistencies students found in the people whom they observed. If you studied specific theories, you might have had students describe a person from the perspectives of two very different theories of personality.

    Moving on to the extension phase, and keeping in mind the upcoming unit, you might have asked the students whether they believe people develop in ways that are consonant with specific theories. If so, how does that happen? If they believe in a particular theory, how does that affect how they look at other people? How might that affect how they would raise their children? Can they guess their own parents' views on personality development? Whether or not you developed similar questions, you want to extend your students' knowledge by raising their curiosity, challenging their understanding, and exploring their attitudes in preparation for the next unit. Can you see how you have strengthened their cognitive structures in the process?

    The other preinstructional materials you developed while proceeding through this chapter similarly can be used as review materials, during a unit or at the end. To use them as review requires preplanning and attention to the two phases described by Hoover.

2. Textbooks can be wonderful sources of review materials. Sometimes they actually label "summary" or "conclusion" paragraphs. Even when not so clearly identified, signal words or phrases within the paragraphs can be easily located, for example, "in review," "the important point," "as a result," "to summarize," or "in conclusion." How often do we actually teach our students to look for such clues? Do our students know how to use these same reviewing hints to preview their reading assignments?

Select a textbook chapter your class will be reading soon. Preview the chapter, searching for helpful review paragraphs and signal words to which you can alert your students; mark these clearly for yourself. This may seem a bit of a reversal, but for this assignment use these selections as a preinstructional strategy to guide your students through the reading materials. You are actually using available review materials to introduce your class to new content, but you need not discard the materials at this point. At the end of the unit, take the class back through those same sections to recall the material presented and then to extend their understanding.

Using the materials available to them and alerting them to signal words, help them develop strategies they can use independently.

Note: Robinson (1978) noted that many mathematics textbooks do not contain summary sections. Instead, they include a list of important concepts at the end of the chapter. In such a situation you can direct your students to use such lists in reviewing what they have learned. They can be redirected to the text for any concepts or ideas that they do not recall or understand.

References

Ausubel, D. P. (1967). *Learning theory and classroom practice.* Toronto: Ontario Institute for Studies in Education.

Barron, R., & Earle, R. A. (1973). An approach to vocabulary instruction at the high school level. *Minnesota Reading Quarterly,18,* 53–65.

Brophy, J., & Good, T. L. (1986). Teacher behavior and student achievement. In M. Wittrock (Ed.), *Handbook of research on teaching* (3rd ed.). New York: Macmillan.

Bruner, J. (1971). The importance of structure. In K. H. Hoover (Ed.), *Readings on learning and teaching in the secondary school* (2nd ed., pp. 32–36). Boston: Allyn & Bacon.

Bruner, J. (1966). *Toward a theory of instruction.* Cambridge: Belknap.

Charlesworth, W. R. (1969). The role of surprise in cognitive development. In D. Elkind & J. H. Flavell (Eds.), *Studies in cognitive development: Essays in honor of Jean Piaget* (pp. 257–314). New York: Oxford University Press.

Clauson, E. V., & Rice, M. G. (1972). *The changing world today: Anthropology curriculum project* (Publication 72–1). Athens, Ga.: The University of Georgia.

Dewey, J. (1938). Progressive organization of subject-matter. In R. D. Archambault (Ed.), *John Dewey on education: Selected writings* (pp. 373–86). New York: Modern Library.

Earle, R. A. (1969). Reading and mathematics: Research in the classroom. In H. A. Robinson & E. L. Thomas (Eds.), *Fusing reading skills and content* (pp. 162–70). Newark, Del.: International Reading Association.

Estes, T. H., Mills, D. C., & Barron, R. F. (1969). Three methods of introducing students to a reading–learning task in two content subjects. In H. L. Herber & P. L. Sanders (Eds.), *Research in reading in the content areas: First year report.* Syracuse University Reading and Language Arts Center.

Flavell, J. H. (1977). *Cognitive development.* Englewood Cliffs, N.J.: Prentice-Hall.

Hartley, J., & Davies, I. K. (1976). Preinstructional strategies: The role of pretests, behavioral objectives, overviews, & advance organizers. *Review of Educational Research, 46,* 239–65.

Herber, H. L. (1970). *Teaching reading in content areas.* Englewood Cliffs, N.J.: Prentice-Hall.

Hoover, K. H. (1971). Review and drill: Valuable but widely misused teaching techniques. In K. H. Hoover (Ed.), *Readings on learning and teaching in the secondary school* (pp. 491–96). Boston: Allyn & Bacon.

Jerrolds, B. W. (1967). The effects of advance organizers in reading for retention of specific facts. (Doctoral dissertation, University of Wisconsin, 1967). *Dissertation Abstracts International, 28,* 4532A. (University Microfilms No. 67–16,963).

Joyce, B., & Weil, M. (1980). *Models of teaching* (2nd ed.). Englewood Cliffs, N.J.: Prentice-Hall.

Keil, F. C. (1984). Mechanisms in cognitive development and the structure of knowledge. In R. J. Sternberg (Ed.), *Mechanisms of cognitive development.* New York: Freeman.

Lawton, J. T., & Wanska, S. K. (1977). Advance organizers as a teaching strategy: A reply to Barnes & Clawson. *Review of Educational Research, 47,* 233–44.

Neisworth, J. T. (1968). The use of advance organizers with the educable, mentally retarded (Doctoral dissertation, University of Pittsburgh, 1967). *Dissertation Abstracts International, 28,* 4539A. (University Microfilms No. 68–7515).

Piaget, J. (1967). *Six psychological studies.* New York: Vintage Books.

Robinson, H. A. (1978). *Teaching reading and study strategies: The content areas* (2nd ed.). Boston: Allyn & Bacon.

Santeusanio, R. P. (1983). *A practical approach to content area reading.* Reading, Mass.: Addison-Wesley.

Smith, F. (1975). *Comprehension and learning: A conceptual framework for teachers.* New York: Holt, Rinehart & Winston.

Steinbrink, J. E. (1971). The effects of advance organizers for teaching geography to disadvantaged black elementary students (Doctoral dissertation, University of Georgia, 1970). *Dissertation Abstracts International, 31,* 5949A. (University Microfilms No. 71–13, 133).

Chapter Eleven

Meaningfulness

Stephanie Hinson
University of Delaware

Definition

The competent teacher knows that learning is facilitated when content is related to learners' interests, to common experiences, or to information with which they are familiar. The importance of meaningfulness in learning has been formally established by research in human learning done in psychological laboratories; practicing teachers have recognized its importance for many years.

Purpose

"Meaningfulness" is one of those concepts in education that seems immediately familiar. Its premise, making lessons relevant to learners, would appear to be based on common sense, but even common-sense concepts like meaningfulness may not be easily translated into teaching. This chapter will facilitate your understanding of the concept by acquainting you with some of the theoretical and empirical literature on topics relating to meaningfulness. The chapter will also assist you in making your lesson content more meaningful by suggesting several pertinent activities for you to incorporate into your teaching.

Background Knowledge

Many educators believe that theory should guide practice or at least guide our thinking about practice. In your preservice course work

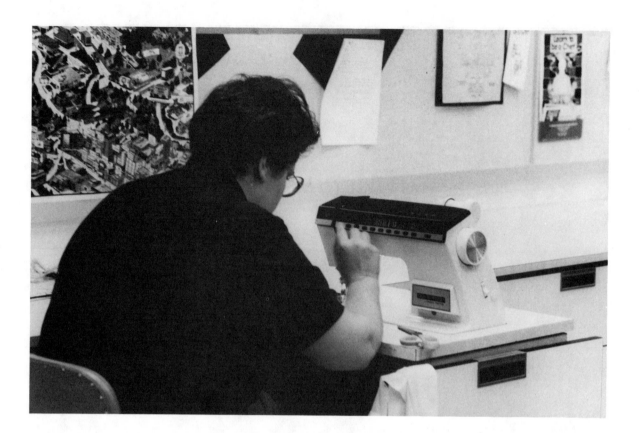

you may have become familiar with educational theorists like John Dewey, Robert Gagne, and Ralph Tyler. Each has offered theoretical support for the concept of meaningfulness.

In his description of an education that draws on select learning experiences, Dewey (1938) states:

> A primary responsibility of educators is that they [not] only be aware of the general principle of the shaping of actual experience by environing conditions, but that they also recognize in concrete what surroundings are conducive to having experiences that lead to growth (p. 40).

It is not enough to be abstractly familiar with the idea that making lesson content more relevant to learners facilitates learning. The idea must be skillfully enacted. We as instructors need to be able to select from the myriad experiences of learners those that will be most beneficial. The term *experiences* used here refers to the broad range of curricular and extracurricular learning sources from which instructors can choose: course work, instructional materials, knowledge of community and the world, and learners' interests and backgrounds. Both Tyler and Gagne agreed that instruction should engage select experiences and advocated that, in choosing experiences to employ within a lesson, teachers draw first on things familiar to the learners. By doing so, they motivate learning and encourage learners to become active participants in the learning process. Tyler (1949) notes:

> The learning experiences must be such that the student obtains satisfactions from carrying on the kind of behavior implied by the objectives. . . . If the experiences are unsatisfying or distasteful, the desired learning is not likely to take place (p. 66).

It was Gagne's belief that the inclusion of external cues to learning—for example, learners' interests—aids recall of verbal information presented during instruction. Accordingly, learners are motivated by the ease of cognitive retrieval of learned material, and this motivation can guide other learning processes, such as performance. A motivated learner may be expected to perform a verbally oriented skill better and receive positive feedback from the teacher for the performance. Thus, a successful learning sequence is completed: The mix of select experiences and lesson content yields motivated cognitive retrieval, which may yield effective performance.

We as instructors, then, need to establish the critical, motivating link between something the learner already knows and what we would like her or him to know. According to Gagne (1976):

> The essential task of the teacher is to arrange the conditions of the learner's environment so that the processes of learning will be activated, supported, enhanced, and motivated. Thus, the teacher needs to be aware of what the processes of learning are and of the specific influences he can exert on them in order to provide successful instruction! (p. 42).

The theorists caution, however, against engaging complementary experiences haphazardly during instruction. We need to know how to use effectively the selected learning experiences within a lesson structure. Dewey (1938) maintained that the beginning of a lesson should include experiences particularly familiar to the learners. The early inclusion of these experiences provides the initial backdrop for further learning.

Tyler (1949) advocated drawing experiences from the learners' own interests and the teacher's knowledge of learners' lives outside school and utilizing them according to "continuity," "sequence," and "integration." By "continuity," Tyler meant that the experiences should be selected and employed so that they exemplify the content at different levels. If you embrace a Piagetian philosophy of child development, you know that children rarely function at one exclusive, clear-cut cognitive developmental level; they are often just a little below or above their predominant level at any given time. It is important, then, that the experiences employed enhance the at-grade presentation of the content and provide a more or less advanced illustration if necessary.

A "sequence" in the employment of experiences means that each experience selected should build successively on the preceding ones.

The experiences also should reflect "integration"; that is, they should illustrate the overall relationship between content units (Tyler, 1949). Material employed to help learners establish a meaningful link may be high in familiarity or capable of logical organization (Gage & Berliner, 1984).

Educational theorists, then, suggest to us at least three things relative to meaningfulness:

1. Linking new and familiar learning is instructionally worthwhile.
2. Choosing learner-satisfying experiences is necessary.
3. Organizing the selected experiences for effective use is important.

Research of these theoretical claims has been primarily in the field of educational psychology. Interestingly, we have learned that some teachers feel that the consideration of learners' interests should be a fundamental element in planning (Taylor, 1973) and that effective teaching requires that the teacher be familiar with the backgrounds of the learners, especially for populations of learners of high socioeconomic status (SES) (Brophy & Evertson, 1974). The major focus of the empirical literature has been, however, the examination of techniques for establishing meaningfulness during instruction. The literature points to several methods teachers can use to assist learners in the encoding of information for ready retrieval. Following are descriptions of several techniques to help teachers establish instructional meaningfulness.

Mediators

Mediators, often in the form of covert verbalizations, create meaningful links between seemingly unrelated items or ideas (Gage & Berliner, 1984). Mediators help learners organize or encode incoming information for faster, more efficient retrieval later. Kendler, Kendler, and Learnard (1962) initially set out to determine whether children more frequently employ mediators in a particular type of learning situation as they grow older. In the study three- to ten-year-old children were asked to choose the "right" picture, given a pictured pair of black and/or white squares. The right choice was determined randomly in advance by the experimenter and depended on the size and brightness of the pictured figures.

In addition to finding out that the number of children who mediated—that is, employed a strategy for choosing between the pictures—did indeed increase with the age of the children, Kendler et al. discovered that the children who mediated seemed to learn faster than those who haphazardly or stubbornly guessed. If the children were able to establish some link between the "right" choices early on and were able to amend their strategy as the test situation warranted, they appeared to be more successful at the task. Post-test questioning revealed greater and more detailed verbalization by the children who mediated, which implies that there is a link between the ability to connect words with actions and the use of mediators (Kendler et al., 1962).

We as teachers can help the mediating process along by providing students with examples of connecting links between seemingly unfamiliar or unrelated bits of information. For example, if a learner has a list of words to remember, the teacher may assist memorization by reading the words aloud and providing sentences that illustrate the use of the words. After reading the words *comb* and *cup*, for example, a teacher might say, "The comb is in the cup" (Gage & Berliner, 1984). This technique may be particularly helpful in learning a foreign language or in advanced science courses where new vocabularies need to be remembered and linked.

Mediators can help students remember key concepts in a lesson. For example, a middle school social studies teacher who wants his students to remember *Delaware* and *chemicals* might say:

> Delaware is important to the chemical industry; Delaware manufacturers supply chemicals for the world; the growth of the chemical industry is reflected in the history of Delaware.

Similarly, a high school English teacher who wants her students to remember *Ophelia* and *rejection* might say:

> Hamlet's rejection of Ophelia led to her unstable condition; seemingly unwarranted rejection left Ophelia delirious; the inability to cope with rejection resulted in Ophelia's suicide.

Practice Activity 11-1

Think about a lesson you intend to teach during the next week. What are the unrelated bits of information to be included? Develop the linking statements you will verbalize to your class.

Advance Organizers

As noted in the preceding chapter, instructors are encouraged to use advance organizers to evoke meaningfulness in lesson content. David Ausubel is often credited with the theory of advance organizers. Ausubel and Robinson (1969) define advance organizers as follows:

> . . . deliberately prepared sets of ideas which are presented to the learner in advance of the body of (meaningful) material to be

learned, in order to insure that relevantly anchoring ideas will be available (p. 145).

These sets of ideas are usually presented in a brief oral or written form and at a high level of generality and inclusiveness. An advance organizer acts as an anchor or "mental scaffolding" upon which to "hang" the subsequently presented content (Gage & Berliner, 1984, p. 314). Like the mediator, the advance organizer attempts to bring familiarity and/or logical organization to material.

Advance organizers differ from the more commonly used overviews and summaries in that they are designed to relate content to students' knowledge, are presented well in advance of the beginning of a unit of instruction, and are presented at a higher level of abstraction, generality, and inclusiveness than the material to be learned.

Early studies of advance organizers have suggested they facilitate learning by the following:

- Drawing out and mobilizing relevant and established anchors, making new material seem more familiar
- Including the relevant specifics of the material under a larger, general principle
- Eliminating the need for rote memorization of the unfamiliar (Ausubel & Robinson, 1969, p. 148).

The early research has also suggested that advance organizers are more effective if the material they precede is factually oriented rather than abstract, if the material is organized from the general to the more detailed, if the amount of advance information covered by the organizers is sufficient, and if the organizers are stated in learnable and familiar terms (Ausubel & Robinson, 1969).

There has been controversy, however, over whether advance organizers are indeed effective. After analyzing 135 published and unpublished studies of advance organizers, Luiten, Ames, and Ackerson (1980) concluded that advance organizers actually did appear to be effective in facilitating learning. Both learning and retention were facilitated and the process of retention increased over the four- to fifteen-week duration of the studies. College and special education students learned more after the introductory passages, but primary and secondary students retained more. The authors found also that students of higher ability benefited most from advance organizers and that oral presentations reaped more rewards than did written ones.

According to Ausubel and Robinson (1969) we can use advance organizers effectively in our classrooms under two conditions. First, when learners lack specifically relevant information pertaining to the desired material, we can use *expository* advance organizers, which introduce new material in terms familiar to the learners. For example, in introducing a completely new arithmetical operation— long division—to an elementary school math class, we can state that division uses all of the operations previously learned, such as addition, subtraction, and multiplication. Or if we taught these operations via set theory (for example, "3 + 4 means combining a set of three objects with a set of four objects"; "3 × 4 means three sets of four objects each"), we can introduce division in the same way. We can review the previous statements and continue, describing division (for example, "12 ÷ 4 means grouping a set of twelve objects into four smaller equal sets"). In this way, we have evoked familiar operations and terminology to introduce the new operation.

Second, when learners are somewhat familiar with aspects of the material to be learned but do not recognize its relevance to previous learning or to their own experiences, we can use *comparative* advance organizers, which clearly point out similarities and differences between the content to be presented and knowledge that the learners have already acquired. For example, physical education instructors might want to introduce a unit on the sports tennis, racquetball, badminton, and squash. It is very likely that all members of the class are at least vaguely familiar with one or more of these sports, so our introduction can point to the similarities among them, for example, the using of racquets, the playing on courts, the scoring determined by volley outcomes. We can point to differences between them also, for example, the length of the racquet handles, the varied balls or shuttlecocks, the kinds of courts. Thus, we have employed a comparative advance organizer to provide initial meaning to a new unit.

Whether you use expository or comparative advance organizers, an advance organizer should be presented for each unit of material. The written or oral introductory statement you present should include a general overview and relevant elements of the material upon which learners can organize any existing knowledge or any subsequently gained knowledge of the subject. By so doing, we help learners avoid attaching the new material to inefficient anchors or irrelevant, tangential points of reference—events that would lead to ambiguity and short-lived internalization of the material.

Practice Activity 11-2

Refer to the advance organizer you wrote for Chapter 10. To insure its contribution to the building of meaningfulness, ask yourself these questions:

- Is it written and will it be presented far enough in advance to orient learners initially to what is to come?
- Is it brief?
- Does it differ from the overviews and summaries you will eventually use in the lesson?
- Does it describe the topic generally yet in enough detail to give learners an adequate preview of the material ahead?

- Is its style more general and inclusive than the actual presentation of the material will be?

Your advance organizer should encompass all of these elements.

Set Induction

According to Schuck (1981), the set induction method was developed at Stanford University in the 1970s. Simply stated, a set is a cognitive readiness to learn. "Set induction," then, is

> ... the initial instructional act on the part of the teacher for the purpose of establishing a frame of reference deliberately designed to facilitate the creation of a communicative link between the experiential field of the pupil and the desired behavioral objectives of the learning experience (p. 228).

Set induction draws on elements of several of the techniques we have discussed already in this chapter. We are encouraged to begin with an orienting period, familiarize learners with the desired content through the use of analogies and pervasive themes (themes that unite the main ideas of the lesson), and encompass the lesson in a relevant context. As can be seen in the example in Box 11–1, set induction provides a familiar anchor upon which to attach new learning.

Schemata-based Instruction

The idea that we should create the contexts or learning sets from which we want learners to work is furthered in research concerning the engagement of "schemata" to establish meaningfulness.

Schemata are abstract cognitive structures. According to Anderson and colleagues (1977), schemata

> ... represent the generic concepts underlying objects, events, and actions. Schemata are abstract in the sense that they contain a "variable," "slot," or "place holder" for each constituent element in the knowledge structure (p. 369).

Schemata specify the relational networks of their constituents. In other words, "schemata" are more general than "concepts" and cognitively surround and interrelate our perceptions of the world. Gage and Berliner (1984) contend that a

> ... general implication for education is that the schemata a person already possesses are a principle determiner of what will be learned from a text) (p. 317).

Box 11-1 *Example of Set Induction for Lesson on Human Respiration*

1. *Orientation:* The teacher begins the lesson by exhibiting a model railroad car for the purpose of starting a discussion of the role of the hemoglobin molecule in the respiratory process.

2. *Transition:* The teacher makes the railroad car analogous to the red blood cell—it takes on and carries an important raw material (oxygen) to the body cells where it plays a key role in the oxidation process producing energy.

3. *Operation:* The teacher introduces the function of the heme molecule in hemoglobin by explaining that it is the iron atoms that bond to the oxygen and that these bonded atoms are carried in the red blood cells to the living cells. Once these molecules reach the cell membrane, they are released giving up the oxygen and taking on carbon dioxide, which is then transported to the cells in the lung tissue for eventual expulsion from the body. Hence, they function like a railroad car bringing raw material to the cells and taking away waste products.

4. *Evaluation:* The teacher then seeks clues to the level of student comprehension through asking questions about the chemical bonding, the oxidation process, etc. Related material such as the role of red blood counts, anemia and its effect upon the human body, the reasons for ingestion of iron, and the role of menstruation in females may be explored depending on the teacher's instructional objectives and the nature and level of the students in the class.

Note: From Schuck, 1981, p. 228. Reprinted with permission of the Helen Dwight Reid Educational Foundation. Published by Heldref Publications, 4000 Albermarle St., N.W., Washington, D.C. 20016. Copyright © 1981.

Instructional materials are rarely exhaustive; therefore, learners' schemata must "fill in the gaps" and make inferences. The problem is that learners, especially inexperienced young ones, may fill in the gaps inappropriately if left to rely on their own limited schemata. The contexts young learners provide for themselves may prohibit them from learning desired material; they may make inappropriate associations between content elements, reducing the material to personally irrelevant gibberish. Teachers, on the other hand, can provide contextual information or relevant schemata for content elements that can enable learners to "cross-list" efficiently new learning with old (Gage & Berliner, 1984, p. 318). As with the set induction method, statements such as "long-term memory is like a giant card catalog" (p. 319) can be used by the teacher to engage desirable schemata in learners.

Anderson et al. (1977) examined the influence of schemata on comprehension of written passages. Sixty college students—music education and physical education majors—were asked to read two

passages and then to answer questions about them. Each passage could be interpreted at least two ways: in terms of a "wrestling match" and of a "music rehearsal." As expected in view of the schemata theory, physical education majors gave more correct wrestling-consistent responses and music majors gave more correct rehearsal-consistent responses. The authors concluded that people's personal histories, knowledge, and beliefs do indeed influence their interpretations of prose.

Additionally, the authors found that high-level schemata not only influence the way people interpret messages but do so to the exclusion of other interpretations. The majority of students in the study were unaware of the alternate interpretations of each passage. Distortions and intrusions (for example, erroneous interpretations, ineffective networks) occur when gaps exist between the material and the learners' comprehension. These gaps can be exacerbated by an incompletely specified text, deliberate distortions by the instructor, disparate schemata of instructor and learner, and the text's appeal to one schema over another (Anderson et al., 1977). In such cases, learners may acquire the information but without efficient internalization or incorporation into their own cognitive schemata.

Carnine and Kinder (1985) found their schemata-based intervention to result in significantly higher reading comprehension scores between pre- and post-tests taken by fourth- through sixth-grade low-performing students. The researchers directed the teachers to ask questions about "the central characters, their goals, obstacles to reaching the goals, and a resolution" (p. 21) for each of three narrative stories and about "specific principles or relationships imbedded in the passages" (p. 22) for each of three expository stories. These questions were posed both before each story and at key stages in the stories.

Significant improvement in comprehension also followed a comparable intervention, "generative learning" instruction, that was employed in the same study. Using this approach, teachers asked students to close their eyes, imagine what was happening at that point in the story, and describe it. Then they were asked to summarize the entire story. The only significant difference between the two methods favored the schemata-based intervention on a maintenance test of the expository stories (Carnine & Kinder, 1985).

Practice Activity 11-3

Help your students become "active" learners. Using Carnine and Kinder's schemata-based intervention approach described above, teach your students the major components of a story and the kinds of questions to ask to help them identify those elements.

Make sure to match the questions to the appropriate type of material. *Narrative* or action stories, such as those found in literature books, take the following kinds of questions:

- Who is the story about?
- What does he or she want to do?

- What happens when he or she tries to do it?
- What happens in the end?*

Expository stories, such as those found in science books, take different kinds of questions:

- What is the rule being discussed?
- How do the examples given fit the rule?
- What other examples fit the rule?*

Hierarchical Retrieval Schemes

Bower and colleagues (1969) examined the ability of certain overriding concepts to include less general concepts. To improve learner recall of categorized word lists, they employed hierarchical retrieval schemes. (Hierarchical arrangements can also be easily used as advance organizers, as is explained in Chapter 10.)

Teaching hierarchically, or presenting material from lower to higher levels of abstraction, provides meaningfulness by supplying learners with a systematic way of organizing material. The increased familiarity with material at the lower levels of a hierarchy aids learners' understanding of higher-level, more complex concepts. Structural information about the material is an important aid to recall.

In the Bower et al. study (1969) structural information was provided by categorizing word lists. The authors asked learners to remember lists of words, some randomly listed, others hierarchically arranged. It was hypothesized that recall can be effectively improved if a learner

> . . . can discover or learn a simple rule or principle which characterizes the items on a list and which relates them to one another, then uses that rule as a retrieval plan in reconstructing the items from memory (p. 340).

Hierarchically presented lists like those prepared by Bower et al. (1969) are distinguished by some structural principle that can be used later to generate the items from memory or to add other appropriate items. Conceptual hierarchies (see Figure 11–1) depict the breakdown of a single category into its subcategories. Associative hierarchies (see Figure 11–2) depict arrangements of items that relate to one another but are not necessarily subcategorized derivatives. Associative hierarchies may be more easily employed in nonscientific subjects such as English, as can be seen in Figure 11–3.

Results of the Bower et al. (1969) experiment revealed very high levels of recall by learners who were given a systematic retrieval plan,

---

*Adapted from Carnine & Kinder (1985).

for example, hierarchical depiction. The authors concluded that the familiar and easily learned retrieval plans "cued" recall of the word lists. Although a goal for advanced learners may be self-discovery of structural rules like hierarchical categorization, we can facilitate learning by describing these rules or by helping learners to discover the rules for themselves.

Practice Activity 11-4

Examine the graphically represented hierarchies in Figures 11–1 through 11–3. Then design one yourself. Let's say you are preparing to teach elementary school students about the structure of their school. Place your principal in the top circle and the two vice principals at your school in the first level of branchings. (This depiction of course assumes that your school has two vice principals, for example, one for discipline and one for scheduling.) Continue the representation, including clerical staff, teachers, learners at corresponding grade levels, and so forth. Now what kind of hierarchical scheme did you prepare—conceptual or associative? If you said "associative," you are right.

Mnemonic Techniques

Teachers can use a variety of techniques to help students recall information. These mnemonic aids, or memory aids, can be taught directly to students.

One type of mnemonic aid is to develop a catchy, easy-to-remember phrase in which the first letter of each word represents the material to be recalled. A familiar example of this is the phrase, "Every Good Boy Does Fine," which is used to recall the names of the lines of a musical staff, E G B D F. Another example is, "James Felt Marvelous And Magnificent; Jim Joined A Spa One Nice Day," to remember the months of the year. To help learners remember and organize zoological classification labels, you might offer the mnemonic "Kings Play Chess On Glass Stools," which represents the categories—kingdom, phylum, class, order, genus, species. Useful mnemonics are often popular with children and are remembered for years. It is surprising to realize how many adults remember from a class long ago at least one mnemonic for recalling, for example, the nine planets or the Great Lakes.

In a study by King and Yuille (1980), young children asked to remember information, such as levels of water in containers (a horizontality task) and the clothing on a picture of a clothesline (a seriation task), were given either operative (functional) or figurative (symbolic) memory aids. For the water-levels task, the operative aid involved a verbal description and a demonstration of the task, while the figura-

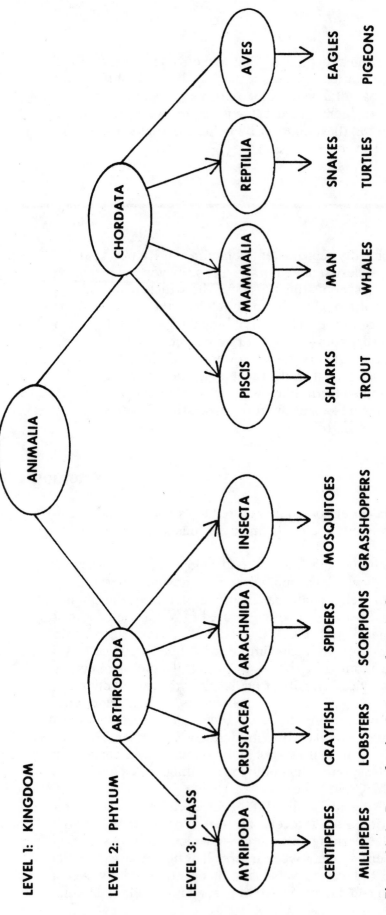

Figure 11-1 *Example of a Conceptual Hierarchy: "Animalia"*

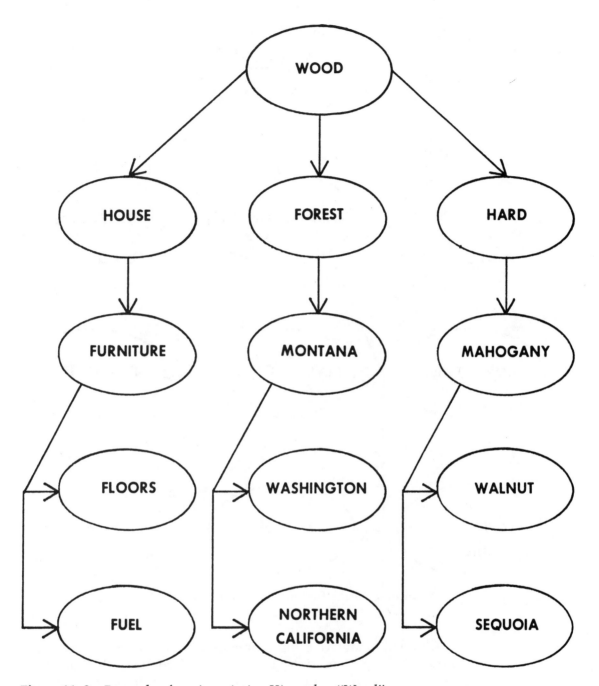

Figure 11–2 *Example of an Associative Hierarchy: "Wood"*

tive aid involved a simple mnemonic. For the clothesline task, two contexts were presented to the children: a story emphasizing the color of the clothing and a story emphasizing the sequence of articles. Findings revealed that the majority (57 percent) of children taught the mnemonic could recall the water levels and a large percentage (93 percent) of those children presented with the "color" context recalled the color of the clothes. The authors concluded that memory

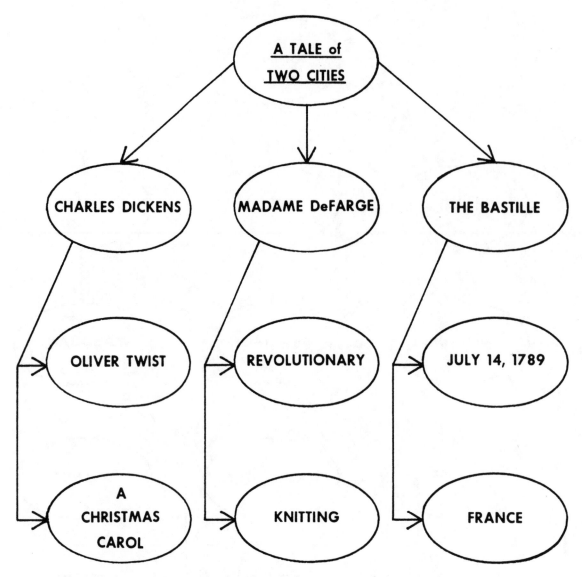

Figure 11–3 *Example of an Associative Hierarchy for an English Unit*

for arbitrary, figurative information, for example, color, can be maintained by the presentation of a meaningful context, for example, a story. They concluded also that mnemonics could be useful in the assimilation of operatively advanced information.

Practice Activity 11-5

Imagine that you must describe the four main functional parts of the brain (the diencephalon, the midbrain, the brainstem, and the cortex) to a classroom of learners. How will you do it? You have at least two choices. You could take the first letter of each part (D,

M, B, C) and incorporate them into a mnemonic like the one for months. Alternatively, you could supply learners with a "house" context, describing each part as you tour the areas of the "house." For example, you could say, "Think of the diencephalon as the 'family room,' because it contains the center of (nerve) activity. Think of the midbrain as the 'hallway,' because it is a connecting organ. Think of the brainstem as a 'busy kitchen,' because it receives and relays (impulse) traffic to other parts of the body. And think of the cortex as the 'roof' of this 'house,' because it covers this site of constant, complex activity."

Conclusions

Meaningfulness requires that teachers do a lot of work during planning and presentation. It requires that you get to know your learners, particularly as a group. Even so, it is not always possible to "get inside learners' heads" to determine which schemata they are bringing to the task. Tyler (1949) suggests that you find out as much as you can about the school community and about the interests and the prior learning experiences of your learners, via the use of such social science research methods as interviewing, questionnaires, observation, and examination of existing documentation, for example, school records.

The keys to meaningfulness are associations—familiar, logical, and numerous associations. The more relevant connections you can draw, both between material the learners already know and new material and between the instructional material and the learners' backgrounds, the more successfully they will learn.

References

Anderson, R. C., Reynolds, R. E., Schallert, D. L., & Goetz, E. T. (1977). Frameworks for comprehending discourse. *American Educational Research Journal, 14,* 367–81.

Ausubel, D. P., & Robinson, F. G. (1969). *School learning.* New York: Holt, Rinehart & Winston.

Bower, G. H., Clark, M. C., Lesgold, A. M., & Winzenz, D. (1969). Hierarchical retrieval schemes in recall of categorized word lists. *Journal of Verbal Learning and Verbal Behavior, 8,* 323–43.

Brophy, J. E., & Evertson, C. M. (1974). The Texas teacher effectiveness project: Presentation of nonlinear relationships and summary discussion (Report No. 74–6). University of Texas: Austin Research and Development Center for Teacher Education. (ERIC Document Reproduction Services No. ED 099 345).

Carnine, D., & Kinder, D. (1985). Teaching low-performing students to apply generative and schema strategies to narrative and expository material. *Remedial and Special Education, 6,* 20–30.

Dewey, J. (1938). *Experience and education.* New York: Collier Books.

Gage, N. L., & Berliner, D. C. (1984). *Educational psychology* (3rd ed.). Boston: Houghton-Mifflin.

Gagne, R. M. (1976). The learning basis of instruction. In R. M. Gagne, *The National Society for the Study of Education Yearbook* (Part 1, pp. 21–43). Chicago: University of Chicago Press.

Kendler, T. S., Kendler, H. H., & Learnard, B. (1962). Mediated responses to size and brightness as a function of age. *American Journal of Psychology, 75*, 571–86.

King, M. A., & Yuille, J. C. (1980, May). *Context effects on children's memory of Piagetian concepts.* Paper presented at the sixtieth annual meeting of the Western Psychological Association, Honolulu. (ERIC Document Services No. ED 192 907).

Luiten, J., Ames, W., & Ackerson, G. (1980). A meta-analysis of the effects of advance organizers on learning and retention. *American Educational Research Journal, 17,* 211–18.

Schuck, R. (1981). The impact of set induction on student achievement and retention. *Journal of Educational Research, 74,* 227–32.

Taylor, P. (1973). *How teachers plan their courses.* New York: NFER.

Tyler, R. W. (1949). *Basic principles of curriculum and instruction.* Chicago: University of Chicago Press.

Chapter Twelve

Individual Differences

Jean Coolican
University of Southern California

Definition

The competent teacher knows that learners progress at different speeds, learn in different ways, and respond to different kinds of motivation. Few generalizations about learning are better established than this one. Research indicates that teaching strategies should be adapted to these differences if all learners are to achieve their full potential.

Purpose

The purpose of this chapter is to help you learn to use information about students sensitively and imaginatively so that you can ensure opportunities for learner success. The chapter will help you select goals and objectives appropriate to learners' abilities, cultural backgrounds, and handicaps and will suggest alternative ways for students to achieve objectives common to the whole group. It will also suggest ways to adapt instruction for your students with special needs, such as those with hearing or vision impairments, physical handicaps, severe learning problems, or unusual talents or abilities.

Background Knowledge

Any school district's statement of philosophy and objectives will almost certainly include a reference to the individual needs and abilities of its students. No matter how it is worded, the intent is to expedite the development of the individual as a fully functioning, autonomous human being. To varying degrees, educators have commited themselves to dealing with learners as people who differ from each other in such areas as ability, age, cultural background, gender, interest, and motivation. This commitment is honored every day in a variety of ways in the classrooms throughout the land.

Practice Activity 12-1

Locate and read both your school division's and your school's statement of philosophy and objectives. How well do you think you are applying the philosophy in your classroom? To what extent are you addressing the objective(s) dealing with individual development?

Indeed, the general public expects its citizens' educational needs, however diverse, to be met in its schools. The public will is often expressed through governmental or legislative action. Public Law 94–142, the Education for All Handicapped Children Act, is a good example of how concern for learners' individual needs affects schools and teachers. In part, this law was enacted because of the disappointing research findings regarding the academic and social effects of placing children in special classes and the negative personal effects of isolating handicapped children from their nonhandicapped peers. The law mandates that free, appropriate public education be made available to handicapped students between the ages of three and eighteen. It explicitly states that these handicapped students be educated to the maximum extent possible, and that they be removed from the regular education environment only when the severity of their problem is such that education in regular classes cannot be satisfactorily achieved. To assure that handicapped students have equal opportunities to be educated, the law dictates that each have a written individualized education program (IEP). Every IEP must include statements of the student's present level of functioning, of annual goals and short-term objectives for achieving the goals, of services to be provided and the extent of regular education programming, and of evaluative procedures and criteria for use on at least an annual basis. A time line of the special education services must also be included.

Recognition of differences among learners, of course, is not limited to special education. To a certain degree, every learner exhibits an individual approach to learning. Educational researchers and practitioners have long realized the importance of recognizing and attending to these individual differences. Indeed, current opinion suggests that educators should aim instruction at particular kinds of students and not at the mythical "average student." The fact that individual differences exist argues for pluralism and for an enlightened opportunism in the use of materials and methods of instruction. No single ideal sequence exists for educating any group of children.

But what does the term *individual differences* mean? How can a knowledge of differences among learners be applied practically by a teacher? To describe what people are like and how they differ from one another and to perceive how one might go about capitalizing on learners' unique abilities are difficult undertakings. Let us for a moment set aside questions of diagnosis—or deciding what learner characteristics should guide instruction—and consider instead how teachers try to adapt their teaching to different learners.

Essentially, a teacher has two general choices when he or she decides to fit instruction to individuals: (a) allow and encourage learners to take different routes to the same objective or (b) permit learners to accomplish different objectives. In other words, individualizing instruction means using various teaching–learning approaches or providing learners with opportunities for attaining different educational outcomes.

Supporting students in alternative ways to achieve the same objective can be accomplished by employing some of the models for teaching concept development in children that are described by Joyce and Weil (1980). These models can help you teach individual students differently by permitting students to achieve objectives by using more of their own initiation and control. In Suchman's Inquiry Training Model, for example, a question or objective is posed by the teacher; following this, the students ask a series of questions to be answered only by "yes" or "no." They then work toward the solution by investigating several ways to process the information needed to answer the original question. If they are trying, for example, to find out why light bulbs suddenly blow out, they might inquire independently by using different kinds of printed material, audiovisual materials, or experimentation. The whole purpose of the model is to guide them in pursuing these different paths. Such models also allow students to generate and test their own hypotheses, thus helping diverse learners reach a variety of goals.

Well-designed basal reading programs that recognize the needs of both slow learners and high-achieving students offer different objectives and different ways to achieve objectives for individual learners. Several programs make provisions for individual differences by offering a wide range of activities, teaching strategies, and materials. Such programs include a component that helps the teacher monitor skill development for each student and prescribe additional practice after each lesson. For students who require additional instruction for remediation and reinforcement, there are repetitive teaching strategies and/or alternative approaches. For students who are ready to extend concepts, there are suggestions for enrichment using a variety of activities, projects, and supplementary readings. These programs are useful resources for beginning teachers because they are formatted for efficient planning and use step-by-step organization, including options for varying ability levels.

As teachers gain experience and develop a repertoire of effective teaching practices, they can expand on this approach to individualization by designing and making operational ways of working with different students, different curriculum materials, and different instructional procedures in order to maximize learning.

Prior Achievement

Differences in learner characteristics can influence both the ends and means of instruction. One excellent perspective on the relationships among learners, teaching, and objectives is offered by Tobias (1976): "[The] higher the level of prior achievement, the lower the instructional support required to accomplish instructional objectives. Conversely, as level of prior achievement decreases, the amount of instructional support required increases" (p. 67). For the classroom teacher this means simply that it is important to understand students' prior levels of achievement or understanding of particular material and to accommodate instruction to variations in such achievement.

Implementation of Tobias's prescription begins with the diagnosis of learner needs. Fortunately, there are many ways to determine whether students have mastered particular concepts or material. For instance, to determine how well a fourth-grade student knows the multiplication tables, a teacher might give a written test or an oral quiz that includes all the tables. A more difficult task for the teacher is to fit instruction to the individual's knowledge of the multiplication tables. Providing more support to a student who scores poorly on a test or quiz does not necessarily mean giving the student more problems to work out. Instead, it might mean providing a series of different activities that are carefully structured to demonstrate concepts of multiplication, for example, grouping manipulative devices, using a calculator, or trying simple thought problems. Providing more support doesn't mean giving learners more of the same; it means helping them structure their thinking in ways they have not yet been able to do for themselves.

Concentrating on prior achievement is important in another way because it suggests a general type of learner characteristic that can serve not only to guide teachers in selecting instructional approaches but also to help them establish goals of instruction. That is, when teachers concentrate on learner characteristics that are modifiable—such as skills, knowledge, and attitudes—as opposed to those that are fixed and uncontrollable—such as race, sex, and age—they may teach with an eye toward helping individuals grow personally, socially, and intellectually (Cronbach & Snow, 1977).

Exceptionalities

Exceptional children are those whose performances deviate from the norm, either below or above, to such an extent that special education and related services are required if these students are to realize their potential. The mandates of PL 94-142, which were described earlier, apply only to students who are handicapped, however, not to non-handicapped students who are gifted or talented. Handicapping conditions recognized under PL 94-142 include mental retardation; learning disabilities; emotional disturbance; hearing, vision, and speech handicaps; physical handicaps; and other health impairments. Keep in mind that there is much variation in both degree and type of disability within each handicapping condition, that handicaps frequently overlap, and that they can change over time. For instance, a child who is physically handicapped may also be mildly retarded and have emotional problems; any of these conditions could improve or worsen, and thus the child's education program would need to be reevaluated.

PL 94–142 mandates not only that handicapped children have the right to free and appropriate education but also that the education be provided in the "least restrictive" learning environment possible.

This means that most mildly handicapped students are spending at least part of their day in the regular classroom. Handicapped students are placed in regular classes according to their identified learning needs. A special education teacher (for example, a resource room teacher) will help you select the special materials, teaching techniques, and/or equipment you may need to implement the handicapped child's educational plan.

It is important to realize that handicapped children are often socially ignored or even ridiculed by their nonhandicapped peers (see Sabornie, 1985). Teachers of mainstreamed students should therefore attempt to establish positive attitudes toward the handicapped and to encourage appropriate interactions between their disabled and nondisabled students. For example, students in a class that includes a hearing-impaired child could be taught the manual alphabet (for "finger-spelling") and rudimentary sign language. To further reduce social isolation of mainstreamed students, teachers might develop a social skills training program or, if necessary, a self-care program. Such a program could be developed with the assistance of the handicapped student's special education teacher.

Many of the educational needs of handicapped children are similar to the needs of other students in your classrooms. As a result of improved identification and placement procedures, emphasis is being directed toward each child's educational characteristics. This could eventually prove to be a useful way of assessing all learners. In addition, the classroom teacher is in a key position to recognize those students who have special needs. A comprehensive diagnosis, however, is not the classroom teacher's responsibility, but that of specialized personnel in the school system. You should be prepared to communicate learners' problems and to work cooperatively with the professionals assigned to diagnose disabilities and prescribe treatments.

Although there is a trend toward noncategorical special education for mildly handicapped children, we will address the areas of exceptionalities using the traditional classifications because most of you will be dealing with these. (It is important to emphasize, however, that labeling children on the basis of any identified deficiency does not enhance self-concept and indeed may lower expectations and reinforce failure in their attempts to achieve.) The following is a survey of the types of exceptionalities you are likely to encounter in your classes and descriptions of teaching strategies appropriate for each. Remember that many of these strategies are appropriate for teaching regular class students as well as mainstreamed special education students.

Physical and Sensory Handicaps

There are many different kinds of physical handicaps, including epilepsy, cerebral palsy, paralysis, and chronic medical conditions. In the absence of other handicaps, physically disabled students should be given the same educational goals and curriculum as nonhandi-capped students (Kneedler, Hallahan, & Kauffman, 1984). They may, however, require adaptive equipment such as special writing instru-ments, chairs, desks, or ramps.

You may have a student with a sensory handicap—that is, a hear-ing, vision, or speech handicap—in your class. Consider the use of some or all of the following strategies for teaching students who are deaf or hearing impaired:

- Seat the student in a good hearing-viewing location. Be con-scious of where and how you teach.
- Speak clearly, and be sure that the student can see your face when you are speaking.
- Use visual signals, techniques, and materials.
- Assign a "hearing buddy" to the student.

If you have a blind or visually impaired student, you might try the following strategies:

- Give the student extra time for assignments and tests. He or she may need to have the material transcribed in Braille.
- Read exams to the student or record them on tape.
- Say aloud whatever you write on the board.
- Encourage the development of listening skills.
- Have other students act as note takers, using carbon paper. Re-source teachers, the student's parents, or volunteers can help transcribe into Braille later.

Students with speech handicaps may demonstrate disorders in ar-ticulation, fluency, and/or voice, or they may be unable to speak at all. Kneedler et al. (1984) suggest the following techniques for teach-ing students with speech or language disorders:

- Be alert to deviations in speech or language, and refer students demonstrating such deviations to a specialist for evaluation.
- Maintain contact with the speech therapist to understand the goals and new speech responses to be reinforced in the class-room.
- Create a relaxed yet stimulating atmosphere conducive to communication.
- Never finish a sentence for a student.
- Reinforce speech-impaired students' efforts to communicate by paying attention to them.

Learning and Cognitive Disabilities

Two groups of exceptional children will be considered in this classifi-cation: the educable mentally retarded and the learning disabled. These students are being educated successfully in the regular classroom. They require additional help because of the seriousness of their learning problems. You will notice that the teaching strategies described are appropriate for all students experiencing learning problems, not just for those children identified as handicapped.

Mainstream programs for mentally retarded children should concentrate on acquisition of basic skills, with special emphasis on functional academic, self-help, personal/social, vocational, and communication skills. Hallahan and Kauffman (1982) offer some specific suggestions for classroom teachers to use with educable mentally retarded students:

- Sequence learning tasks.
- Simplify complex activities.
- Use frequent repetition and drill.
- Help the students verbally rehearse or talk through what they have to learn.
- Maintain a sense of structure and familiarity, but introduce some novelty to increase motivation.
- Help students develop effective school-related behaviors; that is, help them learn to complete tasks.
- Assess continually.
- Provide immediate feedback.

Task analysis offers one way to simplify complex tasks. This technique begins with setting a goal, determining the sequence of steps necessary to reach the goal, starting with what the student can do, and rewarding successful performance of each step. The successful completion of each step motivates the student to perform at progressively higher levels.

Most students identified as learning disabled are taught in regular classrooms and receive part-time resource room services. Defining "learning disability" or delineating a precise set of characteristics of the learning-disabled student is problematic. The absence of universal agreement on what constitutes a learning disability has precipitated widespread controversy. Many children who do not achieve to their full potential in the classroom may be experiencing only minor or temporary difficulties in learning particular basic skills or subjects. Learning-disabled students, according to Kirk and Gallagher (1983), exhibit a severe discrepancy between potential and actual achievement.

Learning-disabled students generally demonstrate near-normal intelligence. Matching curriculum to their abilities is important in helping to close the ability–achievement gap. Providing experiences for success is very important, as it is with all students, especially younger ones. Direct instruction of precisely defined skills, many opportunities to practice, and the same monitoring, evaluating, and feedback used with other students with special needs are the most effective strategies you can implement.

Recent research has indicated that learning-disabled students are deficient in "metacognitive skills"; that is, they do not efficiently select or apply appropriate strategies for successfully completing tasks (see Wong, 1982). They seem to be passive rather than active learners. For example, according to Kneedler et al. (1984), learners who demonstrate good reading comprehension tend to use the following metacognitive strategies (you might want to help the learning-disabled students, or any students with reading problems, in your class to develop these skills):

- They clarify the purpose of what they are reading.
- They focus their attention on important parts of passages.
- They monitor their level of understanding as they read.
- They backtrack or scan ahead for clues when they realize they are not understanding what they are reading.

Many learning-disabled students are also characterized by hyperactivity or a tendency to be distracted. The strategies suggested below for use with students identified as behavior disordered (frequently referred to as "emotionally disturbed") may be applicable for these students, as well.

Emotional or Behavioral Handicaps

Children identified as mildly or moderately emotionally disturbed or behaviorally disordered are most frequently characterized by poor interpersonal relations, poor academic achievement, and poor self-esteem (Kneedler et al., 1984). Some are inordinately shy and withdrawn while others are overly aggressive. Still others behave in ways usually seen in much younger children. They are all handicapped by their inappropriate behavior. Many nonhandicapped children, of course, manifest similar behaviors but not as often and not as extremely (Heward & Orlansky, 1984).

The education of behaviorally disordered children parallels closely good behavior management for students in general (see Chapter 3, "Reinforcement"). Behaviorally disordered students respond well to a structured and predictable environment, with expectations for academic performance and standards of conduct communicated clearly and firmly. They should be able to depend upon consistent, appropriate consequences for their behavior, with the emphasis on reinforcement rather than on punishment.

Remember, behaviorally disordered children, like all others, need to experience success. They also require the kind of warm, accepting environment described in Chapter 14, "Affective Climate."

Giftedness

As noted earlier, the regular classroom is often considered the least restrictive environment for special education students. Advocates of

alternative education for gifted and talented children, however, argue that the regular classroom is too restrictive.

Educators have defined, characterized, and identified gifted children in various ways. Renzulli and Smith (1980) offer a multiple-criterion definition of giftedness (see Figure 12–1):

- High ability (including high intelligence)
- High creativity (ability to formulate new ideas and apply them to the solutions of problems)
- High task commitment (a high level of motivation and the ability to see a project through to its conclusion)

According to the authors, these criteria are interactive rather than exclusive. Like other exceptionalities, giftedness is not fixed or absolute; a student may exhibit the above criteria at different times and under different circumstances.

The most common types of educational services for gifted students are enrichment programs within the regular classroom setting; ability groupings, in which students are placed in special "tracks" according to ability; and accelerated programs that allow students to move more quickly through regular grades. Experts agree that the gifted need both content knowledge and the skills to be able to use that knowledge effectively. The debate over basic skills is not

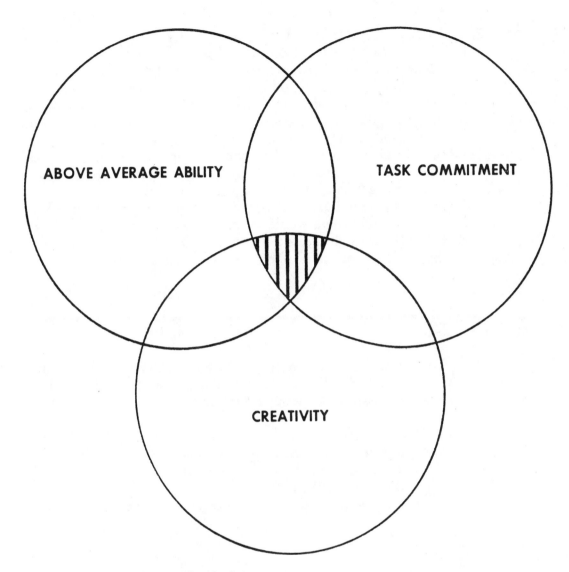

Figure 12–1   *Ingredients of Giftedness*

whether or not to teach them, but how to determine the proper time and emphasis.

One example of a regular classroom program designed to meet the needs of gifted students is Renzulli's "compacting of the curriculum." Essentially, compacting entails (a) determining through formal or informal assessment the curriculum content already mastered and (b) substituting suitably challenging activities and experiences. For example, if a gifted fifth-grader using a grade-level mathematics text-book scores above grade level in mathematics concepts on a test of basic skills, you could assign major checkup sections of the text to guarantee proficiency in basic skills. At that point, you might provide additional activities in one or more of the concepts (causality, probability, analogy, deduction, induction, and so on.) In other words, you offer instruction in areas beyond those typically covered in standard textbooks. The resource personnel in your school or district could assist in selecting materials and pacing the enriched program.

There are many models recommended as guides for gifted education. Schools may have programs based on one model or on a combination. There is no evidence to suggest that any approach is superior to all others. Bloom's Taxonomy of Educational Objectives can be recommended, however, because of its adaptability to the entire range of students in most classrooms. Chapters 9 and 15, "Questioning Skill" and "Evaluation," respectively, describe this approach in detail. Using Bloom's taxonomy, you would develop activities and structure them so that some would be appropriate and required for all students and others would be designated for selected students. Gifted students might be asked to concentrate on those activities at the higher levels of the taxonomy.

Practice Activity 12-2

Do you know the procedure in your school for referring a student who might be in need of services in addition to those offered in the regular classroom? Investigate the following:

1. Who are the specialists, what services do they provide, where are they located, and when are they available?
2. What forms are used, to whom are they submitted, and what is the prescribed time line?
3. How do you as the classroom teacher fit into the procedure?

Cultural Background

Understanding and being sensitive to students' cultural backgrounds and ethnic differences is fundamental for teachers in our pluralistic society. Every student comes to school as a whole person, with a culture and a language, values, attitudes, beliefs, and knowledge. We should make every effort to understand these so as to use them productively in the classroom. Students' learning and behavior are influenced by their cultural and ethnic perspective, as are teachers' actions and behaviors. Garcia (1982) urges teachers to try to understand how other cultural and ethnic groups perceive their social identity rather than view the value of a certain cultural or ethnic group from the perspective of one's own culture—not an easy task, but important if we are also committed to broadening students' awareness and acceptance of diverse cultural heritages.

Employing an ethnic studies instructional model can help increase overall awareness and sensitivity. An ethnic studies model can be utilized in most classrooms irrespective of ethnic or racial composition or of subject matter; the model weaves multiethnic ex-

periences into the classroom and can be used concurrently with other teaching and learning activities. For example, while students are learning to read, they can learn to share cultural interpretations of what they read. Other applications of the ethnic studies model include the following (try to add some ideas of your own):

- In science, students can research famous scientists from several cultures.
- In math, students can study how different ethnic groups, such as the Chinese or the Aztecs, have calculated seasons and time of year.
- Special knowledge of ethnic minority students can be used to build a sense of belonging; for example, sharing ethnic games, songs, or folktales can be done in the native language.
- Depending on the range of ethnic groups in a class, or even in a school, there could be an ethnic food fair or international banquet.

Student Interests

Another factor that affects learning, but is frequently overlooked or not sufficiently emphasized, is student interest. Students' interests in particular areas of inquiry or subject matter are important considerations. Interest may be broad or narrow, intuitive or precisely defined, short-term or long-term.

Interests are developed in many ways. Students may be influenced by each other's interests and by those of parents and teachers. You can gather information about what interests students in a variety of ways. Listening to students is one of the best. If a student talks about "how a space vehicle maneuvers" or "why sports are so much fun," you can begin to identify appropriate subject matter. To enhance the quality of your information about student interests, you should ask questions and observe students at work and at play. Tyler (1974) has suggested that as we try to offer choices based on interests, students will learn to engage in activities they see as appropriate while ruling out those that are not. She contends that the ruling out may be a more important aspect of the developmental process than the selecting. Strong (1958) claims we can sketch or outline individuality when we ask two questions: (1) What *can* the student do? (2) What does the student *want* to do?

We are concerned with the motivating factors in the individual and conditions in the environment that contribute to learning. As teachers we should attempt to meld these successfully by capitalizing on the existing motivation of students and by providing materials and methodologies that will stimulate new interests. For instance, we can make sure that curriculum materials are meaningful, vary the formats of lessons and style of presentation, encourage the use of different senses during lessons, and ask timely questions to sustain curiosity. Frymier (1985) presents a comprehensive view of motivating factors, including a sense of the teacher as a person. He maintains that a teacher who is committed, enthusiastic, and motivated learns to become a more effective facilitator in helping students "learn to want to learn."

Interest inventories are useful instruments for identifying the direction in which an individual is moving or would like to move. The best-known, the Kuder General Interest Survey, published by Science Research Associates (SRA), and similar instruments are closely tied to occupational criteria and are most useful at the middle and secondary levels. The results of these surveys help to predict choices an individual is likely to make based on patterns of past choices. Informal interest surveys can be used with elementary and middle school children. These teacher-made inventories are practical means for beginning to understand what interests students and what they would rather avoid. In addition, teachers can build choice into their daily programs by allowing students to select from a range of learning activities.

Practice Activity 12-3

Study the two samples of classroom interest inventories in Box 12–1. Try them out with your class. Depending on the age, grade,

---

Box 12–1 *Sample Classroom Interest Inventories*

1a. If *you* could decide what you would study in school next week, what would you choose? Why? What would you definitely *not* include? _____

_____

b. If you could magically visit any person from now or from the past, whom would you choose to visit? _____

_____

c. If you were hired to write a new TV show, what would it be about? Who would star in it? Would *you* be in it? _____

_____

d. If you woke up one day and found you had superhuman powers, what would you do? _____

_____

e. If you could somehow become a super-athlete overnight, what would your sport be? What would you do as a super-athlete? _____

_____

2a. I think reading _____ .

b. I wish I could _____ .

c. Someday I _____ .

d. I wish my teacher _____ .

Note: Adapted from Jean Wallace Gillet and Charles Temple. *Understanding Reading Problems*, 2nd ed., pp. 381–82. Copyright © 1986 by Jean Wallace Gillet and Charles Temple. Adapted by permission of Scott Foresman/Little, Brown College Division.

and the reading and writing ability of your students, the items can be completed orally or in writing. You can and probably will want to add questions and items tailored to your students and subject matter.

Cooperative Grouping in Classrooms

Meeting the needs of each individual does not mean that every student has an individualized lesson plan or must spend his or her time engaged in learning activities alone. While learners could engage in a highly individualized curriculum such as PLAN, a computer-managed system marketed by the Westinghouse Corporation, most school divisions, schools, and teachers have neither the resources nor the desire to prescribe instruction for individuals as fully and completely as would a computer-based curriculum. In effective classrooms there is a reasonable mix of individual and group activities.

A substantial body of research evidence that is accumulating suggests that teachers can encourage learners to work with one another in productive, cooperative groups and still protect, perhaps even enhance, the integrity of a learner's individuality. Although the list below is not exhaustive, teachers who are successful at encouraging cooperation and preserving individuality do so by performing these kinds of activities:

- Specifying learners' objectives both for learning and for cooperating
- Making decisions about the size of working groups
- Assigning students to groups, preferably heterogeneous by member ability
- Arranging the room so that group members can communicate with each other and with the teacher
- Planning for the use of materials so as to increase chances for cooperation, for example, giving one copy of directions to a group or giving different materials that require synthesis to various people
- Assigning roles for group members
- Explaining tasks and criteria for success
- Explaining rules for behavior in groups

Teachers who use cooperative grouping also monitor group interactions, often in rather formal ways, and intervene to provide help with the task and to facilitate cooperation (Johnson & Johnson, 1975).

If you were to encourage individuals to cooperate on a task, you might think it wise to overlook differences in performance within the group—in a sense, to avoid differentiating among group members' outcomes. If the group is working on a cognitive task, however, this strategy would not be probable. From a review of the research on cooperative grouping and cognitive achievement, Slavin (1983) argues that cooperation is more effective when group rewards are provided, based on group members' achievement, and when members of such groups are held individually accountable for their performances. It appears that grouping for cooperative learning may be most important for what it can contribute to a student's motivation. When students work together to achieve a group goal, they have opportunities to create certain expectations for one another's behavior, or norms for behavior, and these in turn increase motivation to achieve and help each other (Slavin, 1983). In addition, encouraging individuals of different ethnic groups to work together may promote cross-ethnic relationships among students (Johnson et al., 1984).

Procedures have been developed for students to help each other during seatwork in a variety of subject areas. In some cases students prepare a common product, for example, answers to a drill sheet, and in other situations students study cooperatively in order to prepare for later competition (Slavin, 1980). Benefit seems to derive from the social value of working in groups and the cognitive value gained from explaining the material to someone and/or having it explained.

One such strategy that has been successful is the "jigsaw method" (Blaney, 1978), which is based on fitting pieces of a lesson together like the pieces of a jigsaw puzzle. In the jigsaw approach, students are assigned to teams of equal number. Members of different teams who have the same section form "expert groups" and study together. For example, a biography might be broken down into early life, major setbacks, influences, and so forth. Each then returns to his or her original team and teaches the section to the team. Often, the students are quizzed on the entire set of material. Success depends upon paying close attention to each other's sections; consequently, students are motivated to support and to show interest in each other's work.

To achieve a precise match between learner characteristics and curriculum, you will have to make a number of separate decisions. As you expand your professional repertoire, you will be able to achieve the delicate balance of knowing when to group or individualize and how to incorporate materials and methods that help each child work toward realizing his or her potential.

How might you provide for a wide range of reading levels, developmental levels, interests, and learning styles in classroom instruction? What are some ways to differentiate tasks and assignments and use cooperative learning? To explore the possibilities, let's set a scenario.

You have had your social studies class engaged in a study of politics at the local, state, or national level. You want the students to expand their knowledge of political parties. Here are some suggestions to help you make sure everyone has an opportunity to participate and learn:

- Record or have a student record student questions during the lesson. Use these questions and others as a guide to search for information.
- Elicit possible sources of information from the group: encyclopedias, reference books, classroom texts, television, people, and so forth.
- Make assignments based on the strengths of your students. For example, some less able readers could be assigned to inteview parents, friends, local politicians, and so on; some proficient readers could be assigned the "library" work; several others could be assigned to watch TV news programs and listen to

the radio for any information relevant to the topic. You could be more specific in delineating tasks or have groups go through current radio and TV schedules to decide among themselves the newscasts for which each would be responsible.

- Encourage conversation as a means of gaining information from everyone, and suggest that all use the media as general sources.
- Plan an in-class discussion to center around conversation circles that include students assigned to various sources. This would provide opportunities for successful contribution from all students.
- Expect each circle to formulate one unanswered question to place before the whole class when the lesson continues in the next session.*

An in-class activity for language arts, English, or foreign language at an intermediate level could employ a similar approach of building on students' strengths. Consider the following example and think about adapting some of these suggestions to your classroom.

You have been teaching vocabulary development and sentence structure. You want to see how well each student is understanding these concepts. You can set expectations, differentiate tasks, and provide opportunities for successful oral and written participation:

- Question the group orally on the kinds of sentences—simple, compound, and so forth.
- Have students write in ten minutes as many sentences as they can, and have them use a different number of words in each sentence.
- Circulate and monitor while they write.
- Encourage students to write sentences on the board. Select those who will produce a variety of sentences from simple to compound-complex.
- While students write on the board, call upon many individuals to read their sentences. Ask each to select his or her best, evaluating each effort with constructive enthusiasm.
- Correct the work at the board by having individuals read, identify, and suggest corrections.

Competence in teaching stems from many variables, two of the more important being the capacity to reach out to differing students and to create learning environments that permit them to demonstrate success. Your own success as a teacher will depend on how well you use a variety of approaches, effectively matching them to your students' needs and abilities.

---

*Adapted from Noar, 1972.

References

Blaney, N. (1978). *The jigsaw classroom.* Beverly Hills, Calif. Sage.

Cronbach, L. J., & Snow, R. E. (1977). *Aptitudes and instructional methods: A handbook for research on interactions.* New York: Irvington.

Frymier, J. (1985). *Motivation to learn.* West Lafayette, Ind. Kappa Delta Pi.

Garcia, R. L. (1982). *Teaching in a pluralistic society.* New York: Harper & Row.

Gillet, J. W., & Temple, C. (1982). *Understanding reading problems: Assessment and instruction.* Canada: Little, Brown.

Hallahan, D. P., & Kauffman, J. M. (1982). *Exceptional children: Introduction to special education.* Englewood Cliffs, N.J.: Prentice-Hall.

Heward, W. L., & Orlansky, M. D. (1984). *Exceptional children.* Columbus, Oh.: Merrill.

Johnson, D. W., & Johnson, R. T. (1975). *Learning together and alone: Cooperation, competition, and individualization.* Englewood Cliffs, N.J.: Prentice-Hall.

Johnson, D. W., Johnson, R. T., Tiffany, M., & Zaidman, B. (1984). Cross-ethnic relationships: The impact of intergroup cooperation and intergroup competition. *Journal of Educational Research, 78* (2), 75–79.

Joyce, B., & Weil, M. (1980). *Models of teaching.* Englewood Cliffs, N.J.: Prentice-Hall.

Kirk, S. A., & Gallagher, J. J. (1983). *Educating exceptional children* (4th ed.). Boston: Houghton Mifflin.

Kneedler, R. D., Hallahan, D. P., & Kauffman, J. K. (1984). *Special education for today.* Englewood Cliffs, N.J.: Prentice-Hall.

Noar, G. (1972). *Individualized instruction: Every child a winner.* New York: Wiley.

Renzulli, J. S., & Smith, L. (1980, November/December). An alternative approach to identifying and programming for gifted and talented students. *G/C/T, 11,* 3–8.

Sabornie, E. J. (1985). Social mainstreaming of handicapped students: Facing an unpleasant reality. *Remedial and Special Education, 6,* 12–16.

Slavin, R. (1980). Cooperative learning. *Review of Educational Research, 50,* 315–42.

Slavin, R. (1983). When does cooperative learning increase student achievement? *Psychological Bulletin, 94,* 429–45.

Strong, E. K., Jr. (1958). Satisfactions and interests. *American Psychologist, 13,* 449–56.

Tobias, S. (1976). Achievement treatment interactions. *Review of Educational Research, 46,* 61–74.

Tyler, L. (1974). *Individual differences: Abilities and motivational directions.* Englewood Cliffs, N.J.: Prentice-Hall.

Wong, B. Y. L. (1982). Metacognition and learning disabilities. *Topics in Learning and Learning Disabilities, 2* (special issue).

Chapter Thirteen

Learner Self-Concept

Kathleen Anne Dunne
University of Virginia

Definition

The competent teacher knows that a learner's achievement may be enhanced by improving his or her self-concepts, and that self-concepts are enhanced if teachers' expectations are high and teachers show appreciation of the personal worth of learners.

Purpose

The purpose of this chapter is to help you understand the importance of enhancing a learner's self-concept. Emphasis will be placed on the contribution that teachers make to the development of positive student self-concept. Specific teacher actions that support positive self-assessment will be explored, for example, presenting challenging lessons, encouraging learners' success when dealing with difficult questions, praising difficult accomplishments, and responding appropriately to pupil errors. The chapter will also discuss the importance of developing appreciation of students' cultural heritages.

Background Knowledge

"You're my favorite teacher!" This acclamation is highly prized whenever it comes our way. It is particularly valued when the judg-

ment has stood the test of time. Which of your teachers stands out in your mind? Think about your own school experiences and recall a teacher you'd like to thank. What made that individual so special? Was there a particular quality, a positive attitude, a belief in you that this person communicated?

There has been a "Great Debate" among educators for years about the characteristics of effective teachers. Is the ability to facilitate learning an innate talent, or can teachers be trained? Can we describe objectively what we mean when we talk about an effective teacher? What do effective teachers do? How can we identify them? How can we imitate their behaviors?

Those interested in defining the attributes of effective teachers have been looking in classrooms, recording what they see, and communicating their findings to others. For instance, when teachers let students know they believe in them and expect them to do well, students begin to believe in themselves and do their best to achieve success (Berliner, 1984; Hosford, 1984).

But what is self-concept? Why is it so important to learners? How does it develop? Can it readily be changed once it is formed? If so, how? These and other related questions have guided educational and psychological researchers as well as classroom teachers for years. Like most areas of knowledge about human development, that of self-concept is far from being fully explored. There is some strong evidence, however, for the contention that teachers need to account for self-concept in their interactions with students.

Self-concept can be described as the mental image one has of oneself. This image, of course, may be composed of a host of attributes. For instance, it is rather difficult in a highly visual culture like ours not to think of one's physical appearance as playing some part in one's self-concept. If you doubt this all you need do is visit a weekly meeting of Weight Watchers or spend half an hour watching a television show in which physically beautiful people become rich and famous and loved with amazingly little effort.

There are, of course, other attributes that define our images of ourselves: wit, charm, religiousness, ethnicity, sociability, and success, to mention but a few. Preadolescents and adolescents often tend to see themselves in absolute terms; that is, they think of themselves as either athletic or not athletic, smart or not smart, good or not good, and so forth. Among very young children, these assessments are seen neither as points on a continuum nor as characteristics that are balanced by strengths or weaknesses in other areas. As children grow, they begin to make more distinctions and to think of themselves in more complex ways. This development can be supported with the guidance of teachers.

Self-concept is often defined not so much in terms of what we think of ourselves as in terms of what we think others think of us. Let's try these mental and semantic gymnastics another way. Self-concept works like a mirror: We look at other people to see ourselves. If we think they think we are valuable, we think we are valuable; if we think they think we are deficient, we think we are deficient. Obviously, this definition has direct implications for teachers. Teachers who send clear, positive messages to their students are likely to enhance students' self-concepts, while teachers who berate their students may diminish their sense of self-worth. Teachers' criticism can damage students' self-concepts. Teachers communicate their attitudes about their students' personal worth when, for example, they express their expectations for achievement, respond to their students' work, and react to individual differences among their students.

High Expectations

One characteristic that distinguishes teachers of students who make substantial learning gains from those whose students do not make such gains is the belief of the effective teachers that students can and will learn (Good & Brophy, 1987). In looking for an explanation for this phenomenon, Good and Brophy suggest that teacher expectations are only the beginning of a chain of events. High expectations foreshadow teacher actions that will support the success of learners; teachers often create a warmer affective climate for students whom they perceive to be bright (Cooper, 1979; Cooper & Tom, 1984). Conversely, low expectations lead to classroom interactions that are unlikely to facilitate learning. Teachers' responses, then, are in part a product of their expectations: If we expect students to succeed, we give them every opportunity to do so; if we have low expectations, we may try to protect students from failure by calling on them less frequently and cutting short the amount of time we would usually wait for an answer (Good & Brophy, 1987).

Teachers can use their expectations to support student success. Often the need for teacher support in this area is associated with children who are less capable. In *Giftedness, Conflict and Underachievement*, Whitmore (1980) considers the role of self-concept at length when discussing the underachieving gifted student:

> Studies comparing the characteristics of the achiever with those of the underachiever indicate that negative self-concepts are the central trait distinguishing underachievers from those who are achieving commensurate with their ability (p. 278).

For all learners—not just gifted ones—there is a connection between negative self-concept and failure. Which comes first is not clear.

The message teachers communicate when they set high expectations is that learners are capable. This message, in turn, supports a positive self-assessment on the part of students. If an expectation is so high that a learner is not likely to succeed, the impact of the message can be reversed; that is, it may reinforce the learner's insecurities and diminish his or her sense of self-worth. The trick, if there can be said to be one, is to set learning objectives that are both challenging and attainable. Such objectives will increase the likelihood of success while affirming a positive self-concept.

Let's examine a hypothetical situation to see the results of high expectations in action. It is 8:15 A.M.; the school day doesn't officially begin until 8:30. As you walk through the hallway you notice many children talking, engaging in horseplay, and wandering aimlessly in the general direction of their classrooms. As you enter Mrs. Cashin's sixth-grade classroom you sense a difference in the atmosphere. The generalized energy of children entering school has become directed. Students are talking, smiling, getting started on their school day, but there is a qualitative difference in the tone of their early-morning activity.

As you wander around the room you see John recording the growth of the plants in his science experiment and Susan illustrating the sequence of events of a book she finished reading last night. Other students are similarly engaged. The predominant activity seems to be journal writing. You're impressed.

You return to visit with Mrs. Cashin later in the day, after the children have been dismissed. Mrs. Cashin is flattered by the compliment you offer with your question, "How do you do it?" She responds, "Actually the answer is that I don't do it. Instead, I expect the children to put forth their best efforts, and they do. Not that it's effortless on my part. On the contrary, I help by defining those expectations. The key is challenging each student with a rewarding and accomplishable goal."

She continues: "Take creative writing as an example. Before you stopped by my room this afternoon I was evaluating student writing portfolios. For each member of the class, there is an individual record card that I use to note writing skills as they are acquired. It also helps me suggest to students the skills they should concentrate on in their current writing."

Mrs. Cashin's approach supports the academic progress of each student. The learning objectives she defines are both challenging and attainable, and she has shown a respect for the abilities of each of her students. In short, Judy Cashin is using high expectations to communicate her belief in her students.

Research on effective schools also recognizes the role of high expectations on student achievement (Tursman, 1981). It has been shown that students tend to perform better when teachers communicate a belief in the abilities of students by planning challenging lessons.

Learners receive an assessment message from you based on the degree of difficulty of the tasks assigned. Teachers who have high and attainable expectations are showing a knowledge of and a respect for their students. This message reinforces feelings of personal worth and a positive self-concept.

Practice Activity 13-1

1. Look over your class list to identify a student for whom you have held low expectations. How did you arrive at this judgment? Perhaps past teachers have found the student to be lacking, or test scores indicate he or she is less capable than others in the class. Whatever the reasons, most teachers can readily identify one or more students for whom their expectations are minimal.

2. Now list the strengths of this student, including his or her interests. Look at a specific content area and define the student's current level of achievement. Plan a conference together during which you will help the student identify specific personal strengths and goals. Identify one challenging but attainable goal; you might want to do this cooperatively with the student. Tell the student he or she can accomplish the goal, and you will be there to help if necessary.

3. Keep a journal tracking the student's progress. Notice the frequency with which you give this student opportunities to respond in class. Record the number of times the student volunteers.

Notice interactions with other students. Do these actions indicate an increase, a decrease, or no change in self-confidence?

Praise

Our expectations are evident in the way we respond to students. Let's examine the attributes of one influential category of teacher response: praise.

Verbal praise is an effective device when a teacher's goal is to reinforce newly acquired behavior. The effects of praise on students are greatest in the earliest grades. When students are already motivated to perform in certain ways, however, teacher praise can have the undesirable effect of replacing intrinsic with extrinsic motivation (Good & Brophy, 1987). In other words, students may begin to work for teacher praise when they were previously motivated to demonstrate the desired behavior cn their own. Brophy (1983) sees praise as most effective when used to build intrinsic motivation in students.

Individuals define praise differently. Although many people would judge any positive remark as praise, perhaps the most useful way of assessing the value of a seemingly positive remark is to consider it from the perspective of the person receiving the message. Teacher statements that are very general or are made frequently may have little impact on students. More effective praise, especially after the early years of school, is that which is done well, rather than frequently (Brophy, 1981). What does it mean for praise to be "done well"? Box 13–1 summarizes the attributes of effective praise. As you read it, consider whether or not the positive verbal comments you offer students are characteristically effective or ineffective.

If some praise is good, is more better? The indication is that too much praise can be detrimental. Meyer and colleagues (1979) found that "overpraising" high school students implied that they had low ability. High teacher expectations—and only exceptional praise—were interpreted as a sign of high ability in students for whom they were held.

Practice Activity 13-2

There are many situations that could be used to illustrate the effects of praise on students. Because your colleague, Bertram Smith, has asked you to visit his classroom, let's look at the effects of praise on his students.

Bertram is one of those people you can't help but like. He is a kind and gentle person who sees the good in everyone. You and he met at the orientation meeting for new teachers in your school division. Bert has a high level of commitment to education; he has

---

Box 13–1 *Characteristics of Effective Praise*

Effective praise . . .

- is given contingently.
- explains why some behavior is praiseworthy.
- is credible, spontaneous, and draws attention to the student.
- rewards performance and/or effort.
- suggests why a student's accomplishment is important and provides information about his or her competence.
- helps students appreciate their task-related behavior and their thinking about problem solving.
- describes students' present accomplishments as they relate to past accomplishments.
- is given because the accomplishment was difficult for the particular student.
- attributes success to effort and ability of students, implying similar successes can be expected in the future.
- suggests that students do well because they want to do so.
- focuses students' attention on their own task-relevant behavior.
- helps students appreciate their behavior after task is completed.

Note: Adapted from Brophy. A functional analysis. *Review of Educational Research*, 1981, pp. 5–32. Copyright © 1981, A.E.R.A.

always wanted to teach. He is undaunted in his enthusiasm, but you did detect some concern in his voice when he asked you to visit his class and give him feedback: He senses a problem and is looking for advice. Let's look at Bert's classroom.

The ninth-graders are working in groups on social studies projects that they will present at the end of the week. As you enter, Bertram looks up and smiles your way but does not interrupt his work with the students. He goes from group to group, giving them encouragement:

"Nice job!"

"Good going!"

"Hey, you guys have got it together!"

You also note that the students respond with a pleasant, if passive, "Thanks, Mr. Smith."

Bertram is giving his students "positive feedback," but he senses that something is missing. He is relying on your observation to give him some insights into the situation.

Take a minute to jot down the points you will make when you share your observations with Bert. What is he doing well? What might he do differently?

Responses to Practice Activity 13-2

Did your feedback to Bert include the following points?

- There seems to be a positive atmosphere. The students are engaged in their work and obviously like and respect their teacher.
- Bert's feedback to students, although positive, is very general in nature.
- More specific praise would give the students a clearer sense of what is praiseworthy in Mr. Smith's judgment.
- Is the praise linked with an appropriate goal or past accomplishment of the student(s) involved? Do students know specifically what is meant by "nice" or "good" or "together"?

Practice Activity 13-3

Now it's your turn. Perhaps you would like to have a colleague observe your classroom conversations with students or you might use a tape recorder. However you choose to gather the information, analyze the praise you give students. Define the attributes of the praise you give now and set goals for improving the quality of that praise. Set a time for reassessment so that you can see whether your plan is working.

Appropriate Feedback

How does one protect or enhance a learner's self-concept when the learner is having difficulty? Unfortunately, the research shows that low achievers receive less supportive feedback than do their classmates (Cooper, 1979). In addition, it was noted in one study that teachers gave higher achievers a longer period of time to answer (Rowe, 1969). Can you relate to the frustration of students who, having been asked a question, lose the opportunity to answer just as they are "getting it"? Having that experience repeatedly is likely to lead to a lack of effort. Why invest in a process that will probably end in failure?

There are several things a teacher can do to avoid such frustrating experiences. Consciously call on all of the students in your class during an instructional period. Be sure to give sufficient time for students to formulate their answers. If you have decided that the student will not be able to answer without help, ask another question or rephrase your first one. Structure the situation so that the student can succeed. It is important to encourage the learner to persevere. The

effective teacher defines what learners know and helps them identify what they need to know in order to succeed.

Practice Activity 13-4

You realize the importance of demonstrating concern for students. You also know that the academic growth of your students will have a great impact on how you are perceived by your colleagues and supervisors. How can you improve your impact in these areas?

1. Let's suppose that you are a first-grade teacher and you've just asked the students to add 5 and 2. Johnny raises his hand and, in response to your recognition, confidently states that 5 plus 2 equals 8. How do you respond so that Johnny's sense of self-worth is not diminished but at the same time support his development in math?
   a. "What is the sum of 5 and 3?"
   b. "That's close!"
   c. "Think about it more carefully."
   d. "8 is the sum of 5 and 3. I asked for the sum of 5 [*draws*

five objects on the chalkboard] and 2 [*draws two more objects*]."

2. Randy is usually reserved and unsure of his contributions to class discussions. Today you are discussing the subtraction of whole numbers. The problem stated is the subtraction of 12 from 10. Randy's face lights up. He's sure of this one. You can't subtract a larger number from a smaller one and Randy tells you so. How do you respond to this?

   a. "You believe that it can't be done, Randy."
   b. "Actually there is a way, and that's what we're going to talk about today."
   c. Ask Randy to draw a number line, beginning it at the midpoint of the chalkboard. Have him label the beginning of this line with a number (0). Ask him to tell you what comes before zero.

Responses to Practice Activity 13-4

1. a. This response gives Johnny the opportunity to discover his own error and make a correction based on his own thinking. He knows that "8" can't answer both addition problems.
   b. This response avoids criticism but fails to communicate your belief in the child's ability to solve the problem.
   c. This response might indicate that you think the child is capable, just careless, but you've missed an opportunity to structure a successful learning experience for him.
   d. In this response you have told Johnny the question that corresponds to his answer and have then restated your original question in a way that increases the probability that Johnny will succeed.

2. a. This response recognizes the student, Randy, and is a way of clarifying his response. It may lead the student to develop his answer further or share the thought process through which he arrived at the answer. Too often, this type of response from the teacher is given and received as a neutral recognition of the student's response. It may communicate low expectations because it simply accepts without probing further.
   b. This provides a smooth lead into the lesson but may do so at the expense of the student's self-esteem. More recognition for the logical basis of Randy's conclusion, given the information he has, would support Randy's self-concept and lead into today's lesson. Choice "b" could be restated as, "With the informa-

tion we have discussed in class so far, it does seem that you can't subtract a larger number from a smaller one. Actually, there *is* a way, and that is what we are going to talk about today."

c. The second response would probably be a more supportive one for Randy than this one. Drawing a number line might well be the beginning of your presentation of new information. The student you choose for this might be Randy, or you might involve someone else at this point. Be sure to return to Randy so that he has an opportunity to answer correctly during the lesson. This will let him know that you expect him to meet the challenge presented in this math lesson.

Cultural Heritage

Classrooms are rich and varied in large part because of differences among students with whom we deal. It is possible that all of the thought and effort you invest in developing strategies to support the development of positive self-concepts could be undermined if the cultural backgrounds of the learners are not considered. Ignoring cultural heritage can send a not-so-subtle message that cultural diversity is unappreciated. Chapter 12, "Individual Differences," discusses the concept of cultural differences; in this chapter we will examine the impact of cultural differences on the development of self-concept.

When teachers are ignorant of a student's cultural background, they can misinterpret a student's behavior. For example, we typically expect students to maintain eye contact when we speak with them. Lack of eye contact is often assumed to mean lack of interest, inattention, or defiance. For individuals from certain cultural backgrounds, however, lack of eye contact can signify respect and/or deference (Garcia, 1982).

It is possible that a teacher who is unaware of students' cultural backgrounds will compound the difficulties sometimes experienced by parents from nonmainstream ethnic groups in regard to the public school system. Examples of the effect of cultural background on parents' reaction to a school situation is described in the following paragraphs.

Beginning school is a time of great importance for parent and child alike. School success is often viewed as the precursor to success in life. Early childhood educators are well aware of the high level of concern with which both parents and children approach school. These teachers are also trained in a tradition that values play as an integral part of the learning of young children. If, for example, parents approach their child's teacher with the concern that their child is losing valuable school time by engaging in play, that teacher is likely to discuss with them the benefits of play in the early childhood classroom. If the parents are from the cultural mainstream of the United States, they will probably leave the conference satisfied. The situation is complicated, however, when the parents are from another culture. Some Chinese, for example, may see play as frivolous (Bancroft, 1975); they may believe children should be working. It is difficult for some Chinese parents to see play as an important part of the educational system. The teacher may miss the point entirely by assuming the concern of the nonmainstream parent is the same as that voiced by the parents from the cultural mainstream.

As students progress through school, our expectations of them and the ways in which we organize their experiences change. Many of these changes bring opportunities for a clash of cultural values. For instance, at some point most physical education departments require students to shower after their gym class. If the facilities for showering lack privacy, this requirement might conflict with the cultural or religious values of some students (Bancroft, 1975). It is possible to miss completely the message in students' behaviors. Would you interpret a student's avoiding a group shower as a blatant affront to your authority? If you do so without looking for motives behind the behavior, you might well achieve conformity to your rules while missing an opportunity to create an environment of trust and respect.

There are many assumptions underlying education in the United States. As educators, we need to be aware of these assumptions and to be alert to instances in which they might present barriers to students. Christine Bennett (1979) suggests two important areas for teachers to examine when considering learners' cultural backgrounds: The learner's preferred modes of communication (verbal and nonverbal) and participation.

Have you ever been a member of an audience that responded to a performance in a way that was foreign to you or even rude? Bennett related the following situation to illustrate the importance of knowing the preferred participation style of a "microculture."

In one school, the "Panther Prowl" is an annual homecoming assembly. One year a group of black musicians began to perform, and black students in this school responded enthusiastically with clapping, dancing, and singing. White students, who had been taught to show their appreciation for entertainers by listening quietly and applauding at the end of a performance, found the response of their schoolmates to be rude. They demanded quiet, and many left. Black students perceived the passive response of the white students to be an affront to the performers. Lack of understanding and quick judgments were the precursors to several interracial fights later that evening on the school grounds (Bennett, 1979).

Educators need to reach beyond the comfort zone of mainstream cultural values and mediate the assumptions that might interfere with the education of children from nonmainstream cultures. Bancroft (1975) encourages you to do so by asking yourself the following questions about such children:

- What are the occupational expectations of students in the microculture?
- What form does discipline take? What adjustments are made if the person disciplining and the individual being disciplined are of the same sex or the opposite sex?
- What are the accepted forms of address for persons in authority?
- What are the major symbols and rituals?
- How do people in this microculture express feelings?
- How are loud speech, play, silence, time, work, and leisure perceived?
- How is joking done in this culture?
- What are the norms for behavior between the sexes in the microculture?

We all have a personal sense of identity that includes our cultural heritage. As a nation we have benefited from the contributions of many diverse cultures. For each microculture in society there is a time of adjustment, of finding a place in the larger culture. These adjustments are often traumatic for all involved. As educators, our function is not to convince people to agree with our personal interpretations of U.S. cultural ideals but to affirm the place of many cultures in our society's fabric.

Practice Activity 13-5

Cultural roots are rich sources of motivation for students. Plan an instructional segment through which each member of your class will be able to learn about his or her own heritage and those of his or her classmates. This might be a social studies unit, a writing assignment, or a unit in literature. You might include the areas mentioned in Bancroft's questions. You might also encourage students to use a variety of modes of expression—plays, displays, and the like.

The cultural diversity reflected in your school community could form the basis of a unit of study. Emphasize the contributions of various ethnic groups to the community. Extend the study to other groups and to our national identity.

Personal Worth

We have discussed a number of things you can do to support a positive self-concept. But there are also ways of organizing classroom interactions among students that encourage positive feelings in learners about themselves and about their abilities. Covington (1984) suggests using noncompetitive strategies like the cooperative learning environments described by Johnson and Johnson (1975). These have been shown to support mutual concern among students. The program assigns learners of mixed ability levels into work teams. The barrier that usually exists between students who learn more slowly and their more adept classmates appears to be removed when students work in a cooperative environment. A key characteristic of these environments is their emphasis on team effort while maintaining individual responsibilities. It is possible that the positive effects stem from the affirmation of self reflected by others.

Practice Activity 13-6

The establishment of cooperative learning environments requires a period of planning and skill development before implementation. (Specific suggestions for establishing cooperative learning environments are discussed in Chapter 12.) The following are several techniques you can incorporate in your classroom tomorrow. They will emphasize the value of each individual in your class.

1. Incorporate "Student of the Week" recognition in your classroom. Generate ideas with the students that would become part of this recognition. Possibilities include the listing by classmates of the student's strengths, their interviewing the student, or their writing a biography of the student.
2. Look at *100 Ways to Enhance Self-Concept in the Classroom* by Canfield and Wells (1976). Select a strategy that is appropriate for the learners in your classroom. Here are some of the things they suggest:

   a. *Positive Support Techniques*

      - Positive feedback—students are given an opportunity to recognize the contributions of others after a discussion. This experience can be structured by providing a "stem" for the feedback, for example, "Our group was better because you. . . . "
      - Positive support—students are asked to identify five things that another person can do that give them a good feeling about themselves (p. 111).

   b. *Who's Who*

      - Several students collect biographical data and create a "Who's Who," describing the special attributes, accomplishments, hobbies, and interests of members of the class. Books can be duplicated and a copy given to each student (p. 138).

 c. *Quickies*

- Do well—students identify something they do well and enjoy doing.
- Self-worth—students are asked to write about something they can do to help others feel valuable.
- "Proud-Of" Bulletin Boards—a place is reserved for the display of work, hobbies, ambitions of class members (p. 86).

3. For long-term development, form a study group with other staff members who are interested in building self-concept in students. The members of this group might be fellow teachers, other members of the school staff, and parents. Identify a person in your community (guidance counselor, educator, consultant, and so forth) and arrange to have that person work with your group. Possible programs that can facilitate your goal are Systematic Training for Effective Parenting (STEP) (Dinkmeyer & McKay, 1976), The Human Development Program (Palomares, Ball, & Bissell, undated), and Teacher Effectiveness Training (TET) (Gordon, 1974). Haim Ginott's *Teacher and Child* (Ginott, 1972) may also be helpful.

References

Bancroft, G. W. (1975). Teacher education for the multicultural reality. In A. Wolfgang (Ed.), *Education of immigrant students* (pp. 164–83). Toronto: The Ontario Institute for Studies in Education.

Bennett, C. (1979). Teaching students as they would be taught: The importance of a cultural perspective. *Educational Leadership, 36*(4), 259–62, 264–68.

Berliner, D. C. (1984). The half full glass: A review of research on teaching. In P. L. Hosford (Ed.), *Using what we know about teaching* (pp. 51–71). Alexandria, Va.: Association for Supervision and Curriculum Development.

Brophy, J. (1983). Classroom organization and management. *The Elementary School Journal, 83,* 265–85.

Brophy, J. (1981). Teacher praise: A functional analysis. *Review of Educational Research, 51*(1), 5–32.

Canfield, J., & Wells, H. C. (1976). *100 ways to enhance self-concept in the classroom.* Englewood Cliffs, N.J.: Prentice-Hall.

Cooper, H. M. (1979). Pygmalion grows up: A model for teacher expectation communication and performance influence. *Review of Educational Research, 49,* 389–410.

Cooper, H. M., & Tom, D. Y. H. (1984). Teacher expectations research: A review with implications for classroom instruction. *The Elementary School Journal, 85,* 77–89.

Covington, V. (1984). The self-worth theory of achievement motivation: Findings and implications. *The Elementary School Journal, 84,* 5–20.

Dinkmeyer, D., & McKay, G. D. (1976). *Systematic training for effective parenting: Parent handbook.* Circle Pines, Minn.: American Guidance Services.

Garcia, R. L. (1982). *Teaching in a pluralistic society: Concepts, models, strategies.* New York: Harper & Row.

Ginott, H. G. (1972). *Teacher and child.* New York: Macmillan.

Good, T. L., & Brophy, J. E. (1987). *Looking in classrooms* (4th ed.). New York: Harper & Row.

Gordon, T. (1974). *Teacher effectiveness training.* New York: Wyelen.

Hosford, P. L. (1984). The art of applying the science of teaching. In P. L. Hosford (Ed.), *Using what we know about teaching* (pp. 141–61). Alexandria, Va.: Association for Supervision and Curriculum Development.

Johnson, D. W., & Johnson, R. T. (1975). *Learning together and learning alone, cooperation, competition, and individualization.* Englewood Cliffs, N.J.: Prentice-Hall.

Meyer, W., Bachmann, M., Biermann, U., Hempelmann, M., Ploger, F., & Spiller, H. (1979). The informational value of evaluative behavior: Influences of praise and blame on perceptions of ability. *Journal of Educational Psychology, 71,* 259–68.

Palomares, U., Ball, G., & Bissell, H. (undated). *The Human Development Program.* Human Development Training Institute, 7574 University Ave., La Mesa, Calif.

Rowe, M. B. (1969). Science, silence, and sanctions. *Science and Children, 6* (6), 11–13.

Tursman, C. (1981). *Good teachers: What to look for.* Arlington, Va.: National School Public Relations Association.

Whitmore, J. R. (1980). *Giftedness, conflict and underachievement.* Boston: Allyn & Bacon.

Chapter Fourteen

Affective Climate

Susan O'Connor

Definition

The competent teacher knows that learning occurs more readily in a classroom environment that is nonpunitive and accepting than in one that is hostile or threatening. Teachers need to understand human motivations and behavior—both their own and those of their students. They need to use this knowledge to create the best learning environment possible. The affective, or emotional, climate of the classroom is an important aspect of the learning environment.

Purpose

Our emotions—anger, defiance, joy, enthusiasm, excitement, satisfaction—influence how we teach and how we learn. Research has shown that learning occurs more readily in a classroom environment that is nonpunitive and accepting. It seems reasonable to assume that more effective teaching occurs in such environments as well. It also seems reasonable to assume that a positive affective climate makes teaching and learning more satisfactory human experiences. The purpose of this chapter is to explore strategies for creating an appropriate affective climate, thereby fostering more effective, and satisfying, teaching and learning.

The teacher who would create such an environment should do the following:

- Avoid hostility and punitiveness and use alternative strategies to maintain an orderly learning environment.
- Show courtesy to and consideration for learners.

- Be accepting of learner behavior, drawing upon your knowledge of the principles of human growth and development, individual differences, and group dynamics to develop a variety of interaction strategies.
- Show knowledge of, interest in, and appreciation of cultural

differences and develop a strategy for building a classroom culture; and

- Adapt the physical environment to encourage learning and facilitate learning activities.

Background Knowledge

According to Gagne and Briggs (1979):

> ... the teacher obviously needs to appreciate the importance of his [or her] role as a human model, if for no other reason than the large proportion of time the student spends in [the teacher's] presence. It is likely that those teachers the student later remembers as "good teachers" are the ones who have modeled positive attitudes (p. 89).

Good teachers want to teach, and they like their students. They are active, enthusiastic, and interesting, as well as competent. They communicate the idea that learning can be fun. Good teachers have acquired a variety of positive strategies by which they facilitate learning and maintain order. These strategies are built from a knowledge of their field, a knowledge of themselves, and a healthy dose of imagination.

Practice Activity 14-1

The day started out so well. You made it to school early, so you had time to review your lesson plans for the day and to think about the progress and problems of each of your students. The students arrive, and the school day begins. Things are running smoothly, and you are enjoying your work. You feel competent. About midmorning, one of your students starts to act up and disturb the class. You immediately ask her to stop. To your horror, she throws a temper tantrum right then and there. When she finally calms down, you are exhausted and the class is in an uproar. How can you possibly salvage this day?

Hostility and Punitiveness

Whatever happened to the days of "spare the rod, spoil the child?" What teacher has not wanted to fall back on that old maxim when it has been one of *those* days? Bite your tongue, sit on your hands, count to ten, or what have you—but don't do it!

Much affective experience in the classroom tends to be negative, and negative emotional climates are just not functional. Teacher criticism, teacher or pupil negative affect, and pupil resistance correlate significantly with low achievement and low self-esteem. People achieve more in an environment that is emotionally warm, or at least one that is neutral. Soar (1966, 1973) and Soar and Soar (1972, 1973, 1978) have shown that neutral climates may be as supportive of achievement as warm ones. The rod may serve if control is your primary concern, but it definitely does not work if your goal is higher achievement or improved self-concept. The challenge, then, is to develop and consistently use positive strategies to maintain an orderly learning environment. To stack the deck in your favor, these need to be worked out ahead of time.

The key is prevention. Getting off to a good start is invaluable (Emmer & Evertson, 1980; Emmer, Evertson, & Anderson, 1980; Evertson et al., 1981). This takes careful preparation and organization. Classroom procedures and routines should be formally taught at the outset, and expectations should be precisely stated. Content, method of delivery, and pacing are extremely powerful tools for gaining and holding students' attention. Interested and motivated students are rarely behavior problems. Realistically, however, you cannot control all of the factors that affect each student's level of motivation and interest. For example, if Susie's parents are in the midst of a messy divorce or if Johnny did not have time to eat breakfast on a particular morning, you may find it difficult to hold her or his attention. On the whole, though, the more control you have over the factors within your range of responsibility, the fewer problems you should experience.

What can you do to create and maintain a healthy emotional climate for teaching and learning? There are three areas in which you have a great deal of power and flexibility. These are classroom management, personal management, and interpersonal relations management.

Classroom Management

A great deal of the literature and much of this text focus on classroom management. Classroom management techniques include, among others, the following:

- Holding students accountable (see Chapters 6 and 9, "Accountability" and "Questioning Skill," respectively)
- Modeling appropriate behaviors, praising appropriate behaviors, and reinforcing behaviors incompatible with desirable behaviors (see Chapter 3, "Reinforcement"),
- Modifying the classroom environment (see the section in this chapter on physical environment)
- Using the time-out technique (isolating the disruptive student for a *short* period of time)
- Exhibiting "withitness" behaviors, showing you know what is going on in the classroom (see Chapters 7 and 8 "Close Supervision" and "Awareness," respectively)

One intriguing possibility for managing classrooms is to encourage group cohesiveness in order to foster group cooperation; a cooperative group is more likely to develop productive norms and to be more productive than one that is not cooperative (Johnson & Bany, 1970; Schmuck & Schmuck, 1979; Stanford, 1980; Wallen & Wallen, 1978). Another technique is to establish a contingency contract or token economy (Kelley & Stokes, 1982; Kennedy, 1982). For instance, if students fulfill certain academic requirements, they receive a certain number of points. Once they have accumulated a specified number of points, they get a prize or a special privilege (for example, ten points = one page of stickers; fifteen points = an extra fifteen minutes of art). If you want to use these techniques, you need to study them carefully, of course, before implementing them. (Chapter 3 describes these techniques in greater detail.)

Personal Managment

In contrast to classroom management, personal management receives relatively little attention. What makes you, the teacher, feel irrationally angry or successfully in control? How can you maintain a positive attitude? What can you do to create situations that are professionally and emotionally satisfying? It is just as important to develop a repertoire of personal management strategies as it is to have a repertoire of classroom management strategies.

Practice Activity 14-2

Now is a good time to take a personal inventory. Consider what your strengths and weaknesses are, what you like and do not like about teaching, where you would like to be in ten years, and so forth. One personal management strategy might be to eat a more nutritious breakfast and to take vitamins to prevent the "11:00 A.M. I-am-starving-I-hate-everybody blahs." Another personal strategy might involve recognizing that a certain person annoys you and that this interferes with your ability to teach that person. What can you do? You can concentrate on the positive: Look for things you like and value in the person.

Impersonal Relations Management

Interaction with others is a critical aspect of a teacher's professional skills. A tremendous amount of time is spent interacting with students, parents, other teachers, and administrators. The crux of any and all interactions is communication, both verbal and nonverbal. We lecture, write, discuss, gesture, and so on. The point of all of this is to share messages. Effective teaching is built upon the design and delivery of effective messages. Are certain types of communication more efficient and more accurate than others? In the classroom, two-way communication (discussion) often seems to be more effective than one-way communication (lecture) because in two-way communication students are allowed to ask questions that may help to clarify messages (Ward & Borgers, undated). In addition, two-way communication may foster a more positive attitude among students.

Listening and responding are key ingredients for good communication. It is certainly aggravating to ask someone a question only to receive either no reply or a totally unrelated one.

Ward and Borgers have identified five response styles:

1. *Evaluative.* A response that indicates the responder has made a judgment of relative goodness, appropriateness, effectiveness, rightness. The responder has in some way implied what the speaker might or ought to do.

   - Yes, Mary, I think that's the best way to do it, too.
   - I agree, totally, it should happen in just that sequence.
   - You've done this perfectly, Leanne.
   - That's a possibility, I'm sure John, but do you really think that it is the very best way?

2. *Interpretive.* A response that indicates the responder's intent is to teach, to impart meaning to the speaker, to show him or her. The responder has in some way implied what the speaker might or ought to think.

   - Maybe, Joe, what you really mean is that they weren't as observant as they might have been.
   - Do you think most people really want others telling them what to do—or would they prefer to be in charge of their own lives?

3. *Supportive.* A response that indicates the responder's intent is to reassure, to reduce the speaker's intensity of feeling, to pacify. The responder has in some way implied that the speaker need not feel as he or she does.

   - I'm sure you must feel very angry now, Carl, and find it hard to concentrate on your reading. I understand your not wanting to do your assignment. Why don't we talk about how you feel about the fight you had at recess.
   - I know how disappointing it is when you don't get the grade you thought you would, but let's find out where you made your errors, to be sure you don't repeat them again. I know you will feel better when you understand it.

4. *Probing.* A response that indicates the responder's intent is to seek further information, provoke further discussion along a certain line, to query. The responder has in some way im-

plied that the speaker ought to or might profitably develop or discuss a point further.

- Can you tell me more about the relationship of form to material in sculpting, Ron?
- Will ceramic pottery add to, or detract from, this decor, Perry?
- If you taught the children in your class this lesson, what would you expect them to be able to do when they finished?

5. *Understanding.* A response which indicates the responder's intent is . . . in effect to ask the speaker whether the responder understands correctly what the speaker is "saying," how it "strikes" the speaker, or how the speaker "sees" it.

- Am I right in saying that you think there is no such thing as a "true" democracy, Joe?
- Are you saying that you basically feel you are an optimist, and that explains why you do not study very much before an exam, Cindy?

Practice Activity 14-3

Examine *your* listening and response styles and answer the following:

1. Do you listen? Or is your mind preoccupied with the activities scheduled for fifteen minutes from now?
2. How do you tend to respond, according to the styles described by Ward and Borger? All of these response types have their time and place. Do you use all of them? Or do you rely primarily on one or two?
3. How does the way you respond relate to your teaching goals and objectives?
4. Read the following statements and respond to each according to the five different response styles:

   a. "School seems hopeless. Everyone does okay but me. Maybe something is wrong with me."
   b. "I am really worried about this friend of mine. She is failing all of her courses; she wants to drop out of school and get a job. I'm afraid she will quit school and run away. I don't know what to do."

5. To practice listening skills in your classroom, ask one student to tell a story and another to try to repeat it as closely as possible.

Another ingredient of interpersonal relations management is the leading and facilitating of the group. The teacher is the leader of the class. Group dynamics or processes provide a wealth of resources for a teacher to use to enhance the emotional climate of the classroom. Each group is different, and each group can change. In analyzing your class as a group, you might ask some of the following questions:

- Is the group as a whole cooperative or competitive? Productive or apathetic? Involved or disinterested?
- Who is most influential, and who is least?
- Whom do you influence the most? The least?
- Who influences you the most? The least?
- Is it a struggle for you to maintain leadership of the group?
- Who blocks the group?
- What are the norms of the group?
- How influential are the group norms?
- How do the norms influence how members think and how they feel about things?
- How do the norms influence how members act?
- Do the norms help or hinder group processes?

Ideally, the group is cooperative, involved, and productive. Anything you can do to encourage this will make your job easier and more successful. Strategies for accomplishing this include assigning a group project and stressing learning to work as a group. The final product of a group undertaking should be a symbol of group cooperation, for example, a mural for the hall or a piece of equipment for the school or a local community center.

When you glue together your professional and personal knowledge using a bit of imagination, you will have a growing repertoire of strategies to help you meet the situations that arise daily in teaching. For example, a certain kindergarten teacher who is concerned with teaching personal cleanliness makes a game of teaching her children to comb "Wiggle" and "Squiggle," the "silly salamanders," out of their hair every afternoon. Again, prevention is the key. Why jump into a full-blown power struggle if a little imagination might suffice instead!

Courtesy and Consideration

Courtesy and consideration are common-sense components of a good affective climate. For example, learn and use your students' names, and use polite forms of address. Listen carefully, and don't interrupt them. Try to be aware of any concerns or problems the learners might have, and address those concerns or problems. Since there is only one of you, you might need to develop strategies to help you remember, for instance, all your students' names or sharpen your listening skills.

Learner Behavior

Many factors influence human behavior and thus the affective climate of a classroom. If you do not have a good rapport with a student, it may be because of such factors rather than because of any particular antagonism on the child's part or your own. Good teachers draw upon their knowledge of human growth and development and group dynamics to help them understand their students' behavior. For instance, individual students may behave differently if they are in a cohesive class than if they are in a less closely knit group. Age and stage of development also influence behavior. Very young learners, for example, have relatively short attention spans, tend to be physically active, and thrive in a highly nurturing environment, while older learners are usually able to work independently and for longer periods of time, often like to be allowed to learn in their own way, and are very concerned about peer acceptance.

Teachers should also be sensitive to signs of alienation in their students. Failure to cooperate, antagonism, inattention, and other such behavior suggest that a student is having difficulties committing to class life. Teachers should try to determine the source of alienation and to take remedial action. They should first determine whether some aspect of the teaching–learning situation is leading to alienation. For example, they might pay particular attention to their students' responses to what they say, how they say it, and what gestures or other forms of nonverbal communication they use. If a particular student's alienation is persistent, the teacher should seek assistance from the school psychologist.

Practice Activity 14-4

1. You have just asked your second-grader to recite a poem. All you get is a hostile stare and dead silence. What do you do?
2. Compile a profile of your students' typical behaviors. How do various children affect your teaching style?

Cultural Differences

Membership in a group implies that a person meets certain qualifications in order to belong, and that other persons do not meet those qualifications. Thus, there are boundaries that mark differences between and among groups. In a culturally pluralistic society, cultural groups come in contact with each other and interact socially. That students and teachers from different cultures can and do interact positively in our nation's classrooms is testimony to the success of public education.

Culture is commonly taken to refer to racial or ethnic identity. However, every individual actually belongs to a variety of groups— racial, ethnic, economic, age, religious, and occupational, among many others. Membership in each of these groups affects our assumptions, values, and actions, as well as our use of language and our reliance upon symbols. Thus, how we respond to our world, how we interact with others, and how we learn are shaped by our perceptions of physical and social realities.

In the United States our lives have been particularly enriched by contributions from many different groups. Our cultural diversity has been proven valuable, worthy of recognition and preservation. Cultural diversity is a fact of life. To ignore it is to exacerbate a source of conflict; to utilize it is to tap a valuable resource.

Many groups exist in your classroom. You belong to the occupational group of "teachers," and those you address belong to the group of "students." You are a member of one age group, and they of another. Your students represent various racial, ethnic, economic, and religious groups. As Baptiste, Baptiste, and Gollnick (1980) have noted, "An individual's rights, privileges, and power are directly related to group membership" (p. 12). The teacher has a great deal of influence on the status of groups within the class. The impact of teacher expectations on student behavior is described in detail in

Chapter 13. For example, if a teacher expects or otherwise implies that girls are good at arithmetic and that Asians cannot even add 2 + 2, then that teacher has taken differences based on group membership and used them to define special boundaries for members of each group. In the case of the Asian students in that teacher's class, this boundary becomes a barrier to positive class behavior and the boundary has negative affective consequences. This infringement of rights, privileges, and power leads to the rejection of class values and activities by members of the restricted group.

Knowing that your students are identified with many groups and that these memberships play a significant part in their lives, what can you do to create a positive affective environment? Teachers can build a "classroom culture," being extremely careful not to alienate any of the students because of differences based on their membership in other groups. The idea behind this suggestion is that the teacher and the students develop a sense of loyalty to the class as a group in which they are all functional members. The prevailing sentiment should be, "This is *our* class." Everybody should have a role in formulating the rules of this group (the class) without being penalized for being committed to the values, ideas, and behavior patterns learned in other groups. The purpose of this democratic process is to ensure supportive participation in the group.

Alienation and other negative feelings may result from acts that deny the value of groups to which a student belongs. Such acts can be committed both deliberately and unwittingly. Regardless of the motivation, however, challenging the beliefs, values, or customs that students have been taught to hold dear causes a major conflict to those students. They are forced to reject either their own beliefs or those of the class group. Differences are turned into barriers, and students are hurt.

The beauty of the notion of creating a classroom culture with few barriers caused by individual differences is that its goal is active participation by all members of the class group. Moreover, this participation proceeds in a way that is appropriate to each individual. This is a much different approach from teaching curriculum units about the heritage of different cultures in the hope that students will understand the social demands of cultural pluralism. The cultural classroom approach encourages actual interactions between all members of the class and recognizes the dynamics of group life as a key element in maintaining a positive affective environment.

Practice Activity 14-5

Analyze the group allegiances of the individual members of your class. Based on this analysis, develop a strategy to build a classroom culture.

In summary, using appropriate management techniques, being courteous and considerate, applying your knowledge about group dynamics and human growth and development to your classroom, and being sensitive to the cultural differences of your students will improve the affective climate of your classroom. In addition to employing these interpersonal techniques, you might also consider modifying the physical environment of your classroom, as described in the final section of this chapter.

Physical Environment

The importance of the physical classroom environment is noted in the *Handbook of the Florida Performance Measurement System* (Coalition for the Development of a Performance Evaluation System, 1981):

> Classroom environment can affect student behavior and attitudes, and to the extent that these changes are positive, consistent, and enduring, they do have a chance to improve academic learning. Therefore, the educator should examine these variables and make attempts to enhance the physical context for his/her educational program (p. 191).

There are two ways to approach the physical setting of the classroom. One way is to treat the physical environment as a static structure, allowing the room to control the physical context of the class. The other way is to treat the environment as fluid and dynamic, putting yourself in control. If you realize that the structure is changeable, you will change it to meet the needs of the class. The following are some of the variables to consider when designing the physical environment.

Space

The classroom should be divided into distinct areas that are neatly equipped for specific activities. It should also facilitate monitoring of student activity. Make sure that in your room you can separate work areas from traffic areas, quiet areas from noisy areas, and so forth.

Seating

What is the best seating arrangement for a learning activity? The arrangement of seats should encourage the students to focus their attention and to participate—not to talk with friends or doodle. Totusek (1978) proposed that there are "action seats" in a classroom. Action seats tend to be those in the front and in the center of the room. Students who sit in these seats seems to participate more and achieve higher grades (Becker et al., 1973; Koneya, 1976; Sommer,

1967). Teachers should therefore move about the room while teaching or monitoring to ensure that all students are actively involved in learning activities.

Color

Color plays a part in determining people's moods and attitudes. Because of the traditional design of schools and because of budgetary constraints, room color is not as flexible as some other variables. Still, if your room is an awful, depressing color and you cannot paint it, why not cover it up? Pictures, wall hangings, and student art can add color and texture.

Once you realize that you are not just stuck with a room the way it is, you can arrange the physical environment of your classroom to better suit you and your class.

References

Baptiste, H. P., Jr., Baptiste, M. L., & Gollnick, D. M. (Eds.) (1980). *Multicultural teacher education: Preparing educators to provide educational equity* (Volume 1). Washington, D.C.: Commission on Multicultural Education, American Association of Colleges for Teacher Education.

Becker, F. D., Sommer, R., Bee, J., & Oxley, B. (1973). College classroom ecology. *Sociometry, 36,* 514–25.

Coalition for the Development of a Performance Evaluation System (1981). *Handbook of the Florida Performance Measurement System.* Tallahassee, Fla.: State Education Department, Office of Teacher Education, Certification, and Inservice Task Development.

Emmer, E., & Evertson, C. (1980). *Effective management at the beginning of the school year in junior high classes* (Report No. 6107). Austin: Research and Development Center for Teacher Education, University of Texas.

Emmer, E., Evertson, C., & Anderson, L. (1980). Effective classroom management at the beginning of the school year. *Elementary School Journal, 80,* 219–31.

Evertson, C., Emmer, E., Clements, B., Sanford, J., Worsham, M., & Williams, E. (1981). *Organizing and managing the elementary school classroom.* Austin: Research and Development Center for Teacher Education, University of Texas.

Gagne, R. M., & Briggs, L. J. (1979). *Principles of instructional design* (2nd ed.). New York: Holt, Rinehart, & Winston.

Johnson, L. V., & Bany, M. A. (1970). *Classroom management: Theory and skill training.* New York: Macmillan.

Kelley, M. L., & Stokes, T. F. (1982). Contingency contracting with disadvantaged youths: Improving classroom performance. *Journal of Applied Behavior Analysis, 15,* 447–54.

Kennedy, R. E. (1982). Cognitive-behavioral approaches to the modification of aggressive behavior in children. *School Psychology Review, 11* (2), 47–55.

Koneya, M. (1976). Location and interaction in row and column seating arrangements. *Environment and Behavior, 8,* 265.

Schmuck, R., & Schmuck, P. A. (1979). *Group processes in the classroom.* Dubuque, Iowa: Brown.

Soar, R. S. (1966). *An integrative approach to classroom learning* (Report for NIMH Projects No. 5-R11 MH 01096 and 7-R11 MH 02045). Philadelphia: Temple University. (ERIC Document Reproduction Service No. ED 033 749).

Soar, R. S. (1973). *Follow-through classroom process measurement and pupil growth* (1970–71 Final Report). Gainesville: Institute for Development of Human Resources, University of Florida. (ERIC Document Reproduction Service No. ED 106 297).

Soar, R. S., & Soar, R. M. (1972). An empirical analysis of selected follow-through programs: An example of a process approach to evaluation. In I. Gordon (Ed.), *Early childhood education.* Chicago: National Society for the Study of Education.

Soar, R. S., & Soar, R. M. (1973). *Classroom behavior, pupil characteristics and pupil growth for the school year and the summer.* Gainesville: Institute for Development of Human Resources, University of Florida.

Soar, R. S., & Soar, R. M. (1978). *Setting variables, classroom interaction, and multiple pupil outcomes* (Final Report, Project No. 600432, Grant No. NIE-G-76-0100). Washington, D.C.: National Institute of Education.

Sommer, R. (1967). Classroom ecology. *Journal of Applied Behavioral Science, 3,* 489–503.

Stanford, G. (1980). *Developing effective classroom groups.* New York: A & W Visual Library.

Totusek, P. S. (1978). *The relationship between classroom seating preferences and student personality characteristics.* Paper presented at the annual meeting of the Speech Communication Association, Minn. (ERIC Document Reproduction Service No. ED 169 587).

Wallen, C. J., & Wallen, L. L. (1978). *Effective classroom management.* Boston: Allyn & Bacon.

Ward, G. R., & Borgers, S. B. (undated). *Affective Competency* (Handbook Nos. 1.0–14.0). Houston: University of Houston, Houston Competency-based Teacher Center.

Additional Readings

Anderson, A., Weiner, B., & Prawat, R. S.(1984). *Affective experience in a classroom* (Research Series No. 150). East Lansing: The Institute for Research on Teaching, Michigan State University.

Brophy, J. (1983). Classroom organization and management. *The Elementary School Journal, 83,* 4, 265–85.

Brophy, J. (1981). Teacher praise: A functional analysis. *Review of Educational Research, 51,* 5–32.

Brophy, J. (1979). Teacher behavior and its effects. *Journal of Educational Psychology, 71,* 733–50.

Gollnick, D. M., Osayande, K.I.M., & Levy, J. (1980). *Multicultural teacher education: Case studies of thirteen programs* (Volume 200). Washington, D.C.: Commission on Multicultural Education, American Association of Colleges for Teacher Education.

Good, T., & Power, C. (1976). Designing successful classroom environments for different types of students. *Journal of Curriculum Studies, 8,* 1–16.

Hamilton, S. (1983). The social side of schooling: Ecological studies of classrooms and schools. *Elementary School Journal, 83,* 313–34.

Lee, M. (1980). *Multicultural teacher education: An annotated bibliography of selected resources* (Volume 3). Washington, D.C.: Commission on Multicultural Education, American Association of Colleges for Teacher Education.

Schofield, H. (1978). Teacher effects on cognitive and affective pupil outcomes in elementary school mathematics. *Journal of Educational Psychology, 73,* 462–71.

Woods, P. (1983). *Sociology and the school: An interactionist viewpoint.* Boston: Rutledge and Kegan Paul.

Chapter Fifteen

Evaluation

Harvey Carmichael
Virginia State Department of Education

Michael Caldwell
University of Virginia

Definition

The competent teacher knows that learner progress is facilitated by instructional objectives that are known to the learners and that coincide with the objectives of evaluation. Competence in matching given instructional objectives with informal and formal evaluation contributes to the soundness of the teacher's decisions during the course of instruction.

Purpose

The purpose of this chapter is to help you understand the concept of evaluation and to assist you in coordinating evaluation procedures with instructional objectives and activities. Procedures for planning evaluations while planning instruction will be discussed. The chapter suggests ways to ensure that these procedures are relevant and fair. Strategies for asking appropriate and useful questions, observing learners' work, and checking learners' understanding regularly during instruction to evaluate progress will also be addressed. The chapter will also emphasize the importance of informing learners about their performances and about how their performances will be evaluated.

Background Knowledge

Evaluation—mere utterance of the word strikes terror in the hearts of administrators, teachers, students, and practically anyone facing the prospect of being observed or tested. Teachers plan with vigor in the hope of leaving supervisors with positive impressions about their performances with students. Administrators facing review check every nook and cranny of their schools to guarantee an impression of cleanliness and efficiency. And for students, what is often perceived as the impending doom of exams can trigger a variety of strong reactions.

One wonders why. Why has evaluation become such an important part of our lives, and why do we go to such great lengths to judge our behaviors? Why do we place great importance on testing children, and then often use the information in relatively few ways? Why can't we use unobtrusive methods to collect information about the intellectual growth of children? The pros and cons of these issues continue to be debated. In the end, however, each teacher will be required to address these and related issues on a personal level. As a classroom teacher you will have to assess behaviors for which there are no structured evaluation procedures. You must be aware that although paper-and-pencil tests provide information you will need in order to make judgments about learners, this information is partial at best. The following pages will attempt to provide some direction for you in the hope of making the process of evaluation useful.

Thinking About Evaluation

All too often teachers think about evaluation as something mysterious, something done for someone else—for parents, principals, school boards. Evaluation is also too frequently equated with testing. These ideas unnecessarily restrict the utility of evaluation as a tool of effective teaching. To be sure, formal tests produce valuable information, but teachers generate and use much evaluative information that is not from formal tests.

Given the pervasiveness of the narrow working definitions of evaluation, it is small wonder that many teachers perceive evaluation as an onerous task having little to do with the day-to-day activities of the classroom. Evaluation activities need not be feared or avoided. Evaluation can make a difference in your ultimate effectiveness as a teacher and, therefore, the degree to which you enjoy your work.

Why evaluate? To make yourself a successful teacher. Cutting away the elaborate structure of schools—complicated administrative arrangements, bus scheduling, cafeterias, and the like—one is left with the fact that schools are about learning, and teaching is about helping students learn. Neither occurs in the absence of information about "what works." Evaluation is meant to provide such information.

Though there is much yet to be discovered about the way people learn, we know that learning is facilitated by "knowledge of results." In other words, the learner needs to know that he or she is progressing. When solving math problems or pronouncing words, for example, learners are likely to continue somewhat painfully by trial-and-error until another person or some outside information intervenes. The same may be true for teachers learning to apply their pedagogical skills.

Teachers need to know what works. In fact, one might define a teacher as an individual who is *always* looking for what works. Because human learning is highly variable, what works to help Johnny learn may not work with Mary. Even more troublesome, what worked with Johnny yesterday may not work today.

Teachers are trained to acquire and use information to remove guesswork from their actions. The ability to think on one's feet and to shift directions or activities as new information dictates are major differences between a teacher and "the man on the street." Notice sometime how someone unaccustomed to teaching will make a statement to someone, be misunderstood, repeat the same thing, only more slowly, still be misunderstood, say the same thing a third time, both more slowly and louder, still be misunderstood . . . Well, you get the picture. Adults often have a limited repertoire of "teaching behaviors," consisting only of variation in speaking rate and volume. Continually searching for what works—or evaluating—is how teachers build a repertoire of effective activities and behaviors.

Evaluation involves comparison. Student performance information, test data, for example, are descriptive only; that is, such data describe certain properties of students' responses, like an average response and the variation among many responses. Descriptive information is useful, but it says nothing about the value of students' responses until the description of performances is compared with something else. The "something else" might be a preestablished set of expectations for students' performances or the performances of another group of students.

Evaluating teaching also involves making comparisons. A given instructional activity is not "good" in and of itself, but "good" only when compared to something else. Usually the standard against which teaching is compared is the intent of the teacher or the objective of instruction.

Planning for Evaluation and Instruction

Instruction involves decision making. On a daily basis teachers must select instructional techniques that best match the abilities of their students and the objectives to be accomplished. They must decide how the content to be mastered will be subdivided and presented to offer students the greatest opportunity for learning. Decisions related to time use and emphasis must be considered, and decisions must be made to include and exclude particular topics in the lesson. These decisions are ever-present in teaching and can be problematic even for experienced teachers. It is little wonder that beginning teachers are often troubled by the responsibility.

There are ways to address these problems. One method involves a search for consistency in planning and teaching. This usually means a classroom teacher must examine (a) class objectives, (b) class activities, and (c) assessments of progress. Because classrooms do not exist in a vacuum, however, we would add a fourth, broader area of school goals. Thinking about planning for instruction and evaluation in these terms suggests three broad evaluation questions:

1. To what degree are my classroom objectives consistent with the school goals and purposes?
2. To what degree are classroom activities consistent with the classroom objectives? Or can I expect that these classroom activities will promote the achievement of these objectives?
3. To what degree are assessment activities consistent with the classroom objectives?

Note: These questions are consistent with the earlier contention that evaluation involves comparison. The second element in the question provides the standard against which the first element in the question is to be judged.

As these questions suggest, planning for instruction and evaluation are closely related and should proceed in concert. The notion that planning for assessment can be put off until the end or near the end of the instructional process is counterproductive.

Figure 15–1 provides one handy tool when planning for evaluation. (Chapter 2, "Planning," provides other ideas.) When using this approach, first decide what it is you want to know about student performance or the effectiveness of your instruction; that is, generate some evaluation questions. Remember, it is useful to format such questions with two major elements, as described previously: the element you wish to evaluate and the element to be used as a comparison. Second, think about what kind of information you will need to answer the question. Obviously, you will need descriptive information about the two major elements of the evaluation question and, at this point, you might wish to specify your expectations of an appropriate level of comparison. Third, having decided what information you will need, it will be necessary to consider where and how you can acquire the information.

Evaluation need not be highly technical and/or involve sophisticated statistical manipulations of information. For example, the first sample evaluation question above ("To what degree are my classroom objectives consistent with the school goals and purposes?") requires only that you acquire information about your objectives (from your lesson plans) and about school goals and objectives (from curriculum guides, state standards of learning, discussions with the principal and other teachers, and so forth); compare the two sets of information (something as simple as visual inspection of the two sets); note

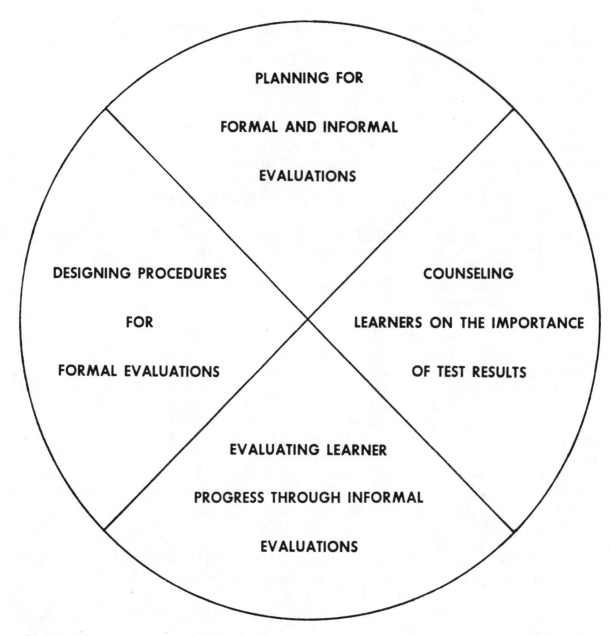

Figure 15–1   *Components of an Evaluation*

areas of similarity and difference; and decide whether you are comfortable with the situation.

Consider for a moment how ill-prepared or well-prepared you could be if pressed by a parent or supervisor for an explanation of your teaching. Your response could be, "Well, the students think it's fun." Or you might say, "I read an article about this technique, talked to other teachers who have used it, and found that this approach shows promise in teaching certain kinds of skills. I have tried it several times and it seems to work." The second response is grounded in some demonstrable knowledge of the situation.

Note: There is nothing inherently wrong with the first statement above, but it does not go far enough. We would argue that positive student responses to instructional content and/or method are much to be desired and are legitimate instructional ends.

A final note about planning for instruction and evaluation is in order. Some of us seem to view planning as a hurdle to be overcome before getting at the "real business" of teaching. But planning is as much a part of teaching as is interacting with students. Planning can establish a rationale for teaching to be considered a professional activity by laying a reasoned and reasonable base upon which to construct teaching activities. Thinking about your teaching is necessary but not sufficient for success. Write your teaching intentions in your plans. Even though you might not refer to the plan either immediately before or during the conduct of the lesson, the fact that you have written what you intend to do will help you to remember.

Practice Activity 15-1

1. Use the second general evaluation question stated earlier to construct a specific evaluation question about the effectiveness of some aspect of an instructional activity you have planned, and write this question in Figure 15–1.

2. Decide what information you will need to answer the question, "What is the best source of this information, and what is a reasonable approach for collecting the information?" Write the result of your decisions in the appropriate columns in Figure 15–1.

Evaluating Learner Progress Through Informal Assessment

Although much emphasis in education today is placed on the importance of test results, it is equally important for the beginning teacher to master strategies of informal assessment, because many instructional decisions are based on information gathered through examination of student products such as presentations, papers, homework, and discussions. These informal assessments of student work help teachers determine instructional goals and select strategies for instruction *and* evaluation. An organized and systematic method of informal assessment can enhance a teacher's ability to understand students and to make appropriate instructional decisions.

Unlike most formal evaluations, informal assessments are ongoing. Information gathered about students is not referenced to a particular question or fixed point in time. The degree to which teachers can develop and refine their intuitive skills will determine the amount and utility of the information collected. Informal assessments are most useful when students are actively involved in the processes. Such active involvement can result in greater student participation in planning and instruction and in improved student motivation. Instruction tends to be teacher dominated when information about students is not shared, thus sometimes forcing students to play a passive role in the classroom.

One strategy for involving students in the instructional and evaluational processes, is to discuss an upcoming unit with the class and ask the students to research particular topics related to the unit. You can provide them with an outline of issues to be explored, but encourage them to explore the topic fully and to expand the outline. Allow time for these research activities, since many students will have to rely on resources located in the school library. Once this activity has been completed, the students can share the results of their research. You can then devise an instructional plan, incorporating the ideas and information provided by the students into the overall instructional plan for the unit.

It is important to note that assessments have traditionally focused on students. Student assessments often provide the most easily accessible information. The danger in relying on student assessments is that judgments will be too narrow, that we will set our boundaries for data collection at points that do not include events outside the classroom, thereby limiting our perceptions of students' abilities to perform well in class. The quality, and consequently the usefulness, of data collected will depend on the teacher's ability to set meaningful limits for data collection. These data should provide as thorough an understanding of the learners' experiences and abilities as possible.

The number of techniques teachers might use to assess learner progress informally is limited only by imagination and experience. Most teachers, however, will ask questions and observe learners as they work, so as to check learner understanding.

Asking Questions

The information teachers collect will be only as good as the questions they ask. It is important that teachers ask questions that solicit the information needed to make appropriate decisions. Bloom and his colleagues (1956) have identified six levels of objectives that can be applied to informal evaluation (Chapter 9 discusses Bloom's approach in detail). In Box 15–1 the taxonomy has been modified to provide a framework for generating questions to be used to examine a student's level of thinking. Each level of this taxonomy represents an important component of student achievement. Answering knowledge or recall questions helps students acquire information with which to think about, formulate, and verify conclusions. Questions at this level should be used as a foundation for higher levels of analysis and synthesis.

Box 15–1   *Blueprint for World History Test—Tenth Grade*

Process Objectives	Content Areas				Number of Items
	The Roman Empire 50%		The Golden Age of Greece 50%		
Recognizes vocabulary and key terms	–Pax Romana –senate –patrician –plebeians	legion tribunes veto aqueducts	–democracy –propaganda –minotaur –labyrinth	calvary tyrant helots spartan	
20%	4 or 5 items		4 or 5 items		8
Identifies specific facts related to . . .	–establishment of Roman Empire –importance of the Roman Senate –Roman leaders –Punic Wars		–types of democracy –reasons for importance of sea trade –city-state rivalries –Greek contributions to Western culture		
40%	7 or 8 items		7 or 8 items		16
Identifies principles, concepts and generalizations from content	–relationships between Roman leaders and the fall of Rome –struggle between the Christians, Hebrews, and Romans –literature and the Greco-Roman culture		–development of a flourishing culture –colonization as a result of sea trade –Persian Wars threatened Greek civilization		
40%	7 or 8 items		7 or 8 items		16
Number of items:	20		20	Total:	40
Total time for test:	50 minutes				

Note: Percents indicate weight of objective.

Questioning skills can also be a valuable tool for students as they attempt to learn material covered in class. One strategy for teaching students to ask questions might be to supply them with the information shown in Box 15–1 and to ask them to write several questions at each cognitive level. After discussing their questions and explaining misconceptions, the teacher could give the students a series of questions to classify into the categories presented in the taxonomy. This activity should be reinforced frequently.

A second strategy might be to have children arrive at the answer to a problem by asking questions. Torrance and Myers (1970) cite an example of a teacher who instituted an "I [for *Inquirers*] Club" for

Box 15–2   *Types and Examples of Test Items*

The Essay Question

Essay questions allow students to use their own words and style of writing. Because of time constraints, there are usually a small number of questions to sample student achievement. Students are required to supply organization and detail. Answers to essay questions will vary in degrees of completeness and accuracy.

Example: Compare the administrations of President Nixon and President Reagan in terms of significant developments in international relations. Cite specific examples.

True-False, Matching and Multiple Choice Items

These items, typically referred to as "objective," provide students with a limited number of choices from which to select their answer. Examples of each type are given below.

True-False

T   F   Measles is caused by a virus.

Matching

Column A   Column B

( )   1.   Cairo   ( )   a.   Ganges
( )   2.   Calcutta   ( )   b.   Mississippi
( )   3.   New Orleans   ( )   c.   Nile
( )   4.   Paris   ( )   d.   St. Lawrence
( )   5.   Quebec   ( )   e.   Seine
                          ( )   f.   Thames

Multiple Choice

Who were the Huks in the Philippines?
a.   A tribe of primitive headhunters.
b.   A community-supported rebel group.
c.   Wealthy landowners and industrialists.
d.   Members of the minority party of the legislature.

students who explained a puzzling event by asking questions. They provide the example reproduced in Box 15–2.

Practice Activity 15-2

1.   Select a topic from a lesson you plan to teach. Make a list of questions you might use in a discussion with students. Try to write a question at each of the six levels shown in Box 15–2.
2.   Consider why students should learn to ask good questions.

Checking Understanding

A more detailed discussion of questioning strategies as they relate to instruction is presented in Chapter 9. For the purposes of evaluation, using questions to check learners' understanding of the concepts presented in a lesson can be an important measure of whether or not the lesson objectives have been met. It would be difficult to test students at the end of each lesson. But a teacher needs to seek feedback about the progress being made by learners so that appropriate lesson modifications can be made. It is important that puzzled looks, unusual replies, protests, the lack of performance, and other responses not go unnoticed (Fraenkel, 1973). Any of these cues can provide valuable information on how well students are responding to the lesson being taught and can help the teacher answer that very important question, "Have my students learned what they need to learn in order to move on to the next objective?"

Designing Procedures
for Formal Evaluation

Collecting reliable information about learners is an important part of decision making. It is essential to design evaluations that are relevant to the objectives of the lesson and fair to the students being evaluated.

Preparing and Administering Tests

Educators place great emphasis on test scores. We promote, fail, or provide remediation for children in response to their performances on teacher-made tests. Yet perhaps the most generous statement that might be made about teacher-made tests is that they are generally defective evaluation devices (Thorndike & Hagen, 1969). This section will discuss teacher-made tests. It will deal specifically with ideas for developing a blueprint for a test, constructing test items, and administering a test.

Preparing a test blueprint.   As noted earlier in this chapter, planning for instruction and evaluation should occur simultaneously. There are several reasons you should try to do both before instruction. The most obvious is that it is relatively simple to develop a test blueprint, or plan for a test, from a well-constructed lesson plan. This will not only serve as a means of ensuring that all parts of the lesson are assessed, but will also save hours of agony when the time comes to produce a test.

The most important step in planning a test is to define the objectives of the lesson. Many volumes have been devoted to the usefulness of stated objectives as a means of identifying and presenting content and developing skills. For the purposes of this discussion, however, let's simply note that appropriately stated objectives will make it easier to decide what to include on a test.

Box 15–3 gives an example of a blueprint for an examination in world history for a ninth-grade class. The three categories of objec-

---

Box 15–3   *Informal Evaluation Based on Bloom's Taxonomy of Educational Objectives*

Topic: Primitive Tribes

Level of Objective	Sample Item	Sample Student Response
Knowledge: Ability to recall or recognize ideas, facts, etc., when certain cues or signals are given	"Name one primitive tribe of people."	"The Yanomamo Indians of South America."
Comprehension: Ability to receive and understand what is being communicated	"Describe how they live."	"They hunt wild game and gather fruits and vegetables."
Application: Ability to use questions, rules, principles, ideas, and methods in particular situations	"Give an example of how their way of life is similar to the way people live in our country."	"We both depend on plants and animals for survival. We only differ in the way we get them."
Analysis: Ability to break down information into components or parts	"Explain how primitive families divide the work."	"The men were hunters and warriors, and the women took care of the children."
Synthesis: Ability to work with pieces of a whole	"Determine what a person from a primitive culture would need to do to prepare for a meal."	"Find meat and vegetables; build a fire; prepare food; cook food; and eat."
Evaluation: Ability to make quantitative and qualitative judgments about the usefulness of ideas and information	"Assess the benefits of living in a primitive culture."	"It is good to be free to hunt, but bad when game is scarce."

tives in the box have been weighted to total 100 percent. These weights are determined somewhat arbitrarily by the teacher; however, a rule of thumb is to assign the greatest weight to those topics that receive the most attention during instruction (for example, two weeks of instructional time on a particular topic might be translated into roughly 30 percent of a unit, thereby weighting the material in that section of the test as 30 percent of the exam grade).

Constructing test items.   There are a number of concerns to consider when constructing a test. One of the first questions to be addressed is how many items to include. Teacher-made tests should be "power" tests rather than "speed" tests; that is, it is important to construct a test that will allow most of the students a chance to attempt each item. The greater the number of objectives covered by the test, the greater the number of items required to measure achievement.

Because most class periods average forty to fifty minutes, it will be important to make a determination about the type of items based on the time constraints. For instance, if you want to measure ten process objectives, three of which relate to student writing skills, you might decide to limit the number of objective items on the test to allow students enough time to give you an accurate sample of their writing abilities. But if you want to measure fifteen to twenty process objectives, each being defined by several items, it might be necessary to use more objective items (multiple choice, matching, checklist, and so on). It might be helpful to note that a typical student might require thirty to forty-five seconds to read and attempt a fairly simple multiple choice or true–false item, while he or she might require seventy-five to one hundred seconds to read and attempt a more complex item (Thorndike & Hagen, 1969).

Several types of test items have been used effectively over the years. The types of items that are most often constructed by classroom teachers are essay questions and true–false, matching, and multiple-choice items (see Box 15–4). Each of these item types allows students to operate within a completely structured situation. Students respond to a large sample of items and receive a score for each item based on a predetermined answer key.

Both essay and objective items should be used to evaluate most types of student learning. The number of items in each category will be determined by time constraints, pupil ability, and the process objectives listed in the lesson/test blueprint.

Administering the test.   The medium for administering a test will depend on the facilities available in school. Teachers will invariably encounter administrators who are conscious of the ever-increasing costs of purchasing supplies, and thus may be instructed to use paper sparingly. In such cases, the chalkboard provides a practical solution for administering essay questions. Space on chalkboards is

Box 15-4   *The "I Club" Approach to Teaching Children to Ask Information-gleaning Questions*

TEACHER: Several years ago a Japanese ship left port and headed for the open sea. When it had reached a spot about five hundred miles from the nearest point of land, the captain gave a signal and the crew spilled a half-ton of pearls over the side. What questions can you ask that might help you explain this apparently unreasonable (and true) happening? Ask only questions that can be answered by "yes" or "no." Each of you can keep up his questioning until he decides to "pass" to someone else.

VICKI: Were they crooks who were being chased by the police and wanted to get rid of the evidence—the pearls—so they would not be jailed?

TEACHER: No.

VICKI: I pass.

HARRY: Was the captain driven crazy by a mysterious drug, and then he forced his crew to throw the pearls overboard?

TEACHER: No.

HARRY: I pass.

JENNY: Did the Russians break a Japanese code and then follow them in a sub, and then they surfaced and were about to get the pearls, and so the captain told the men to throw the pearls overboard?

TEACHER: No.

JENNY: I pass.

MARY: Were they doing anything illegal?

TEACHER: No.

MARY: Uhh . . . I pass.

JEFF: Was the captain following orders from someone?

TEACHER: Yes.

JEFF: From the Japanese government?

TEACHER: Yes.

JEFF: Was it the war or defense department?

TEACHER: No.

JEFF: Was it the part that has to do with trade with other countries?

TEACHER: Yes. That is half of it. Can you get the rest?

JEFF: Uhh. Gosh, I don't know.

TEACHER: Go head—try another question.

JEFF: Was it because they wanted to keep the price of pearls high?

TEACHER: Yes. You are in the "I" Club.

Note: From Torrance & Myers, 1970, pp. 241–42.

usually too limited when presenting multiple-choice and matching items.

It is possible to administer a test orally; however, this procedure may not be appropriate for all groups. Differences in student abilities make it difficult to set a tempo that allows enough time for all students to decide on an answer to a problem and then to record it. True–false and short-answer items seem to fit this medium best. Multiple-choice questions may be too difficult to follow easily when presented orally (Thorndike & Hagen, 1969).

Practice Activity 15-3

1. Prepare a statement of the objectives for a unit you plan to teach. Which of these objectives might be measured by a written test?
2. Use these objectives to prepare a blueprint for a test to evaluate your students' progress.
3. Using your blueprint as a guide, construct a test for your unit. Include essay, multiple-choice, matching, and true–false items on your test.

Assigning Grades

Educators have debated for years the advantages and disadvantages of grading students' efforts. A number of researchers have concluded that grading students is detrimental and undesirable (Holt, 1969; Purkey, 1970; Marshall, 1969), while others have stated that evaluation and grading are inescapable and worthwhile (Osgood, Suci, & Tannenbaum, 1957; Fitch, Drucker, & Norton, 1951). No doubt both positions have merit and should be given consideration.

Regardless of one's position, however, we can remain somewhat certain that tests and grades will be with us in the future, for they are part of most educational systems, and children are conditioned at an early age to consider grades as social and personal rewards (recall the discussion about accountability in Chapter 1). Teachers can use grades not only as indicators of student progress but also as incentives to help students reach higher levels of achievement. Because grades are used to evaluate student progress and are thus part of the process of retention or promotion, they automatically affect students' desire to do well. Teachers must ensure that each student has opportunities to succeed and that tests are neither too difficult nor too easy. Care should be taken to explain test results to students and to ensure that students who have performed poorly understand that low grades are neither indicators of personal worth nor proof that they are low achievers.

The literature is inconclusive about the effects of strict or lenient grading on low- and high-achieving students (Goldberg, 1965). A safe rule for beginning teachers might be to construct a reliable and valid test for a particular group of learners and use the results to encourage children to learn. To some degree tests will determine when, what, and how students will study. Well-constructed examinations can give students an opportunity to test their knowledge and, with prompt and constructive feedback, can motivate students to improve their performances. Tests that are poorly constructed or used as punishment for misbehavior can just as effectively discourage learning and have extremely negative effects on a student's self-concept.

It is important to realize that for some students, grading requires special procedures. Bender (1984), for example, suggests the following guidelines for grading handicapped children in the mainstream:

- Base grades on the objectives found in the student's Individual Educational Plan (IEP). It is important that the mainstream teacher participate in the formulation of the handicapped student's IEP to ensure that the IEP objectives are consistent with those in the mainstream class.
- Grade student performance on a logical sequence of objectives. The objectives should follow, as closely as possible, the sequence of objectives in the mainstream class.
- Grade learner performance on individualized instruction of these objectives. Planning for instruction should reflect an understanding of the academic abilities of the handicapped child.
- Explain all grading practices on the IEP. If, for instance, a mainstream student is receiving good grades on work below grade level, it is important to explain this verbally and in writing at the IEP meeting.
- Grade student performance on state or district competency test objectives *only as a last resort*. If this is required by your school district, the IEP objectives should be constructed so as to include state or local competencies.
- Seek guidance from principals and other teachers in grading handicapped students' performances. Use experts in the field or other professionals who have dealt with similar questions.

Counseling Learners on the Importance of Test Results

Thus far we have discussed the importance of planning evaluations when planning for instruction. We have noted the need to ensure that formal and informal evaluations are both relevant to class activities and fair for all students. We have also stressed the importance of evaluating learner progress on an ongoing basis to check their comprehension and understanding. In this section we will explore the issue of counseling children on the importance of test results.

From the primary grades to graduate school, students frequently ask questions about the importance of material on which they will be tested. The frequency of these questions indicates that students perceive tests to be an important guide to what they need to know in order to be successful and, indeed, to define what they need to learn. In light of this, the successful teacher will use this motivational factor to the greatest advantage by counseling students on the necessity of performing well on a particular test.

By definition, counseling learners on the importance of test results involves explaining the purpose of the test and how the results will be used. In addition, students should understand why a particular test is relevant to them personally.

The perceived importance of a test appears to affect student performance. Yamamoto and Dizney (1965) found that children performed better on a test when it was called a "standardized" test than they did when it was called an "achievement" test. Naughton (1968) showed that students who were informed of how test results would be used performed better than those who were not so instructed.

Research has indicated that examiners should try to be positive and approving in a testing situation and should attempt to convey the idea that there is an important task at hand. Shannon (1980) found that student attitudes toward reading were more positive when students were counseled on the nature and purpose of the testing before the test was administered than when they were not. Communication of the test's importance thus affects the overall score received by the learner.

Communicating test results.   What teachers say to students and what they communicate may be entirely different. If, for instance, a teacher says, "Frank, you made a stupid mistake," what she communicates may very likely be "I don't care for you." The objective of sound communication is to alter, in a positive manner, learners' self-images and to give them a sense of the importance of results to them personally.

Thorndike and Hagen (1969) offer three suggestions for presenting test data. First, although individual test results are vital to the instructional process, teachers should attempt to present an overall picture of the student's standing on an ongoing basis. Teachers should realize that the benefits of using test results to alter self-perceptions in students will be a gradual process.

Second, teachers should attempt to relate the significance of the test to the student's activities and experiences outside the classroom. The greater the congruence between these two experiences, the more successful the bid to relate the importance of the test to the student. For instance, Jimmy wants to join the navy after graduation. His career goals include attending the navy's nuclear submarine program. His physics teacher takes extra time to stress the relationship of physics to his career goal and points out that one factor to be considered by the admissions board will be his mastery of physics principles. In essence, Jimmy's teacher has made a connection that is clearly relevant to his life experiences and has increased the importance of his doing well in physics class.

Third, students should take an active role in relating test results to themselves and their plans. The acceptance of the information communicated depends on the student accepting as true what has been said. This depends in part on the student making a conscious effort to relate test results to his or her situation. Thus in regard to our earlier example, Jimmy should take an active role in interpreting the meaning of a low score on a particular test and the relationship of that score to his chances of being accepted in the nuclear submarine program. In summary, teachers and students working together in an honest and open atmosphere should be able to use tests to enhance the learning experience.

Practice Activity 15-4

Consider the following:

1. Why is it important to counsel learners on the use of test results?
2. What steps should you take in presenting test data to students?

Pulling It All Together

Again, it is crucial that as teachers plan for instruction they also plan for formal and informal monitoring of learner progress (Tyler, 1950; Zahorik, 1975; Morine-Dershimer & Vallance, 1976). Let's look at a situation in which a teacher would be required to make a decision regarding a student's progress.

Anna Fontaine, a sixth-grade teacher, noticed during mathematics drills that George was having trouble keeping up. She wondered whether she should move him to a slower math group or place him in a remedial class. She decided that she needed more information before she could accurately judge George's mathematics ability.

Her first step was to plan a strategy for collecting the needed data. Over a period of several weeks Ms. Fontaine collected considerable information regarding George's mathematics aptitude. She gave him a series of standardized and informal tests. She observed George during recitation drills in an effort to detect behaviors that might indicate particular attitudes toward mathematics. She used flash cards to check his knowledge of facts.

After analyzing the information collected from these formal and informal evaluations, Anna drew the following conclusions:

- George's mathematics aptitude was slightly above average.
- George understood addition; however, he seemed to have some difficulty with subtraction.

- George was shy around the children in his math group and tended to be less aggressive than the other members during recitation drills.
- George was very athletic and tended to rush out of the room when the bell signaled the beginning of physical education class, which immediately followed George's math group.

On the basis of her data, Anna decided to make several changes in her approach to teaching mathematics. George's aptitude indicated that he should remain in the same group. His shyness in the group suggested that he was somewhat insecure; thus, she decided to work with him individually on subtraction. She also decided to praise George's athletic abilities in an effort to channel his more aggressive traits into the academic setting. Finally, Anna changed the meeting time of George's group so that it met immediately after physical education.

Ms. Fontaine used both formal and informal evaluation procedures in her instructional planning. She noticed a problem with one of her students and, basing her judgments on reasonable data, designed a procedure for dealing with the situation. Clearly, in this example instructional planning was shaped by the evaluation procedure, resulting in informed decisions.

The overlap of instructional planning and evaluation planning does not stop here. As noted earlier, it is important to recognize that the identification of content to be included in a lesson automatically assigns it value and shapes to some extent how a learner's ability to grasp specific concepts can be evaluated. Establishing methods for evaluating student progress when planning instruction gives direction and purpose to teaching–learning activities. The successful teacher strives for consistency between these activities and the evaluation criteria so that students are given every opportunity to master what is being taught.

Practice Activity 15-5

Joanne, an energetic third-grader, is extremely disruptive during class. Her grades in mathematics and reading are below grade level. She excels, however, in art and music. She is popular with her classmates and, except for her disruptions, is well-liked by her teacher.

1. How might Joanne's teacher collect useful information about Joanne's performance?
2. What very tentative conclusions might be drawn relative to Joanne's behaviors?

References

Bender, W. N. (1984). Daily grading in mainstream classes. *The Directive Teacher, 6* (2), 4–5.

Bloom, B. S., Englehart, M. B., Furst, E. J., Hill, W. H., & Krathwohl, D. R. (1956). *Taxonomy of educational objectives: The classification of educational goals. Handbook I: Cognitive domain.* New York: Longmans Green.

Fitch, M. L., Drucker, A. J., & Norton, J. A. (1951). Frequent testing as a motivating factor in large lecture classes. *Journal of Educational Psychology, 42,* 1–20.

Fraenkel, J. R. (1973). *Helping students think.* Englewood Cliffs, N.J.: Prentice-Hall.

Goldberg, L. R. (1965). Grades as motivants. *Psychology in the Schools, 2,* 14–17.

Holt, J. (1969). *On testing.* New York: Pitman.

Marshall, M. (1969). *Teaching without grades.* Corvallis: Oregon State University Press.

Morine-Dershimer, G., & Vallance, E. (1976). *A study of teacher and pupil perceptions of classroom interaction* (Technical Report, Beginning Teacher Evaluation Study). San Francisco: Far West Laboratory for Educational Research and Development.

Naughton, J. (1968). A modest experiment on test motivation. *Personnel and Guidance Journal, 46,* 606.

Osgood, C. E., Suci, G. J., & Tannenbaum, P. H. (1957). *The measurement of meaning.* Urbana: University of Illinois Press.

Purkey, W. W. (1970). *Self-concept and school achievement.* Englewood Cliffs, N.J.: Prentice-Hall.

Shannon, A. J. (1980). Effects of methods of standardized reading achievement test administration on attitudes toward reading. *Journal of Reading, 23,* 684–86.

Thorndike, R. L., & Hagen, E. (1969). *Measurement and evaluation in psychology and education.* New York: Wiley.

Torrance, E. P., & Meyers, R. E. (1970). *Creative learning and teaching.* New York: Dodd, Mead.

Tyler, R. W. (1950). *Basic principles of curriculum and instruction.* Chicago: University of Chicago Press.

Yamamoto, K., & Dizney, H. F. (1965). Effects of three sets of test instructions on scores on an intelligence scale. *Educational and Psychological Measurement, 25,* 87–94.

Zahorik, J. (1975). Teacher's planning models. *Educational Leadership, 33,* 134–39.

Index

Academic learning time (ALT), 81–95
  accountability and, 97–99
  background knowledge for, 82–89
  definition of, 81, 83
  purpose of, 81
Accountability, 97–108
  background knowledge for, 97–99
  clear expectations and, 103–104
  definition of, 97
  establishing consequences and, 104–106
  monitoring students and, 106–108
  purpose of, 97
  task assignment and, 100–103
Achievement, student, 111–112, 214–215
Ackerson, G., 198
Active teaching (see Supervision, close)
Advance Organizer Model (advance organizers), 171–175
Advance organizers:
  comparative, 172, 173, 199
  expository, 172, 198–199
  meaningfulness and, 197–200
Affective climate, 247–261
  background knowledge for, 249
  courtesy and consideration, 254
  cultural differences and, 256–258
  definition of, 247
  hostility and punitiveness, 249–250
  learned behavior and, 255–256
  management and, 250–254
  purpose of, 247–249
Alberto, P. A., 55, 59
Allocated time, 83, 85–86, 88–91
ALT (see Academic learning time)
Ames, W., 198
Analysis, in Bloom's taxonomy, 151, 153, 275
Anderson, C., 99
Anderson, G. L., 129
Anderson, L., 70, 71, 250
Anderson, R. C., 147, 200–203
Antecedent Conditions, 123–130
  classroom and school environment and, 128–130
  information about students and, 123–125
  nature of the instructional task and, 126–128
Application, in Bloom's taxonomy, 151, 153, 275
Arlin, M., 68
Associative hierarchies, 204, 207, 208
"At-risk" students, 10–11

Austin, G. R., 16
Ausubel, David P., 171–174, 197–198
Awareness, 121–144
  antecedent conditions and, 122–130
    classroom and school environment, 128–130
    information about students, 123–126
    nature of the instructional task, 126–128
  background knowledge for, 122–123
  Classroom Interactions and, 123, 130–142
    student cues, 131–135
    teacher actions, 138–142
    teacher interpretations, 135–138
  definition of, 121
Aylesworth, M., 100–101

Ball, G., 245
Bancroft, G. W., 242
Bandura, A., 59
Bany, M. A., 251
Baptiste, H. P., Jr., 256
Baptiste, M. L., 256
Barron, R. F., 174, 176
Basic skills, 220–221
Becker, F. D., 258
Beginning Teacher Evaluation Study (BTES), 84, 86, 99
Behavioral contracts, 52–54
Behavioral handicaps, 219
Behaviorism, 45
Being, language of, 133, 134
Bender, W. N., 279
Bennett, Christine, 242
Berliner, D. C., 11, 39, 82, 86, 196, 198, 200, 201, 232
Bernal, E. M., 11
Bissell, H., 245
Blaney, N., 227
Blind students, 217
Bloom, Benjamin S., 25, 137, 150–155, 222, 271, 275
Blueprints test, 272, 274–276
Borg, Walter R., 41
Borgers, S. B., 252
Borko, H., 29
Bossert, S. T., 17
Bower, G. H., 204–205
Boyer, E., 10
Brandt, R., 86
Briggs, L. J., 249
Brooks, D. M., 135–136
Brophy, J., 44, 68, 76, 78, 85, 98–101, 105, 110,

Brophy, J. (*continued*)
    112–113, 126, 169, 196, 233, 234, 236, 237
Bruner, J., 171

Cagne, R. M., 249
Canfield, J., 244
Carnegie Forum on Education and the Economy, 4
Carnine, D., 203
Carrier, C. A., 92–93, 106–107
Carroll, John, 83–84
Catholic schools, 16
Census Bureau, U.S., 16
Charlesworth, W. R., 171
Children's Defense Fund campaign, 10
Clarity of structure, 167–191
    background knowledge for, 169–170
    definition of, 167
    structuring strategies and, 170–190
        advance organizers, 171–175
        advantages, 170–171
        outlines, 181, 183–187
        review, 187–190
        structured overviews, 174, 176–182
Classroom Environment Scale (CES), 129
Classroom Interactions, 123, 130–142
    student cues and, 131–135
    teacher actions and, 138–142
    teacher interpretations and, 135–138
Classrooms, 250–251 (*see also* Affective climate)
    arrangement of, 126
    cooperative grouping in, 225–228
    environment of, 128–130
Clauson, E. V., 172, 173
Climate (*see* Affective climate; Environment)
Climate surveys, 129–130
Clinical interview, 124
Closed questions, 155–156
Close supervision (*see* Supervision, close)
Coalition for the Development of a Performance Evaluation System, 258
Cognitive behavior modification (CBM), 58
Cognitive development, 123–126, 171, 195
Cognitive disabilities, 217–219
Cognitive structure, 171–172
Cohen, M., 5
Coker, H., 99
Coleman, J. S., 16, 83
Color, affective climate and, 259
Comparative advance organizers, 172, 173, 199
Comprehension, in Bloom's taxonomy, 151, 152, 275
Conceptual hierarchies, 204, 206
Consequences, establishing, 104–106
Consideration, 254

Consistent rules, 67–79
    age levels and, 76, 78
    background knowledge for, 67–72
    definition of, 67
    overlap ability and, 70
    purpose of, 67
    "withitness" and, 70
Continuity of experiences, 195
Contributing, 133–134
Cooper, H. M., 233, 238
Cooperative grouping, 225–228
Corcoran, T. B., 17
Courtesy, 254
Covington, V., 244
Craig, R., 45
Crawford, J., 99
Cronbach, J. J., 215
Cues, student, 131–135
    teacher interpretation of, 135–138
Cultural differences, 136, 222–223
    affective climate and, 256–258
    self-concept and, 241–243

Daily review, 112
Davies, I. K., 146, 147, 155, 170
Davis, John, 27
Deaf students, 217
Dewey, John, 171, 194, 195
Dinkmeyer, D., 245
Discussions:
    full class, 159–165
        designing appropriate questions, 161
        familiarity with the material, 161
        objectives, 161–162
        strategy for question construction, 162, 163
        student responses, 162–165
    small group, 157–158
Dizney, H. F., 280
Dropouts, 10–11
Drucker, A. J., 278

Earle, R. A., 173, 176, 182
Early, M., 184*n*
Ebmeier, H., 110
Educable mentally retarded students, 217–218
Effect, Law of, 45
Eisner, E. W., 24
Emmer, E., 68, 70, 72, 75, 250
Emotional handicaps, 219
Engaged time, 83, 86–87
Engaging, 133–134
Environment (*see also* Affective climate):
    classroom and school, 128–130
    physical, 258–259
Essay questions, 273, 276
Estes, T. H., 174

Evaluations, 151, 153, 201, 263–283
  background knowledge for, 264–265
  components of, 267, 268
  definition of, 263
  formal, designing procedures for, 274–276,
      278–281
    administering, 276, 278
    assigning grades, 278–279
    blueprints, 272, 274–276
    constructing test items, 273, 276
    counseling learners on the importance of
      test results, 279–281
    test preparation and administration, 274–
      276, 278
  of learner progress through informal assess-
      ment, 270–275
  planning for, 266–270
  purpose of, 263
  synthesis of information in, 281–282
  thinking about, 265–266
Evaluative response style, 252
Evertson, C., 68, 70–78, 99, 112–113, 196, 250
Exceptional children (*see* Handicapped stu-
      dents)
Exercise, Law of, 45
Expectations, 114
  clear, 103–104
  high, 233–236
Experiences:
  select learning, 194–196
  use of term, 194
Expository organizers, 172, 198–199
Extinction, 62–64

Fading, 57–58
Feedback, 238–241
Feistritzer, Emily, 4, 5
Fischer, B., 9
Fisher, Carles, 82, 86
Fitch, M. L., 278
Flavell, J. H., 171
Formal evaluation, designing procedures for,
      274–276, 278–281
  assigning grades, 278–279
  counseling learners on the importance of
      test results, 279–281
  test preparation and administration, 274–
      276, 278
Fraenkel, J. R., 159, 161, 274
Fraser, B. J., 129
Frederick, W. C., 87
Frymier, J., 224
Fuller, F. F., 25
Futrell, Mary Hatwood, 11

Gage, N. L., 11, 39, 196, 198, 200, 201
Gagne, E., 111, 112
Gagne, Robert, 194–195

Gallagher, J. J., 218
Garber, H., 16
Garcia, R. L., 222, 241
Generative learning instruction, 203
Georgia, University of, 172
Gifted students, 11–12, 219–222
  definition of, 220, 221
  self-concept and, 234
Gillet, Jean Wallace, 225
Ginott, Haim, 245
Goldberg, L. R., 279
Gollnick, D. M., 256
Good, T. L., 72, 85, 98–101, 105, 110–112,
      113, 169, 233, 234, 236
Goodwin, S. S., 164
Gordon, T., 245
Gordon, Thomas, 138–140
Goss, S., 87–88
Governor's Task Force on Readiness, 10–11
Grades, assigning, 278–279
Grant, B. M., 140–142
Grant, V., 16
Grouws, D., 110–112

Hagen, E., 274, 276, 280
Hallahan, D. P., 217, 218, 219
Handicapped students, 12
  exceptionalities and, 215–219
    emotional or behavioral, 219
    learning and cognitive disabilities, 217–
      219
    physical and sensory, 216–217
Harnischfeger, A., 84
Hartley, J., 170
Hayman, M., 71
Hearing impaired students, 217
Heightening, language of, 133, 134
Hennings, D. G., 131–133, 137, 140–142
Herber, H. L., 189
Heward, W. L., 219
Hierarchical retrieval schemes, 204–208
Hoffer, T., 16
Hollifield, J., 10
Holt, J., 278
Homework assignment, 112
Hoover, K. H., 188, 189
Hosford, P. L., 232
Hostility, 249–250
Human Development Program, The, 245
Hunt, David, 1
Hyman, Ronald T., 147

"I Club" approach, 272–273, 277
I-messages, 139–140
Indirect messages, 139
Individual differences:
  accountability and, 100–103

Individual differences (*continued*)
  background knowledge for, 212–214
  cooperative grouping in classrooms and, 225–228
  cultural background and, 222–223
  definition of, 211
  giftedness and, 219–222
  prior achievement and, 214–215
  purpose of, 211
  student interests and, 223–225
Individualized education program (IEP), 213, 279
Individualized questions, 158–159
Input, 131–135
Instruction, planning for, 266–270
Instructional and management strategies, 111, 112
Instructional task, 126–128
Integration of experiences, 195, 196
Interest inventories, 224
Interests, student, 223–225
Interpersonal relations management, 251–254
Interpretive response style, 252
Inventing, 137

Jackson, P. W., 24
Jefferson, Thomas, 14
Jerrolds, B. W., 173
Johnson, D. W., 226, 227, 244
Johnson, L. V., 251
Johnson, R. T., 226, 227, 244
Joyce, B., 172, 173, 214

Karlin, R., 184*n*
Karweit, N. L., 83, 85, 87
Kaskowitz, D., 84
Kauffman, J. K., 217, 219
Kauffman, J. M., 218
Keil, F. C., 171
Kelley, M. L., 251
Kendler, H. H., 196, 197
Kendler, T. S., 196, 197
Kennedy, R. E., 251
Kilgore, S., 16
Kinder, D., 203
King, M. A., 205
Kirk, S. A., 218
Kneedler, R. D., 217, 219
Knowledge:
  in Bloom's taxonomy, 151, 152, 275
  of results, 265–266
Koneya, M., 258
Kottcamp, R., 5
Kounin, 106
Kounin, J. C., 130, 131
Kounin, J. S., 68–71
Kounin, S. J., 92–94, 106
Kuder General Interest Survey, 224

Language disorders, 217
Lawton, J. T., 173
Learned behavior, 255–256
Learning:
  meaningfulness in (*see* Meaningfulness)
  meaningful verbal, 171
  time and (*see* Academic learning time)
Learning disabilities, 217–219
Learning Environment Inventory (LEI), 129
Lesson planning, 169–170
Lessons:
  clarity of the structure of (*see* Clarity of structure)
  structure and sequence of, 126, 127
Linder, B., 185*n*
Lortie, D., 4
Luiten, J., 198

McCutcheon, G., 25
McGauvran, M. E., 29
McKay, G. D., 245
McNergney, R., 92–93, 106–107
Mager, R. F., 27
Mainstream programs, 218
Management, 250–54
Marland Report, 11
Marshall, M., 278
Matching test items, 273, 276
Meaning, covert, 137, 138
Meaningfulness, 169, 193–210
  advance organizers and, 197–200
  background knowledge for, 193–196
  conclusions, 209
  definition of, 193
  hierarchical retrieval schemes and, 204–208
  mediators and, 196–197
  mnemonic techniques and, 205, 207–209
  purpose of, 193
  set induction and, 200, 201
Mediators, 196–197
Medley, D., 99
Meichenbaum, D. H., 58
Metacognitive skills, 219
Mills, D. C., 174
Minority students, 10
Mnemonic techniques, 205, 207–209
Modeling, 56–57
Moos, R. H., 129
Morine-Dershimer, G., 25, 281
Morrison, H. C., 24
Moskowitz, G., 71
Motivation, 195
Multiple choice tests, 273, 276
Myers, R. E., 272–273, 277

Narrative (or action) stories, 203–204
National Commission on Excellence in Education, 2, 82

National Education Association, 4
National Governor's Association, 4
Nation at Risk, A: The Imperative for Educational Reform, 3, 82
Naughton, J., 280
Negative punishment, 62, 64–65
Negative reinforcement, 45–46, 62
Neisworth, J. T., 173
Nonverbal language:
  of students, 131, 133–135
  of teachers, 140–142
Noonkester, M., 100–101
No response at all, 164
Norton, J. A., 278
Nurss, J. R., 29

O'Brien, P., 129
100 Ways to Enhance Self-Concept in the Classroom (Canfield and Well), 244
Open questions, 155–156
Operation, in set induction, 201
Orientation, in set induction, 201
Orlansky, M. D., 219
Osgood, C. E., 278
Outlines, 170, 181, 183–187
Output, 138–142
Overlap, ability to, 70

Palomares, U., 245
Participation, language of, 133–134
Pearson, P. D., 147
Perloff, B., 59
Personal attacks, 164
Personal management, 251
Personal worth, 243–245
Peterson, P. L., 127
Physical handicaps, 216–217
Piaget, Jean, 124, 171
PLAN (computer-managed system), 226
Planning, 23–42
  Antecedent Conditions and, 123
  background knowledge for, 24–26, 44
  definition of, 23
  evaluating the success of, 39–40
  for evaluation and instruction, 266–270
  goals and objectives of, 26–29
  lesson, 169–170
  purpose of, 23, 43
  student needs identified in, 29–35
  teaching procedures formulated in, 35–37
  when things go wrong in, 37–39
Plisko, V., 2, 10, 12
Positive reinforcement, 45
Praise, 236–238
Primary reinforcers, 46–47
Private schools, 16
Probing response style, 252–253
Problem solving, collaborative, 105–106

Procedures, teaching, formulation of, 35–37
Processing decisions, 135–138
Projecting, 137
Prompting, 54–58
Provenzo, E., 5
Public Law 94-142 (Education for All Handicapped Children Act), 12, 213, 215–216
Pulaski, M. A., 124
Punishment, 62–65
  affective climate and, 249–250
  extinction and, 62–64
  negative, 62, 64–65
  response cost and, 64
Pupil-observation system, 92–93
Purkey, S. C., 16–17
Purkey, W. W., 278
Put-down messages, 139

Questioning skill, 145–165
  background knowledge for, 146–147
  definition of, 145
  full class discussions and, 159–165
  in informal assessments, 271–273
  purpose of, 145
  strategies for classroom use of, 157–159
    individualized questions, 158–159
    small group discussions, 157–158
    student questions, 159
    tutorial questions, 159
    written questions, 157
  teachers' use of, 148–156
    functions, 148–150
    levels and types of questions, 150–155
    open and closed questions, 155–156

Reading, close supervision in, 112–113
Recalling, 137
Reflecting, 137
Reinforcement (reinforcers), 43–66
  conclusion, 65–66
  continuous, 61
  data collecting and recording for, 61–62
  definition of, 43
  delivering, 60–61
  guidelines for, 51
  increasing desirable behavior and, 52–60
    behavioral contracts, 52–54
    fading, 57–58
    modeling, 56–57
    prompting, 54–58
    self-management, 58–60
    shaping, 57–58
    work plans, 54
  learned, 47
  negative, 45–46, 62
  positive, 45
  primary, 46–47

Reinforcement (reinforcers) (*continued*)
  punishment and, 62–65
  secondary, 47–48
  selection of, 48–51
  theory of, 44–51
  token, 47–48
Reinforcement schedules, 60–61
Renzulli, J. S., 220, 221
Reprimand, 164
Response cost, 62, 64
Responsiblity, lack of, 101
Review, 187–190
Rice, M. G., 172, 173
Robinson, F. G., 197–198
Robinson, H. A., 177, 190
Robinson, V., 3
Rodman, B., 4
Role-taking skill, 126
Rosenshine, B. S., 127
Rowe, M. B., 238
Rules system (*see* Consistent rules)

Sabornie, E. J., 216
Sanford, J., 72
Santeusanio, R. P., 173, 175
Sarcasm, 164
Schemata-based instruction, 200–204
Schmuck, P. A., 251
Schmuck, R., 251
School environment, 128–129
Schools, 13–20
Schottman, T. A., 184n
Schuck, R., 200, 201
Schuman's Inquiry Training Model, 214
Science Research Associates (SRA), 224
Seating, affective climate and, 258–259
Seatwork, 112
Secondary reinforcers, 47–48
Self-concept, learner, 231–246
  background knowledge for, 231–233
  cultural diversity and, 241–243
  definition of, 231–233
  feedback and, 238–241
  high expectations and, 233–236
  personal worth and, 243–245
  praise and, 236–238
  purpose of, 231
Self-control, 58–60
Self-management, 58–60
Selman, Robert, 126
Sensory handicaps, 216–217
Sequence of experiences, 195–196
Set induction, 200, 201
Shanker, Albert, 3
Shannon, A. J., 280
Shaping, 57–58
Shavelson, R. J., 122
Skinner, B. F., 45

Slavin, R., 226, 227
Small group discussions, 157–158
Smith, F., 171, 178, 179
Smith, L., 220
Smith, M. C., 16–17
Snow, E. E., 215
Snyder, T. D., 16
Soar, R., 99
Soar, R. M., 250
Soar, R. S., 88, 250
Social cognition, 125–126
Social perspective-taking abilities, 126
Socioeconomic status (SES), 196
Socrates, 150
Soloman, G., 36
Solution messages, 139
Sommer, R., 258–259
Space, affective climate and, 258
Spaulding, Robert, 86–87, 114–115
Special reviews, 112
Speech disorders, 217
Stallings, J., 84–86, 113
Stanford, G., 251
Steinbrink, J. E., 173
Stern, J., 2, 10, 12
Stern, P., 122
Stimulus-response theory (S-R), 45
Stokes, T. F., 251
Strong, E. K., Jr., 224
Structured overviews, 174, 176–182
Structure of lessons (*see* Clarity of structure)
Students, 9–13
  accountability of (*see* Accountability)
  achievement of, 111–112
    prior, 214–215
  cues of, 131–135
    teacher interpretation of, 135–138
  evaluation of (*see* Evaluations)
  individual differences of (*see* Individual differences)
  information about, 123–125
  learning time of (*see* Academic learning time [ALT])
  misbehavior of, 93, 139–142
  needs of, 29, 100–102
  progress of, informal assessment of, 270–275
    asking questions, 271–273, 277
    checking understanding, 274
  questions of, 159, 164
  reinforcement of (*see* Reinforcement)
  responses of, in full class discussions, 162–165
  rules for (*see* Consistent rules)
  self-concept of (*see* Self-concept, learner)
  supervision of (*see* Supervision, close)
  task assignment and, 100–103
  uninvolvement or disruption by, 37–39

Suci, G. J., 278
Supervision, close, 109–120
  background knowledge for, 109–115
  characteristics of, 110–111
  definition of, 109
  instructional and management strategies
    for, 111, 112
  philosophical base of, 113–114
  purpose of, 109
Supportive response style, 252
Swing, S. R., 127
Synthesis, 151, 153, 275
Systematic Training for Effective Parenting
    (STEP), 245

Tanenbaum, P. H., 278
Tarrance, E. P., 277
Task analysis technique, 218
Tasks, assignment of, 100–103
Taxonomy of Educational Objectives, 150–
    155, 222, 271, 275
Taylor, P. H., 25, 196
Teacher and Child (Ginott), 245
Teacher Effectiveness Training (TET), 245
Teachers (*see also specific topics*):
  characteristics of, 2–3
  shortage of, 3–4
Teaching:
  active (*see* Supervision, close)
  context of, 1–21
  planning as, 269
Technology, 109–110
Temple, Charles, 225
Tests, 272–281
  counseling on results of, 279–281
  grading of, 278–279
  preparing and administering, 274–276, 278
    administering, 276, 278
    assigning grades, 278–279
    blueprints, 272, 274–276
    constructing test items, 273, 276
    counseling learners on the importance of
      test results, 279–281
  types and examples of items on, 273, 276
Texas Teacher Effectiveness Study, 99
Textbooks, review and, 190
Thinking level, six-category system analysis
    of, 137
Thorndike, R. L., 45, 274, 276, 280
Time:
  academic learning (*see* Academic learning
    time [ALT])
  allocated, 83, 85–86, 88–91

  engaged, 83, 86–87
  wait, 147
Tobias, S., 214–215
Token reinforcement, 47–48
Tom, D. Y. H., 233
Torrance, E. P., 272–273
Totusek, P. S., 258
Tracks, 220
Transition, 201
Trickett, E. J., 129
Troutman, A. C., 55, 59
True-false test items, 273, 276
Tugend, A., 10
Tutorial questions, 159
Tyler, L., 224
Tyler, R. W., 24, 194–196, 209, 281

Underachievers, 101
Understanding response style, 253
Updike, John, 161–162

Vallance, E., 281
Valuing, 137
Visually impaired students, 217

Wadsworth, B. J., 124
Wain, John, 147
Wait time, 147
Walberg, H. J., 87, 129
Wallen, C. J., 251
Wallen, L. L., 251
Waller, W., 2
Wanska, S. K., 173
Ward, G. R., 252
Watson, J. B., 45
Weil, M., 172, 173, 214
Wells, H. C., 244
West, E., 164
Whitmore, J. R., 234
Wiley, David, 83–84
Wise, A., 5
"Withitness," 70, 106, 131
Wong, B. Y. L., 219
Woolfolk, A. E., 135–136
Work plans, 54
Worth, personal, 243–245
Written questions, 157

Yamamoto, K., 280
Yinger, R. J., 25, 38
Yuille, J. C., 205, 207–208

Zahorik, J. A., 25, 39, 281